READING TEXTS, SEEKING WISDOM

Reading Texts, Seeking Wisdom

SCRIPTURE AND THEOLOGY

edited by

David F. Ford & Graham Stanton

William B. Eerdmans Publishing Company
Grand Rapids, Michigan / Cambridge, U.K.

First published 2003 in the United Kingdom by
SCM Press
9-17 St Albans Place, London N1 0NX
SCM Press is a division of
SCM-Canterbury Press Ltd

This edition published 2004 in the United States of America by
Wm. B. Eerdmans Publishing Co.
255 Jefferson Ave. S.E., Grand Rapids, Michigan 49503 /
P.O. Box 163, Cambridge CB3 9PU U.K.

Printed in the United States of America

09 08 07 06 05 04 7 6 5 4 3 2 1

ISBN 0-8028-2763-2

www.eerdmans.com

Contents

Notes on the Contributors

Richard Bauckham is Professor of New Testament Studies and Bishop Wardlaw Professor in the University of St Andrews, Scotland. He is a Fellow of the British Academy and a Fellow of the Royal Society of Edinburgh. His recent books include: *James: Wisdom of James, Disciple of Jesus the Sage* (1999); *God and the Crisis of Freedom: Biblical and Contemporary Perspectives* (2002); *Gospel Women: Studies of the Named Women in the Gospels* (2002); and (with Trevor Hart) *Hope against Hope: Christian Eschatology in Contemporary Context* (1999).

Markus Bockmuehl is Reader in New Testament Studies in the University of Cambridge, and a Fellow of Fitzwilliam College. His recent books include *Jewish Law in Gentile Churches: Halakhah and the Beginning of Christian Public Ethics* (2000) and *The Epistle to the Philippians* (1997); he has also edited *The Cambridge Companion to Jesus* (2001).

James D. G. Dunn is Lightfoot Professor of Divinity at the University of Durham. Recent publications include: *New Testament Guides: 1 Corinthians* (1995), *Epistles to the Colossians and to Philemon* (1996), *The Acts of the Apostles* (1996), *The Theology of Paul the Apostle* (1998) and *Christianity in the Making. Vol. 1: Jesus Remembered* (2003).

David F. Ford is Regius Professor of Divinity in the University of Cambridge and a Fellow of Selwyn College. His teaching and research are in the areas of systematic theology, hermeneutics, modern theology, and interfaith theology. His recent works include: *Self and Salvation: Being Transformed* (1999), *Theology: A Very Short Introduction* (1999, 2000), *The Shape of Living*

(1999, 2002), and (as editor) *The Modern Theologians: An Introduction to Christian Theology in the Twentieth Century* (2nd edn 1997).

Daniel W. Hardy was Director of the Center of Theological Inquiry in Princeton until 1995. Prior to that he was Van Mildert Professor of Divinity at the University of Durham and Residentiary Canon of Durham Cathedral. He now teaches and supervises in the Faculty of Divinity at the University of Cambridge. His most recent books are *Finding the Church* (2001) and *God's Ways with the World* (1996), and he is completing a book on the social theory of the Church.

Martin Hengel was Professor of New Testament and Ancient Judaism at the University of Tübingen and Director of the Institut für antikes Judentum und hellenistische Religionsgeschichte until his retirement in 1992. Recent books include: *Studies in Early Christology* (1995), *Paulus zwischen Damaskus und Antiochien* (1998), *The Four Gospels and the One Gospel of Jesus Christ* (2000), *Kleine Schriften,* Vol. I–III (1996, 1999, 2002), and *The Septuagint as Christian Scripture* (2002).

Morna D. Hooker is Lady Margaret's Professor Emerita in the University of Cambridge, and a Fellow of Robinson College. Her recent books include: *From Adam to Christ: Essays on Paul* (1990), *A Commentary on The Gospel according to St. Mark* (1992), *Not Ashamed of the Gospel* (1994), *The Signs of a Prophet* (1997), and *Paul: A Short Introduction* (2003). She is editor of *Black's New Testament Commentaries*, and has been joint editor of the *Journal of Theological Studies* since 1985.

William Horbury is Professor of Jewish and Early Christian Studies in the University of Cambridge, a Fellow of the British Academy, and a Fellow of Corpus Christi College, Cambridge. He has written on ancient Judaism, the New Testament, the early church, the history of Hebrew and biblical study, and the history of Jewish–Christian relations. His books include *Jewish Messianism and the Cult of Christ* (1998), *Jews and Christians in*

Contact and Controversy (1998), and, jointly with David Noy, *Jewish Inscriptions of Graeco-Roman Egypt* (1992).

Paul M. Joyce is University Lecturer in Theology in the University of Oxford. He is author of *Divine Initiative and Human Response in Ezekiel* (1989) and the *New Century Bible Commentary on Ezekiel* (forthcoming). He contributed the commentary on Lamentations for the *Oxford Bible Commentary* (2001) and is preparing the Lamentations volume for the new Blackwell Bible Commentary series, which focuses on the reception history of biblical texts. He has also published widely on method and on hermeneutics.

Diana Lipton is Director of Studies in Theology at Newnham College, Cambridge, an Affiliated Lecturer in the Faculty of Divinity, Cambridge University, and a part-time lecturer at Leo Baeck College – Centre for Jewish Education. Her publications include *Revisions of the Night: Politics and Promises in the Patriarchal Dreams of Genesis* (1999). She is currently co-editing with Janet Soskice an Oxford Reader in *Feminism and Theology*, and working on a book on prophecy and divine kingship in the Hebrew Bible.

Robert Morgan is priest-in-charge of Sandford-on-Thames, Reader in New Testament Theology at the University of Oxford, and Vice-Principal of Linacre College. He edited *The Religion of the Incarnation* (1989), and wrote *Biblical Interpretation* (with John Barton) (1988) and *Romans* (1995).

Walter Moberly is Reader in Theology in the University of Durham, and his research interests focus on the theological interpretation of Scripture. His books include: *The Old Testament of the Old Testament* (1992) and *The Bible, Theology, and Faith: A Study of Abraham and Jesus* (2000).

Christopher Rowland is Dean Ireland Professor of the Exegesis of Holy Scripture at the University of Oxford. Recent books include a commentary on the Book of Revelation for the New Interpreter's

Bible (1998) and *Radical Christian Writings: A Reader* (2002). He has just completed a commentary on the reception history of the Apocalypse (with Judith Kovacs), which will be published as part of the new Blackwell Bible Commentaries series focussing on the history of interpretation.

Graham Stanton is Lady Margaret's Professor of Divinity in the University of Cambridge, and a Fellow of Fitzwilliam College. He is most recently the author of *A Gospel for a New People. Studies in Matthew* (1992), *Gospel Truth?* (1995), *The Gospels and Jesus* (2nd edn 2002), and *Jesus and Gospel* (forthcoming, 2003). He is a General Editor of the International Critical Commentaries.

Denys Turner is Norris-Hulse Professor of Divinity at the University of Cambridge, and a Fellow of Peterhouse. His books include *Marxism and Christianity* (1983), *Eros and Allegory: Medieval Exegesis of the Song of Songs* (1995), *The Darkness of God: Negativity in Christian Mysticism* (1995) and *Faith Seeking* (2002). He has edited with Oliver Davies, *Silence and the Word: Negative Theology and Incarnation* (2002). In progress is *Proving God*.

John Webster is Lady Margaret Professor of Divinity at the University of Oxford and will shortly take up a post as Professor of Systematic Theology at the University of Aberdeen. His recent books include *Word and Church* (2002), *Holiness* (2003) and *Holy Scripture* (2003).

Rowan Williams is the Archbishop of Canterbury, and a former Lady Margaret Professor of Divinity at Oxford. Among his books are *Arius: Heresy and Tradition* (1987, 2nd edn 2001), *On Christian Theology* (2000) and *Lost Icons: Reflections on Cultural Bereavement* (2000).

Frances Young is Edward Cadbury Professor of Theology in the University of Birmingham. A recent publication is: *Biblical Exegesis and the Formation of Christian Culture* (1997).

Introduction

DAVID F. FORD AND GRAHAM STANTON

What is Scripture? What did it mean in the past and what sense does it make now? What is its truth? How is it related to God, to communities of believers, to academic disciplines and to current concerns? How is biblical scholarship related to past insights and modern methods? What is the significance of the history of scriptural interpretation? Above all, when account is taken of attempts to answer such general questions, how are specific texts to be understood today?

The questions raised in this book are not only broad and complex but are also important in several respects. They involve fundamental issues of meaning and truth that relate to reality as a whole. These are clearly vital to the religious traditions and communities whose Scriptures are at issue – in the present set of essays the focus is mainly on Christian Scripture, with Jewish Scripture as its most 'significant other'. Those communities are woven into the history of many parts of the world, and are at present of global importance. For example, how the estimated two billion or so Christians interpret their Scriptures has effects far beyond their own boundaries. Even more broadly, the interpretation of Scriptures is just one instance of a pervasive problem facing all religions, cultures and frameworks of meaning: how is the past to be related to the present and the future? Recent centuries have brought many changes, and the practices, values, traditions and texts that embody long-term memory have repeatedly been challenged and often ignored or distorted. Are there appropriate ways to re-examine them, appreciate their past and present meanings, interrogate and test them, and allow them to contribute to the shaping of a future that has roots in the best of the past? Yet such vast matters cannot be adequately addressed by generalities. They of course need to be thought about and discussed in many contexts and at all levels, including the most popular. But they also call for the sort of detailed attention and intensive discussion that may be found among those whose lives are dedicated to them in academic settings. The irony, however, is that such people often shy away from the larger questions and from attempts to make significant connections across the boundaries of academic disciplines. So part of the significance of this book is that it has brought together a group of biblical scholars and theologians committed both to practising their disciplines as rigorously as possible and also to keeping in view the broader horizon of the past and present significance of Scripture.

There are four key features of this book.

The first is, as already suggested, that it is written by a team of experienced academics who try to distil what they have learnt over many years about fruitful ways to relate Scripture and theology.

The second is the combination of thought about theoretical and methodological questions with attention to specific texts.

The third is less obvious: the process of writing included a good deal of conversation, seminar discussion and debate in the context of a conference. These are not essays produced in isolation from one another. They have already been through discussion both among the authors and with wider groups, especially joint sessions of the Cambridge University senior New Testament and Systematic Theology seminars, the Cambridge Theological Society, and the conference held in 2002 to celebrate 500 years of the Lady Margaret's Professorship of Divinity.

The fourth feature is a common concern with wisdom. Wisdom is of course a theme in Scripture, and many of the essays deal with that explicitly. More widely, wisdom is about trying to integrate knowledge, understanding, critical questioning and good judgement with a view to the flourishing of human life and the whole of creation. Theological wisdom attempts all that before God, alert to God, and in line with the purposes of God. The desire for such theological wisdom is at the heart of all the essays.

Those four features by no means lead to a unified common position. Indeed, given the differences in disciplines, methods, philosophical and theological positions, scholarly judgements and much else, they were almost guaranteed to leave much diversity and many unresolved issues. Yet perhaps wisdom is just as much a matter of learning to relate together through our differences as it is of coming to common statements and positions. Certainly, at the end of this process we as editors are greatly encouraged both by the extent of worthwhile engagement and even convergence in the course of the discussions and debates and also by the deep desire of the participants to take this much further.

We see the challenge of that 'much further' as one of the most urgent matters facing both Christian theology (in ecclesial and in academic settings) and the field of theology and religious studies in universities. The health of Christian understanding and living is vitally connected with the richness and wisdom of its interpretation of Scripture. The health of theology and religious studies in universities is vitally connected with the quality of its engagement with classic texts, above all the Scriptures of the various religious traditions. Too often that engagement is constricted in method and content, and is unwilling to face the larger questions of truth, practice and the significance of the reception of Scriptures down the centuries and around the world today. We hope that this collection will make a small contribution both to Christian theology and to the field of theology and religious studies, but above all we hope that both contributors and readers will be inspired to take much further this seeking of wisdom through intensive study and discussion of Scripture.

1. Jesus Christ, the Wisdom of God (1)

DAVID F. FORD

'Oh, how foolish you are' says the risen and still incognito Jesus in Luke 24 to Cleopas and another disciple on the way to Emmaus, referring to their failure to interpret rightly the recent events of Jesus' ministry, death and reported resurrection in relation to the Scriptures. The understanding of Jesus in relation to the Scriptures, both those referred to by Luke and the Christian New Testament in which his own Gospel was later included, is clearly vital to Christian theology. In this essay I will focus on that through the lens of wisdom.

Some assumptions about theology, scriptural interpretation and Jesus

A short essay on a large topic needs to assume some things which would require to be discussed at greater length if space permitted. Here, in brief, are a few of the assumptions which I will be making in what follows. They relate to the nature of Christian theology, the Christian interpretation of Scripture, and the understanding of Jesus Christ.

Theology as wisdom

I am conceiving Christian theology as a seeking of wisdom that asks not only about meaning, interpretation and truth but also, inextricably, about living life before God now and about how lives and communities are shaped in line with who God is and with God's purposes for the future. In short, it is about lived meaning directed towards the kingdom of God.[1] Because of the nature of God and of the reality of which God is creator, this wisdom is in principle both available and endlessly rich. There can be no human overview of it, and its pursuit is prayerful, collaborative, and transformative. In the setting of a university it requires full engagement with a wide range of disciplines and traditions (both secular and religious) in order to learn from them, converse with them, and try to discern and realize their meaning in relation to God and God's purposes. This involves being simultaneously affirmative, critical and transformative in relation to the Christian and other traditions, and also in relation to the university, so as to enable that to be a place for the pursuit of wisdom as well as of information, knowledge and know-how.

The senses of Scripture

The interpretation of Scripture has a special importance within this. In other chapters of this volume (especially those by Bockmuehl, Hardy, Young, Horbury, Turner and Williams) there are a number of variations on the theme of multiple approaches to the meaning of Scripture. The richness of scriptural meaning is not exhausted by its literal sense (or plain sense or historical sense or original sense – though these do not necessarily all have the same sense as each other, and there are also many ways of construing each of them!) and there is need for other senses and various interpretative methods in order to try to do justice to texts whose 'surplus of meaning' seems endless as they are approached

[1] This is a rather different conception of wisdom from that used by Robert Morgan in his essay. His is a provocatively narrow conception which especially focuses on the mythological dimension of the personified figure of wisdom being identified with the risen Jesus Christ. Mine tries to take account of that but differs in not contrasting wisdom with doctrine, but seeing wisdom as an attempt to explore the deep connections of reality in relation to God – in Morgan's terms this would include trying to think through the relationship of *mythos* and *logos* (and also *ethos*). My conception sees it as a wise development of Christian theology to have made wisdom one of its key theological concepts in relation to God, Jesus Christ and the nature of theology.

in different periods, cultures and contexts, through various disciplines and 'interests', with new questions and conversation partners, or in long-term worshipping communities.

The concern to explore both the literal and the other senses, however described, might be termed the 'theological interpretation' or even, in line with the notion of wisdom used in this essay, the 'wisdom interpretation' of Scripture.[2] Christian wisdom interpretation is, of course, indebted to Jewish interpretation (for example, combining *peshat* and *midrash*; engaging with both written and oral Torah, and developing the latter in a contemporary wisdom tradition) and there are analogues in other scriptural, legal and literary traditions. In these traditions there are also debates and conflicts about the appropriate interrelation of senses, which can be instructive and even inspirational for those involved in analogous debates. These efforts of other traditions to find wisdom through intensive conversation (and often conflict) around their texts are among the most promising places for learning how better to seek wisdom in one's own.

Jesus Christ according to Scripture

Within the Christian interpretation of Scripture the figure of Jesus Christ is especially significant. Among the array of construals of him, the following four positions are most relevant to this essay.

First, there is the relationship of what he is reported to have said, done and undergone to his person. The deepest structure of the testimonies to him is, perhaps, the pattern of ministry, death and resurrection, and this is correlated with the inextricability of his words and actions from his person. The question of who he is is unavoidable, and the meaning of his message and activity in proclaiming the kingdom of God is as inseparable from what happens to his person as it is from who God is and what God does. The culmination of this is in his death and resurrection.

[2] Morgan's use of 'theology' and 'theological' therefore has much in common with my use of 'wisdom'. I see one of the tasks of wisdom being to interrelate what he calls the doctrinal, historical and literary approaches to the Bible.

Second, there is the question of the historical status of those testimonies. Here I would follow Robert Morgan's perceptive summary and appraisal of the quests for the historical Jesus in recent centuries.[3] He examines key issues such as John the Baptist, the kingdom of God, parables, discipleship, healing, exorcism, authority, ethics, eschatology, death and resurrection, and assesses the results of the waves of scholarly activity and its approaches through historical, literary, and sociological methods. He articulates well a recurring paradox. He writes:

> At almost every point it is possible to challenge the historicity of individual narratives, and in the systematic analysis of a Strauss this builds up an impression that very little can be known about Jesus. But that has always been contradicted by the impression of many readers of the gospels that when all allowance is made for the peculiarities of the tradition this Galilean charismatic can be known surprisingly well.[4] Apart from the context and the extraordinary impact of his life, a picture of the man emerges in his relationships with friends and followers, enquirers and opponents . . . How well we can ever know another human being, especially one from a distant time and culture, may still be questioned. Historians and biographers bring much of their own expectations and experience to their narrative task, and there is always room for conflicting interpretations of the data. And some will continue to doubt whether that frame of reference can ever be adequate for interpreting a religious master who became an exclusive focus for so much later religious devotion.[5]

That is another way of suggesting the need for something more than a quest for knowledge of the literal historical reference of the testimonies. That quest leads to irresolvable diversity among

---

[3] For a summary of Morgan's position see 'Jesus', in John Barton, (ed.), *Biblical World*, Oxford: Oxford University Press, 2002, pp. 223–57, together with an excellent bibliography.

[4] That is what I would call a wisdom judgement, taking into account the available knowledge and theories and then making a higher-level judgement.

[5] Morgan, 'Jesus', p. 241.

scholars. In my terms, it is the task of wisdom to cope with this dilemma, taking into account the available knowledge and theories and then making a higher-level judgement. There will of course be a diversity of wisdoms too, but at least the discussion has moved on beyond the foolish expectation that it is resolvable by some agreement about the facts.

All those are points that might apply to the testimonies to many historical figures. They are none the less important for that, but Morgan's account is also helpful in identifying the core problem specifically in relation to Jesus, and why (in my terms) this is of such a nature as to require theological wisdom as well as scholarly precision. It is to do with God. Morgan argues that the distinctive voice of Jesus is heard in relation to God and the kingdom of God. Jesus affirmed the nearness of a God of compassion and generosity, and had a strong sense of God's present activity in the world and of trust in God's future victory over evil, and also of his own role in God's purposes.[6] If Jesus' relationship with God is as central to his identity and message as Morgan says, then the historical truth of Jesus is inextricable from the truth of God.

This is intensified and given its ultimate distinctiveness in the climax of the Gospel story, the resurrection of the crucified Jesus.

---

6 Morgan understands Jesus' ethics and eschatology, for example, in the context of his God-centredness. E.g.:

> The future eschatological aspect of Jesus' uncommon phrase 'the kingdom of God' (the metaphor is scarcely to be found outside Daniel in apocalypses) is better coordinated with his understanding of God translated into convictions about the future of the world. Unlike some modern social thinkers, his focus was on God and so on this world, rather than this world and so its need for transformation. His thinking was theocentric, with all the actions that implied on behalf of the neighbour. ('Jesus', p. 246)

> Against Matthew's tendency to moralize Jesus' proclamation of God's rule (and so subordinate eschatology to ethics), and against Schweitzer's implausible subordination of ethics to an imminent eschatological expectation (making ethics a short-term instruction for the 'meantime', an *Interimsethik*), it seems best to explain both these aspects of Jesus' teaching as arising out of his overwhelming experience of the reality and nearness of God. ('Jesus', p. 249)

The testimonies to this are simultaneously about something happening to this person and about this being ascribed to God. God acts, Jesus appears. The person of Jesus is in this way identified with the action[7] of God. There is a great deal more that could be said about this. With respect to the question of history, I just want to note my agreement with the approach of Markus Bockmuehl in his recent treatment of the resurrection of Jesus.[8] He says that here 'the conscientious historian – *qua* historian – is necessarily entangled in a matter of theological significance'[9] in grappling with testimonies that speak of an event that both is in historical time and space and yet cannot be straightforwardly understood as an event in historical time and space.[10] It suggests 'a generative event of irreducibly colossal magnitude' which 'stretched inherited explanatory categories to breaking point',[11] and 'in the end, the only available category big enough to fit the reality was the theocentric, eschatological affirmation of resurrection, one that is rooted in the living God, the Holy One of Israel: "This Jesus God raised up" (Acts 2.32; cf. Keck 2000: 137–44).'[12]

This combination of testimony to a God-sized event, for which the person of Jesus is constitutive, with the God-centred Jesus portrayed by Morgan, together show that truth-seeking attention to 'the Jesus of history' no less than to 'the Christ of faith' has to question the adequacy of non-theological categories, and in the process question the adequacy of that Jesus of history/Christ of faith distinction.

Finally, there is the question of how all this relates to Jesus and wisdom. In broad outline, the position on this that I find

---

[7] Though 'action' is not an adequate category – or rather, one has to be especially careful with terms such as this that seem, as Morgan suggests, non-mythological, to remember the analogical character of all our language about God.

[8] Markus Bockmuehl, 'Resurrection', in Markus Bockmuehl, (ed.), *The Cambridge Companion to Jesus*, Cambridge: Cambridge University Press, 2001, pp. 102–18.

[9] Ibid., p. 115.

[10] Ibid., p. 109.

[11] Ibid., p. 111.

[12] Ibid., p. 113.

most convincing is as follows. It amounts to trying to find a way between the minimalism of Morgan and the maximalism of Witherington.[13] In his ministry Jesus might be described as a 'prophetic sage' (Witherington),[14] teaching a God-centred wisdom and even perhaps being identified with, among many other things, wisdom. The conception of him as wisdom personified is intensified by his resurrection. The risen Jesus Christ can be described by Paul as 'the wisdom of God' (1 Cor. 1.30),[15] by the later Pauline tradition of Colossians as one 'in whom are hidden all the treasures of wisdom and knowledge' (2.3), by John as the Logos (whose relationship to wisdom is much debated, but seems to me close),[16] and by the book of Revelation as the Lamb that was slaughtered and is worthy 'to receive power and wealth and wisdom and might and honour and glory and blessing' (5.12). This hardly amounts to wisdom being the master category through which to identify Jesus Christ, but it is a significant one; its close, even coinherent relation with others (such as creation, law, prophecy, kingship and teaching) increases its pervasive

[13] It is most in line with contributions such as those of R. W. L. Moberly, 'Solomon and Job: Divine Wisdom in Human Life'; James D. G. Dunn, 'Jesus: Teacher of Wisdom or Wisdom Incarnate?'; and Stephen C. Barton, 'Gospel Wisdom', in Stephen C. Barton, (ed.), *Where Shall Wisdom Be Found? Wisdom in the Bible, the Church and the Contemporary World*, Edinburgh: T. & T. Clark, 1999; for Witherington see Ben Witherington III, *Jesus the Sage: The Pilgrimage of Wisdom*, Minneapolis: Fortress Press, 1994, 2000.

[14] Witherington, *Jesus the Sage*.

[15] Morgan questions whether Paul was developing a 'wisdom Christology' here, but in my broad sense of wisdom he was certainly thinking, with profundity, dialectical intensity and practicality, about the meaning of Jesus Christ crucified. He even claims to have the mind of Christ.

[16] For two summary treatments, both strongly in favour of interpreting the Fourth Gospel in wisdom terms, see Witherington, *Jesus the Sage*, ch. 8 and Sharon H. Ringe, *Wisdom's Friends: Community and Christology in the Fourth Gospel*, Louisville: Westminster John Knox Press, 1999. Cf. Martin Scott, *Sophia and the Johannine Jesus*, Sheffield: Sheffield Academic Press, 1992; Elizabeth Schüssler Fiorenza, *Jesus: Miriam's Child, Sophia's Prophet: Critical Issues in Feminist Christology*, New York: Continuum, 1994; Elizabeth A. Johnson, *She Who Is: The Mystery of God in Feminist Theological Discourse*, New York: Crossroad, 1994.

importance; and for theology it has the added attraction of being a guiding idea for its own discourse, well suited to developing dimensions that go beyond its literal biblical senses while not being discontinuous with them. There are many New Testament puzzles with regard to it, such as the apparent lack of interest by the traditions of Paul and the Fourth Gospel in details of what Jesus taught. But there is more than sufficient to encourage a theologian to develop wisdom as a christological category, and the story of Christian theology after the New Testament shows its continuing the fruitfulness.[17]

Foolishness and wisdom on the way to Emmaus

Within the horizon that has been sketched I will now return to consider the last chapter of Luke's Gospel.

I have deliberately chosen a passage that does not mention wisdom explicitly, but, in its references to the disciples being foolish and slow of heart to believe what the prophets said, to Jesus' interpretation and opening of the Scriptures, to knowing that goes beyond the historical facts, and to the opening of minds to understand the Scriptures, there is sufficient indication of concern for what I take as a wisdom appropriate to the life, death and resurrection of Jesus Christ. Within Luke-Acts this is borne out by other references and resonances, in specifically Lucan material as well as in that shared with Mark and Matthew. Zechariah's prophecy is of one who will 'guide our feet into the way of peace' (Lk. 2.79; cf. Prov. 3.17 on wisdom: 'all her ways are peace', and Lk. 24.36 'Peace be with you'). Jesus as a boy was 'filled with wisdom' (Lk. 2.40), amazed the teachers in the Temple with 'his understanding and his answers', and 'increased in wisdom' (Lk. 2.52). It is at least worth discussing to what extent wisdom even in the narrow sense (associated explicitly with the genre and the personified figure in OT and intertestamental literature) is reflected in various features of Jesus' ministry (especially in 'Q')

[17] Cf. on the patristic period the contribution of Frances Young to this volume.

such as the announcement of his coming, the Spirit coming upon him, his testing, his teachings in various forms such as beatitudes, parables, aphorisms, pronouncements on the law, and apocalyptic sayings, his wonder-working, his debates, his rejection, and his gathering of followers called 'learners'.[18] The sayings about what is here being greater than Jonah and greater than Solomon (Lk. 11.29–32 and par.) show in relation to prophecy and wisdom the complexity of applying categories and titles to Jesus – these are here applied simultaneously alongside each other and are also transcended. If it is the case that both Jesus and those who testified to him were shaped by an intertestamental Judaism in which 'there was a tendency for the old categories to be merged – law and wisdom, but also wisdom and prophecy or apocalyptic vision',[19] then identifying pure genres is less important than doing justice to the reality of Jesus Christ who invites a convergence and transformation of categories.

The key wisdom question in Luke 24 is therefore about the simultaneous multiple transformation occasioned by the resurrection of Jesus, with special reference to its cognitive aspect. I will attempt to formulate its wisdom from various angles.[20]

A new beginning of wisdom?

If 'the fear of the Lord is the beginning of wisdom, and the knowledge of the Holy One is insight' (Prov. 9.10) then it is wise to pay attention to the role of God in this chapter. The event that opens it, the resurrection, is so obviously attributed to God that this is not even mentioned. The responses to the resurrection include perplexity, amazement, startled terror, fear, wonder and joy. All of this culminates in the disciples worshipping the ascending Jesus and then being continually in the Temple blessing

---

18 For a very strong statement of the connections in these respects and many more, see Witherington, *Jesus the Sage*, ch. 5.

19 A. N. Wilder, *Jesus' Parables and the War of Myths: Essays on Imagination in the Scriptures*, Philadelphia: Fortress Press, 1982, p. 79.

20 The main way will be something like Morgan's third type of New Testament theology.

God. And God is literally the last word of this Gospel. So we have the fear, and we have the Lord; and the focus on God is inseparable from the focus on Jesus, who is concerned, among other things, with overcoming foolishness and opening minds to the right understanding of Scriptures. All of this in biblical terms amounts to the conditions for what one might call a new beginning of wisdom in response to what is beyond its previous conceptions.

The person who at the beginning of the Gospel is filled with wisdom and amazes the teachers in the Temple here interprets the Scriptures. Yet, even as he does this and their hearts burn within them, the vital recognition of who he is does not occur through this conversation: it happens only through the breaking of bread. The main point of the teaching about himself is not contained in the teaching: that just opens the way for the recognition and vanishing in the breaking of bread. There is here perhaps a wisdom about the limits of wisdom – even when it is taught by Jesus – and *a fortiori* about the limits of textually-conveyed wisdom; also about the strange realities of absence and presence, and about what later tradition called word and sacrament.

The contemporaneity of the living Jesus Christ (and of the Spirit that, he says, 'I am sending upon you' – Lk. 24.49) with all attempts to understand him and what happened to him does not amount to a safe rule for sound interpretation of history or of Scripture. Forms of theological or interpretative closure, whether in method or content, are disturbed and opened up by this living presence. Luke repeatedly makes this point in Acts, where Peter has his scripturally-grounded conceptions of uncleanness and the limits of the people of God revolutionized by a vision (Acts 10—11); and Stephen, in the longest piece of scriptural interpretation in Luke-Acts, so profoundly challenges his audience's understanding of the meaning of Scripture and recent history that they stone him to death – and it is worth noting that just before this speech his wisdom is emphasized twice.[21] Here in the last chapter of

[21] He was one of seven 'full of the Spirit and of wisdom' (Acts 6.3) and his opponents 'could not withstand the wisdom and the Spirit with which he spoke' (6.10). Within his speech he says that 'Moses was instructed

Luke's Gospel the ultimate surprise of the resurrection signalled by the opened tomb is followed by the opening of the Scriptures (v. 32), the opening of eyes (v. 31), and the opening of minds (v. 45). One might also say that there was an opening up to the whole world ('to all nations' – v. 47) and an opening of heaven ('power from on high' – v. 49; 'he withdrew from them and was carried up into heaven' – v. 51).[22] Taken together this amounts to a new transformative dynamic, most vividly described by Luke as the rushing mighty wind and tongues of fire at Pentecost in the first chapter of Acts.

At the heart of this dynamic in Luke 24 is a transformative exchange or transfer. The chapter is not just about Jesus but also about what happens between him and the disciples, and *in* the disciples. There is walking together, conversation, blessing, touching, feeding, and great joy. The opening of eyes, minds and Scriptures is part of a transfer of responsibility by Jesus to the disciples, a commissioning as witnesses, followed by a blessing that both seals this and begins a new period in which the absence or ascended presence of Jesus leaves them with new responsibility. But it is not only about new responsibility. The ones who carry the responsibility are to be transformed and to carry a message that requires repentance and forgiveness of sins. This is a further dimension of what has already been going on during their discipleship, and the decisive event is to be the 'power from on high', the sending of the Holy Spirit. That is the ultimate transfer, a sharing of life from God, and it is about whole persons and communities being transformed. Again Stephen, who in Acts is the one who most nearly re-enacts the pattern of Jesus Christ,[23] is a key figure, showing how closely wisdom is linked

in all the wisdom of the Egyptians and was powerful in his words and deeds' (7.22), which resonates through later patristic commendation of borrowing from Greek and Roman thought (often called 'spoiling the Egyptians' by analogy with the Israelite 'borrowing' of jewellery before their Exodus from Egypt).

[22] I am grateful to Rachel Muers for the significance of this theme of 'opening'.

[23] Stephen in Acts 6—7 is 'full of the Spirit', serves at table, does 'great

to being filled with the Spirit, to the interpretation of Scripture, and also to good living, service, community-building, personal transfiguration, and good dying.

Figuration and fulfilment: supersession or transformation?

The Scriptures have appeared several times in what has just been said. How might their significance be summed up? Clearly they are integral to the transfer of understanding, responsibility and transformative power, and Acts shows their continuing role in the early Church. But this raises huge questions, above all about the central thrust of the biblical interpretation in this chapter: that the Scriptures Jesus is interpreting are about him and are fulfilled through him. For Christians, the christological interpretation of the Old Testament in the New Testament is of great significance for their identity, and is especially so in relation to Jews. What does one say if (to refer to the two leading figures in Morgan's essay) one is not completely happy with Barth's way of understanding this and is definitely unhappy with Bultmann's?

John David Dawson begins his book, *Christian Figural Reading and the Fashioning of Identity*,[24] by asking 'whether there is a kind of Christian reading of the Old Testament that might express Christianity's relation to Judaism while respecting the independent religious identity of Jews, and, more broadly, the diverse identities of all human beings'.[25] He finds the possibility of this kind of biblical interpretation in various ancient and modern Jewish and Christian thinkers who have faced the issue of the Christian figural or typological interpretation of the Old Testament.

---

wonders and signs among the people', is a powerful controversialist, is plotted against and accused (with the participation of elders and scribes) of blasphemy and attacking the Temple, is tried and accused by false witnesses, his face appears transfigured, he accuses the council of repeating the persecutions of their ancestors, while he is being stoned he prays that the sin not be held against his killers, and then he is killed.

[24] John David Dawson, *Christian Figural Reading and the Fashioning of Identity*, Berkeley: University of California Press, 2002.

[25] Ibid., pp. 3f.

Dawson begins with two stories told by Luke, the disciples meeting Jesus on the road to Emmaus and Philip meeting the Ethiopian eunuch on the road to Gaza. He ends his own journey (which takes him through thinkers such as Origen, Augustine, Calvin, Erich Auerbach, Hans Frei and Daniel Boyarin) at a place that I find more habitable and potentially fruitful in this respect than either Barth (key aspects of whose position on christological interpretation Dawson deals with through engagement with Hans Frei) or Bultmann (whose position as regards the transformative potential of Scripture bears some more distant resemblances to that of Origen of Alexandria, but whose theological engagement with the Old Testament is radically different).[26] In brief, Dawson argues for a position that gives a theological account of figural reading as being not primarily about texts and meanings but about rendering God's historical, transformative action intelligible. Dawson says provocatively:

> Whether we still think naively that texts 'have' their meanings, the way capitalists own their property, or – with more sophistication or readerly effort – that textual meaning is forever distanced and deferred – we still instinctively bring to Christian figural reading the assumption that, whatever else it may be about, it must concern texts and meanings. The question about the intelligibility of a divine performance is something we would rather not consider, for the idea that the prophet Isaiah had, in his own right and not only as a consequence of some later Reader's strange interpretation, once referred in some oblique fashion to the person of Jesus who had not yet appeared in history and, in so doing, sought to render *intelligible* a certain divine performance, is, for most of us, historiographically absurd; it is, in fact, the height of *unintelligibility*. Yet any effort to understand Christian figural reading as fundamentally a matter of texts and the presence or absence of meaning, rather than a matter of rendering God's

[26] Dawson is concerned to rehabilitate major elements of Origen's biblical interpretation, which unlike Bultmann's builds a great deal of Old Testament interpretation into its theology.

> historical performances intelligible, is doomed to theological irrelevance, however much contemporary theoretical sense it might make.[27]

Figural reading is concerned about historical reference and the literal sense, and also about God's transformative presence in history and directly in human lives now, with an orientation to a radically transformed humanity in the future:

> The charge of hermeneutical supersessionism, the fear of it, and the defenses against it are all embedded in this conflicted dynamic of past realities and future possibilities. The overwhelming presumption of classical Christian figural reading, at least as it has been characterized in the writings examined in this book, is that the Christian Bible is read Christianly when it is seen to depict the ongoing historical outworking of a divine intention to transform humanity over the course of time. Moreover, Christian figural readers insist that the history of Israel, Jesus of Nazareth, his immediate followers, and the Church are all somehow ingredients in this overarching divine intention. That intention and its outworking in history are regarded as alternately clear and obscure, reliable and unpredictable. Figural readers turn to the text of the Bible for clues and models useful for unravelling as much as they can of what they think they discern as the mysterious working of God in the lives of people over time. What is always ultimately at stake is the reality and the proper characterization of a divine performance in the material world of space and time, a performance that defines the personal, social, ethical, and political obligations of Christians in the present, as well as their stance toward past and future.[28]

There are ways of reading Scripture, and of championing the literal sense, which resist the continual transformation of what already exists (including the literal reading) into something different, due to fear of the destabilizing novelty that makes all

27 Dawson, *Christian Figural Reading*, p. 6.
28 Ibid., p. 216.

things new. There are also ways of reading Scripture that lose touch with the literal sense through an interpretation in which the letter does not remain in the spirit. The latter is especially vulnerable to supersessionism in relation to Judaism. Dawson's position extends without supplanting former Jewish meanings, and concludes with what he calls the 'unexpected claim that fulfilments are more, and yet again are not more, than their figures'.[29]

In relation to Luke 24, the implications of Dawson might be to inspire a theology that succeeds in combining Barth's concern for the Old Testament, the person of Jesus Christ, and the reality of God with Bultmann's concern for personal transformation and the possibilities of history, while doing better justice than either to the ongoing significance of Judaism. Such a theology would be worthy of the new beginning in wisdom that I have discovered in the chapter.

Other ways of seeking wisdom

A wisdom interpretation of Luke 24 might explore other paths too. I will simply sketch four of them in bare outline to indicate some of the possibilities.

First is the historical way. This would especially involve historical examination of the resurrection stories in Luke and other sources, taking into account the vast secondary literature. It would be too much to expect what are sometimes called 'assured historical results' from this (above all for the reasons suggested by Bockmuehl and Morgan above), but it is not necessarily only the end point that makes a journey worthwhile. Morgan has summed up well the value as well as the appropriately modest expectations of theologically significant results that we should associate with historical inquiry into such matters. In Luke, it is noteworthy that the two disciples seem to have all the historical facts but are still called foolish by Jesus. History is about far more than trying to prove or disprove certain facts. The whole historical enterprise is a major modern resource for wisdom. It embraces historical

[29] Dawson, *Christian Figural Reading*, p. 218.

philology, textual criticism, critical examination of multiple sources, redaction criticism, the history of the reception and theological understanding of texts, contextual studies conducted by many disciplines, attempts to get inside the 'common sense' of a period, efforts to portray people, events, institutions, cultures, or developments, and acknowledgement of lacunae, uncertainties, ambiguities, and apparently irreconcilable conflicts of interpretation or judgement. The complexities, the multiple dimensions, the interplays of light and shade, the irreducibly different standpoints, the abundant surplus of meanings, and the intensities of suffering and joy both call for wisdom and expose the inadequacies of anything less.

Faced with all this, claims of historical reliability, clarity and factuality may have to be modest and subject to many qualifications, but that chastened confidence is in the name of the broader, richer reliability of a wisdom that is alert to the contributions as well as to the limitations of historical reasoning. Scriptural reasoning seeking the wisdom of God might find in Luke 24 a paradigm of how events and texts become signs that are open to continually fresh extensions, connections and implications when interpreted in the Spirit of the risen Jesus Christ.

Second is the imaginative way. One thinks here of the arts, such as painting, literature in prose and poetry, theatre, music or film. There is wisdom to be learnt from these, and each has its own distinctiveness that communicates its perceptions in ways irreducible to other forms.[30] It is also worth considering the more imaginative modes of interpretation. These are common in sermons, meditations, and a range of practices in spirituality – the Exercises of St Ignatius Loyola are widely used, for example, and many other Christian traditions have their own characteristic ways of engaging imaginatively with Scripture in order to distil its wisdom for living. One of the most provocative interpreters of Scripture in recent centuries has been Søren Kierkegaard. His multiple retellings of the story of Abraham in *Fear and Trembling*

---

[30] Cf. Jeremy Begbie, (ed.), *Sounding the Depths*, London: SCM Press, 2002.

are profound interpretation in the subjunctive mood: what might have happened, how characters might have responded. The historian is inevitably primarily concerned with the indicative, however many hypotheses are considered. The artist or imaginative interpreter can try to recreate the conversation on the road to Emmaus, can experiment with 'what if . . . ?' scenarios, or can assume that Cleopas's companion was a woman disciple – and/or his wife.

Third is the interscriptural way. I have already mentioned Dawson's concern to bring Christian figural interpretation into dialogue with Jewish ways of interpreting their Scriptures. The wisdom potential in interpreting our Scriptures in dialogue with each other – Jews, Christians, Muslims, Hindus and others sitting down together to read and interpret in dialogue – is immense. It may be that the apparently roundabout way of listening to each other wrestle over our Scriptures would prove the surest way to understand something of the richness, depth and hermeneutical subtlety of our different traditions. Each has had forms of study and collegiality gathered round their own Scriptures; there are now signs of new forms of joint collegiality being developed, where participation in one's own community is seen as compatible with and even enriched by such joint study.[31]

Fourth is the way with which Morgan concludes his essay: what might be called the devotional way. The formation of liturgies, lectionaries, the Church Year, and patterns of prayer, meditation and spirituality, and the composing of hymns, disciplines, ethical maxims, and so on, might be seen as the sphere in which the lived meaning of Scripture has been most thoroughly embodied over the centuries in corporate and more personal practices that have tried to distil the wisdom of Scripture and the wisdom of living before

[31] For the past six years I have been part of the Society for Scriptural Reasoning which meets at the Annual Meeting of the American Academy of Religion, and gathers Jewish, Christian and Muslim scholars, philosophers and theologians to interpret their various Scriptures in conversation with each other. While it is still young, members of the Society are already convinced of the great potential of this form of engagement between the three Abrahamic faiths and their interrelated Scriptures.

God in our world. Luke 24 has had more than its fair share of attention in this sphere, and we would have to immerse ourselves in the study and even inhabiting of such practices in order to begin to take the measure of its still-growing significance.

God

In conclusion, I return to that last word of Luke's Gospel. I am acutely aware that I have discussed the topic of 'Jesus Christ the Wisdom of God' with no direct exploration of what wisdom in God might be. Yet this is the biggest issue that faces theological discussion of the topic. I would only say that the multi-volume work which this requires is unlikely to find a better motto than that given by Augustine in Book XV of his *De Trinitate*: 'Just, then, as we distinctively call the only Word of God by the name of wisdom, although the Holy Spirit and the Father are also wisdom in a general sense, so the Spirit is distinctively called by the term love, although both Father and Son are love in a general sense.'[32] It is in the love of this wisdom and the wisdom of this love that the Christian interpretation of Scripture finds its distinctive fulfilment.

---

32 Saint Augustine, *The Trinity*, introduced, trans. and ed. Edmund Hill OP, New York: New City Press, 1991, p. 420.

2. Jesus Christ, the Wisdom of God (2)

ROBERT MORGAN

Lady Margaret and John Fisher would surely be puzzled by the shape of our modern theological faculties, with their academic specialisms and carved up syllabuses. More than that, they would surely be shocked if our conference pairings of biblical teachers with systematic theologians were taken to imply that as historical critics the former merely hand over their 'results' to the latter – who then cook them into real theology, or speaking of God today. It is true that many biblical scholars modestly or indignantly deny that they are theologians, and that some systematic theologians are unduly deferential to biblical scholarship, but however differently we understand our work David Ford and I will agree with our ancient benefactors and with Schleiermacher[1] that systematic theologians do their own exegesis, in friendly and sometimes critical conversation with biblical specialists, and that Old and New Testament theologians can also do contemporary theology, albeit with different accents, in and through their historical and exegetical scholarship. We are therefore both concerned (from different angles) with contemporary Christian reading of Scripture, and talking responsibly today of the God whom we worship.

The relationship of this theological interpretation of Scripture to a normal biblical scholarship which says little directly about that theological task calls for some attention here. What follows

[1] 'Every theologian must do one's own exegesis . . . There is very little here, too, one can allow oneself to take over directly from the specialists.' Friederich Schleiermacher, *Brief Outline on the Study of Theology* §89 (1830²), ET Richmond: John Knox Press, 1966, p. 46.

will therefore say less than is needed about the intricacies and uncertainties in the biblical data on Jesus as God's Wisdom,[2] and more about how these texts are appropriated by those who speak of God confessionally while also inhabiting a culture that is generally sceptical about such discourse.

The historical exegesis cultivated by normal biblical scholarship is indispensable to any critical theological interpretation of Scripture (and therefore integral to theological education), but it does not always coincide with, much less exhaust, Christians' engagement with their Scriptures. Part of its attraction both to a church that seeks to communicate with those outside its doors, and to the modern university which imposes no religious tests on its members, is that it can be done as well by unbelievers as by believers. However, that poses a question about the relationship between this exegesis and the way that Christians read their Scriptures on the assumption that these speak of the God whom they themselves worship. What believers discover in Scripture may be influenced by their attempts to shape their own living and thinking and praying in accord with its witness.

The usual (unstated) assumption about this relationship is that we all use the same exegetical methods and share broadly similar interpretative aims, but that the believer in addition accepts the truth of the texts' witness, and perhaps seeks to apply it to the needs of a congregation. *Applicatio* is quite separate from *explicatio*.

In most matters that is surely right. We have to understand what a text is saying before we can decide whether it has anything important to say to our situation. But where the subject-matter is as elusive as it often is in religious texts one may ask how far two readers occupying different standpoints are even seeing the same 'thing'. Personal alignment with the witness of a text may lead a believer to describe quite differently what it is about. Even the agreement that it is a 'religious' text may be deceptive, given the very different theories about religion which that label

---

[2] See, e.g., J. D. G. Dunn, *Christology in the Making*, London: SCM Press, 1980, ch. 6.

covers. The particular aims which guide how a text is read, and the wider context present to the interpreter, may affect how it is assimilated and described. Value-judgements are not separate from the whole range of possible meanings. Those who reject the apparently plain meaning of a scriptural text that conflicts with their religious convictions, for example, may be appealing to what they consider the sense of Scripture as a whole. One may disagree with their judgement and disapprove of their reading strategy, but the debate that follows would then reveal disagreement about the real subject-matter of the text being discussed.

Definition of the subject-matter becomes important as soon as this is disputed. Until quite recently there was in English faculties of theology, even in secular universities, enough tacit agreement about the reality of God to make such a discussion seem unnecessary.[3] In fact the problem had already been signalled in late nineteenth-century liberal Protestant theology by the shift from describing the biblical texts in doctrinal terms to a preference for talking about Israelite, Jewish, and early Christian 'religion'. The implications of this modern turn to 'religion' were not obvious because the ways in which liberal theologians understood much of the biblical (prophetic) 'religion' corresponded to their own beliefs and values, and what they disliked about it also had analogues in the Catholic Church nearby. 'Religion' was thus a category enabling them to understand the Bible in their own terms, both sympathetically and critically, as well as placing it in the historical distance. A change of perspective was taking over biblical studies, but because biblical religion was studied historically in a culture where history could still be thought of as a vehicle of God's Spirit, and this research was situated in Christian theological faculties, the change was assimilated without difficulty. It was, however, a change. 'Religions' invite analysis and description. The term allows an outsider's standpoint, whereas 'theology', when properly used with an adjective identifying the community whose talk of God is intended, is a more confessional

---

[3] A good indication of this was the custom of some (not many) of our university teachers (i.e. not too long ago) who began lectures or courses with public prayer and others who half apologized for not doing so.

term, despite often consisting largely of historical description[4] and philosophical analysis.

Christian theological interpretation of Scripture, that is, talking of God by interpreting these texts, presupposes some alignment of the interpreter with their religious witness.[5] That does not (quite) mean that only a believer can do it, as though faith were always so clear-cut, but it implies a sympathetic openness to what the authors were trying to say and do which has a different texture from what is normally required by historical exegesis, description or reconstruction.

Such an imprecise and metaphorical indication of the difference (of 'texture') between historical and theological exegesis is intended to suggest that the interpreters' differences of standpoint are often invisible in scholarly work. Historians of religion (usually) show sensitivity and empathy for the texts they are interpreting, and biblical theologians do not have to make their own confessional standpoint explicit when the texts are themselves explicitly confessional. Exegesis of such texts can of itself be 'theology', corresponding to the exegete's own contemporary talk of God. Whether or not in any given case this is so, the exegete is under no obligation to say. Further, someone reading a piece of New Testament exegesis can read it as theology (i.e. as genuinely speaking of God) even if the exegete intended no more than explicating the words, and actually was quite sceptical about their reference. Theology, like beauty, is at least partly in the eye or intention of the reader or author, and this allows some historical and theological exegesis to coincide.[6] It is only where an interpreter disagrees with the way a text articulates its theological subject-matter, and so engages in *Sachkritik* (criticism of the inadequate formulation in the light of the *Sache*, or theological

4 *Brief Outline* §28, p. 26. In acknowledging a debt to Schleiermacher I remember with gratitude also the conduit, the late Professor Gerhard Ebeling.

5 For a classic expression see the Prefaces to Barth's *Epistle to the Romans*, 2nd edn, 1921, ET London: Oxford University Press, 1933, esp. pp. 17, 19.

6 Cf. R. Bultmann, 'The Problem of a Theological Exegesis of the New Testament' (1925), ET in *The Beginnings of Dialectic* (sic) *Theology*, Richmond: John Knox Press, 1968, p. 256.

subject-matter itself), that theological interpretation is seen to go beyond historical exegesis, and to involve a kind of evaluation which exceeds the historian's brief.

This allusion to the theological 'subject-matter' (*Sache*) of Scripture, and implicit appeal for interpretations which align themselves with this, recalls where Barth and Bultmann were united over *Sachexegese*, and where they were divided over *Sachkritik* in the 1920s.[7] From an inner-theological perspective their disagreements loomed large at the time, but in the context of the secularization of biblical scholarship, visible at the end of the nineteenth century[8] and more aggressive today, their shared aim to communicate the Christian gospel is far more significant than their disagreements. The same can be said about the different approaches of David Ford who owes more to Barth, and myself who owes more to Bultmann, as we reflect on how to understand and communicate the witness of Scripture to the revelation of God in Christ, making contemporary Christian sense of what we read, if need be against the cultural stream of a biblical scholarship which is under no obligation to speak of God today.

The Psalmist's lament, 'How shall we sing the Lord's song in a strange land?' (Ps. 137.4), poses a challenge which Barth, followed by Hans Frei, answered by describing the Church's faith and letting the theory catch up with the practice. Bultmann, on the other hand, looked for a general theory and so led his pupils into deep hermeneutical waters (of Babylon). Barth's approach rejuvenized narrative theological interpretation of Scripture (as well as dogmatics), and Bultmann's rejuvenized New Testament theology, properly so-called. My contribution to our theme aims to elucidate the latter, using our Jesus Wisdom topic as an illustration.

---

[7] See Barth, *Romans*, pp.16–20 and Bultmann, *The Beginnings*, pp. 119, 240. Also R. Bultmann, *Faith and Understanding* (1933), ET London: SCM Press, 1969, pp. 72, 81, 86, 92, 218, 240, 280.

[8] The classic expression of this shift from New Testament theology as 'doctrine', to the history of religion is W. Wrede, *On Task and Method of 'New Testament Theology' (so-called)* (1897), ET in R. Morgan, *The Nature of New Testament Theology*, London: SCM Press, 1973. New edition forthcoming.

Christian theological interpretation of Scripture has always had *doctrinal*, *literary* and *historical* components, on account both of the texts being interpreted (religious literature from the ancient world) and the aims of these interpreters (to clarify Christian *belief* which centres on a *historical* person illuminated by the witness of these *texts*). This activity, usually called 'New Testament theology', grew out of an older 'biblical theology' at the start of the nineteenth century when a newly developed historical consciousness put pressure on the traditional interpretations of these texts. The proof-texting (*dicta probantia*) of the old Protestant biblical theology gave way to historical description of the New Testament authors' beliefs, but these were typically described and organized in Christian doctrinal terms. That clarified the subject-matter and assisted Christians' appropriation of their Scripture and use of it to scrutinize contemporary belief and practice.

By the end of the nineteenth century the idealist metaphysics of history which had made F. C. Baur's historical theology genuinely theological was so attenuated, and historical research in theology had become so independent of dogmatics, that a case could be made for dissolving New Testament theology into the history of early Christian religion.[9] Some doctrinal language might be useful in describing, say, Paul's thought,[10] but the belief that it referred to a genuinely theological subject-matter was becoming optional, and therefore abandoned in the practice of the now more historical and less hermeneutical discipline, even though most practitioners personally adhered to it. Where the discipline's historical methods and tasks implied historical *aims* Wrede was right to place a 'so-called' before the name of the discipline, and (better) to change it to 'the *history* of early Christian religion and theology'.[11] The justification for the traditional name New Testament *theology*, lies in the aim of interpreters like Bultmann and his pupils (against Wrede, p. 115) to speak of God today

---

[9] Wrede, *Task and Method.*
[10] Ibid., pp. 76, 87, 107.
[11] Ibid., p. 116.

through the interpretation of these texts. That requires using historical methods and performing historical tasks in the interests of a more than 'merely historical' aim. It resists allowing these methods and tasks to substitute a 'purely historical' *aim* for the traditional theological ones. Historical research stands guard against distorting the witness of these ancient writers, and can contribute much towards understanding them, but it cannot dictate the terms of reference without removing the theology from New Testament theology, and so losing a main reason for studying this collection of religious literature.

When the pretensions of historical research are cut back, New Testament theology moves on into its most natural frame of reference, a frame implied by the phrase *interpretation* of (religious) *texts*, or literature. The *literary* aspects of Christian theological interpretation of Scripture were always dominant until the nineteenth century. The *doctrinal* type of biblical theology, introduced in Protestant orthodoxy and pietism, was only a small part of scriptural interpretation even there. The literary interest has now recovered a prominent place in biblical scholarship and can be expected to influence future New Testament theologies.

When our New Testament theological theme 'Jesus Christ the Wisdom of God' is viewed through these three (ideal) types of New Testament theology, the weaknesses of the first and second are as clear as the fruitfulness of the third. The theme itself is attractive,[12] especially in places of learning. Wisdom is even more fashionable than goodness and honesty, though true wisdom surely includes both (the reverse does not hold). Practical wisdom (σωφροσύνη) holds a central place in religious ethics and *sophia* is also rightly treasured for being a feminine word in Greek (and Hebrew and Latin and German and French – the English and Welsh are no help for obvious reasons), and so offering a balance

---

[12] See, e.g., E. Schüssler Fiorenza, *In Memory of Her*, New York: Crossroad / London: SCM Press, 1983; eadem, *Jesus: Miriam's Child, Sophia's Prophet*, New York: Continuum / London: SCM Press, 1994; S. Schroer, *Wisdom has Built Her House*, Collegeville: Liturgical Press, 2000, with further bibliography; Celia M. Deutsch, *Lady Wisdom, Jesus and the Sages*, Valley Forge: Trinity Press International, 1996.

to the predominantly masculine and patriarchal imagery for God in the Judaeo-Christian tradition. It is unfortunate that the erotic Lady Wisdom seeks out only male disciples,[13] but the potential of this language is far-reaching.[14] It is, of course, *imagery*. That warns us against literalism and suggests that literary critical types of interpretation are likely to be most appropriate.

The New Testament itself has no problems with the tradition's masculine imagery for God and a male saviour, but readers rightly bring their own questions and concerns to a text. Only that is no substitute for hearing what the text itself is getting at. Authorial intention, where it can be inferred with some probability by historical study, remains the best control against arbitrary interpretations which do violence to a text by imposing the interpreter's beliefs on it. Talk of God's wisdom helped some to express the truth of the gospel, not by redressing gender imbalance but proclaiming the now risen Lord's unity with God. Identifying Jesus as personified Wisdom, God's instrument in creation who made her abode in Israel, is mythological speech which expressed, and helped some to hold in their imaginations, their basic belief in Jesus as the revelation of God. Whether this basic belief is expressed less mythologically in the language of agency, or more metaphysically in a logos theology, it requires some theory of the unity between Jesus and God his Father. But these Wisdom passages in the New Testament probably originated in liturgical contexts and were not part of a worked-out incarnational theology. They were not intended to explain *how* Jesus could be the saving revelation of God. This wisdom idea is *mythos* not *logos*, and therefore not, strictly speaking, a Christology which expresses conceptually what the myth narrates pictorially. The phrase 'Wisdom Christology' is therefore potentially misleading,[15] a product of a one-sidedly doctrinal emphasis in New Testament theology. When this 'makes doctrine

---

[13] I owe this observation to Dr Teresa Morgan.

[14] See E. A. Johnson, *She Who Is*, New York: Crossroad, 1992.

[15] 'Christology' in this context is shorthand for 'christological language and imagery'. It is admittedly difficult to avoid the word when referring to any specific example.

out of what is not doctrine'[16] and turns myth into metaphysics instead of interpreting these texts in accord with their intention to *celebrate* Jesus as the saving revelation of God, rather than define his nature, it is open to the charge of misreading the New Testament. Finding the later *doctrine* of pre-existence or incarnation in these hymnic passages is anachronistic and involves a category mistake.

This way of speaking of God doctrinally by interpreting the Bible in doctrinal terms is what those who have not followed Bultmann in his move beyond (not behind) Wrede usually mean by 'biblical theology', and it partly explains the ill-repute into which the phrase fell as a result of the 1960s reaction against the 'biblical theology movement'. The doctrinal type of New Testament theology, still powerful in conservative circles, makes the transition from biblical text to contemporary theology too easy. It expects its doctrinally articulated interpretations to provide a substitute for systematic theology instead of allowing these two forms of contemporary theology to complement and stimulate one another. Its value and partial validity lie in the way its use of doctrinal categories preserves some sense of the Christian subject-matter of Scripture, and helps Christians appropriate these texts by relating them to their own religious life and theological thinking, but it seems artificial to those whose understanding of Scripture is enriched by a historical sense and literary sensitivity.[17]

One way of deflating the doctrinal claims made for the wisdom texts is by labelling them 'myth'. This calls for a literary type of theological interpretation less reductive than demythologizing but more credible than interpretations which assume that strong cognitive claims are being made by these liturgical formulations. 'Myth' engages the imagination; its truth claims are elusive. Its early Church contexts are doxological rather than argumentative. Failure to respect that distinction between doctrine and

[16] Wrede, *Task and Method*, p. 75.

[17] Wrede, *Task and Method*, p. 78, savages such New Testament theology as 'an arid and boring subject. It means that the thought of the New Testament is not reaching us in the living freshness which belongs to it.'

myth prompted the 1970s English debate about 'the myth of God incarnate'.[18] This common confusion between myth and theology or doctrine was probably partly caused by the doctrinal type of New Testament theology.

That emphasis had long been superseded in liberal theology, if not in conservative congregations, by the *historical* type of New Testament theology (so-called) advocated by Wrede. This could make little theological use of the myth of Jesus as Wisdom. Liberal theologians were understandably unsympathetic to myth at a time when their literalist opponents were reading it as doctrine, and our wisdom theme was virtually ignored in Bousset's history of religions classic *Kyrios Christos*.[19] Bultmann recognized the importance of the wisdom myth in the background of the Johannine prologue[20] and recent scholarship has found it elsewhere in John and in Matthew,[21] in addition to 1 Corinthians and some probably liturgical fragments, but the big question for theological interpretation is not whether historically sensitive exegetes are right to find the theme in all these New Testament writings, but how it might be relevant for speaking of God today. The answer of some liberal and now some more conservative theologians who hope to draw theology out of their historical study is to be found in a newly popular topic of historical Jesus research: Jesus the Sage.[22]

---

[18] See M. F. Wiles in J. Hick, (ed.), *The Myth of God Incarnate*, London: SCM Press, 1977. Other contributors to this debate, both radical and conservative, added to the confusion.

[19] On the different evaluations of myth, see R. A. Johnson, *The Origins of Demythologizing*, Leiden: Brill, 1974.

[20] The not very prominent key texts are Jn 11.19 (contrast Lk. 7.35), 11.28–30, and 23.34 (contrast Lk. 11.49). See n. 21.

[21] E.g., M. A. Scott, *Sophia and the Johannine Jesus*, Sheffield: JSOT Press, 1992; Deutsch, *Lady Wisdom*.

[22] B. Witherington, *Jesus the Sage*, Minneapolis: Fortress Press, 1994, combines this motif with Jesus as prophet, unlike B. Mack and G. Downing who see Jesus as a Cynic preacher. See also B. B. Scott, 'Jesus as Sage: an innovating voice in common wisdom', in J. G. Gammie and L. G. Perdue, (eds.), *The Sage in Israel and the Ancient Near East*, Winona Lake: Eisenbruns, 1990.

This new trend highlights aspects of the style and content of Jesus' teaching which had been underestimated. The criteria of dissimilarity and coherence have sometimes been used to bury aspects of the Gospels' pictures of Jesus. He evidently used aphorisms and appealed to ordinary experience in a proverbial but also paradoxical way. Egyptian and some Jewish wisdom is socially conservative, upper-class, and academic. Even Kierkegaard's conservative and privileged academics can see that Jesus of Nazareth was very different from Jesus ben Sirach, who was devoted to the law, the Temple and the priesthood. But that did not justify the twentieth-century recovery of eschatology blinding scholars to this other aspect of the gospel evidence. Greek counter-cultural wisdom is a more relevant model for the Galilean preacher of the kingdom, and John's presentation of Jesus' riddling discourse might preserve more historical echoes than is usually allowed. But whether or not this model does justice to the eschatological urgency of Jesus' talk of God, the main question is how (if at all) historical reconstructions of Jesus can combine with the New Testament christological witness to inform Christian talk of God today. For Jesus to be confessed in faith as the Wisdom of God he must have been at least a wise man, and that is a historical claim, but Paul's contrasting human and divine wisdom in 1 Cor. 1–2 makes this an unpromising way forward. Historical judgements about Jesus are important. They may erode or undermine christological claims. But they will not on their own bear much theological weight.

The historical type of New Testament theology seems unable to move beyond its discovery of wisdom (and other theological) ideas in and behind the New Testament witness. In trying to return Jesus to his first-century witnesses it could not keep him (or them) in our modern theological time.[23] The historical judgement that Jesus was a wise man (cf. Mk 6.2, par. Mt. 13.54; Jn 2.25, and even Josephus, *Ant.* 18.63) is congruent with the biblical witness to him as the wisdom of God (cf. Mt. 11.19,

[23] Albert Schweitzer said this about historical Jesus research: *The Quest of the Historical Jesus,* London: SCM Press, 2000, pp. 478–9, but it is equally applicable to a 'purely historical' descriptive New Testament Christology.

28–30; 23.34, 37),[24] but it does not lead even to this, let alone to a modern Christology. Constructions of the 'historical Jesus' (so-called) provide no ladder to what the New Testament writers and subsequent Christian orthodoxy have said about him, and often lead to versions of Christianity which break decisively with this, as Ritschl, Kähler, Dean Church and others observed. The methods of historical Jesus research (valid as they are) make it a potential enemy of orthodoxy and are always in some tension with Christian reading of Scripture. Apologists engage in this research as much to unmask their opponents' concealed polemics against Christianity as to learn anything new about Jesus. They make proposals which they claim are more true to the evidence than damaging reconstructions masquerading as 'the real Jesus'.[25]

It seems clear that New Testament theology must start at the other end, with the witness of these literary texts, and interpret them in a way that is both historically responsible and theologically suggestive today.[26] Proclamation elicits faith (where and when God wills) by communicating the biblical message about God in Jesus. In its search for understanding faith might then ask behind the texts about their congruence with what can be known about Jesus by critical historical methods. This will not demonstrate the truth of their witness but may enhance their credibility and clarify their meaning.

---

[24] Not that the theme is explicit in Matthew (or John), or likely to be noticed by anyone without a synopsis and a strong view of Matthew's redaction of Q. Even if Matthew expected his readers to catch his allusions to wisdom he does not link Jesus the teacher and Son who reveals the Father to those he wants to (11.27), with the myth of his agency in creation echoed in the hymnic passages. The pre-resurrection roots of both Matthew's and the hymns' Christology lie in Jesus' authority, reflected in his activity, including his use of wisdom forms, but probably most apparent in the theological substance of his message and (implicitly) his person.

[25] J. P. Meier, *A Marginal Jew*, vol. 1, New York: Doubleday, 1991, p. 21, rightly distinguishes between 'the real Jesus' and 'the historical Jesus'. Martin Kähler's classic and one-sided polemic, *The So-Called Historical Jesus and the Historic, Biblical Christ* (1892), ET Philadelphia: Fortress Press, 1964, has been attractively repristinated by Luke T. Johnson, *The Real Jesus*, San Francisco: Harper, 1996.

[26] An outstanding recent example is R. W. L. Moberly, *The Bible, Theology, and Faith*, Cambridge: Cambridge University Press, 2000.

The historical component in theological interpretation of the New Testament is essential if Scripture is to remain definitive of Christian belief. It helps preserve the givenness of revelation *ab extra* and makes possible some degree of consensus about valid meanings by excluding arbitrary interpretations from doctrinal contexts. But this component should no more determine the nature of the enterprise and the character of its products than the doctrinal component should. Bultmann's elevation of his hermeneutical interest over the historical, so that 'the reconstruction stands in the service of the interpretation of the New Testament writings under the presupposition that they have something to say to the present'[27] points towards a literary frame of reference for theological interpretation. This will show how the texts refer to the historical figure but say more about him than historians as such can say. It will seek to communicate their theological claims as binding today. It will recognize and appreciate the mythological echoes of Jesus as Wisdom of God without making them do more than they do in the texts (which is not very much), and without justifying them by appeal to history. It can highlight the wisdom overtones in John's account of the sending of the Son, and the grain of historical truth in the Johannine Jesus' riddling speech. Once disciplined by the literal sense, a New Testament theology consisting of literary critical interpretations of the witnesses will be open also to more figural interpretations of Scripture (like those of feminist theology) which can nourish faith without defining Christian identity.[28] How this literary emphasis in the theological interpretation of Scripture might develop receives rich suggestions in David Ford's and other essays in this volume. A concluding observation on the

---

[27] R. Bultmann, *Theology of the New Testament*, vol. 2, London: SCM Press, 1955, p. 251. Even this New Testament *theology* only occasionally breaks out of the historical paradigm which (rightly) dominates New Testament *scholarship*.

[28] I argue (with Aquinas, *ST* 1.1.9) that using Scripture as a doctrinal norm presupposes the literal sense of the New Testament, in 'The New Testament Canon of Scripture and Christian Identity' in J. Barton and M. Wolter, (eds.), *The Unity of the Canon and the Diversity of Scripture*, BZNW, Berlin: de Gruyter, 2003.

wisdom theme which has provided an example illustrating the argument of this essay will therefore suffice.

The literal sense of the texts is fundamental for the literary type of New Testament Theology, and it is reinforced today by our own historical sense. When Paul on one occasion called Jesus the wisdom of God, and wisdom for us from God (1 Cor. 1.24, 30) he was not developing a 'wisdom Christology' and perhaps not even echoing his opponents' Christology. Rather, he was subverting their boasting by finding God's wisdom paradoxically revealed in the cross. Theological interpretation of this text on Christian presuppositions (including that it will 'have something to say to the present') may suggest that it subverts much modern talk of wisdom as well. Even Lady Margaret's and our own 'love of learning and desire for God'[29] is put in question by the cross, and by those poor in spirit (Mt. 5.3) and simply poor (Lk. 6.20) who bear it in the world today. Christians still attracted by the call of Wisdom and wanting to understand Jesus as the revelation of God in these terms remain subject to that foolish *Grund und Mass der Christologie*.[30] Our New Testament theologies will have to be as dialectical as Paul and Mark and maybe John when we speak of Jesus as divine Wisdom. They will accept what the New Testament hymns are saying about Jesus being the revelation of God, even though the myth gives no direct support to the doctrine or theology. These passages are part of the scriptural foundations of Christian belief, but they contribute to theology *in*directly by quickening the Christian imagination that reads Scripture to strengthen its faith, and is then better equipped to build its theology on what the myth and other New Testament materials are getting at, not on this myth itself, nor on the doubtful history of 'Jesus the Sage'.

---

[29] The echo of the title of Dom Jean Leclercq's study of monastic culture (1957), ET New York: Fordham University Press, 1961, is intended to underline the ecclesial context of theological interpretation, even when done in a modern secular university which is proud of its medieval origins and renaissance stars.

[30] So Martin Kähler, *Schriften zu Christologie und Mission*, Munich: Kaiser, 1971, pp. 292–350.

The truth of the myth of the Wisdom of God incarnate will emerge (if at all) in living the life, which includes singing the songs – Pliny's *carmen Christo quasi Deo* – and reading the Scriptures. Only a historicist and positivist Scrooge will fail to enjoy the myth at Christmas, so it is perhaps appropriate to end by recalling some of the liturgical passages of Scripture that see Christ as Wisdom without using the word, and one liturgical context in which they are regularly heard.

Those who start Christmas Day at 8 o'clock with the Book of Common Prayer hear the opening of the Epistle to the Hebrews celebrate Jesus as the revelation of God. The passage echoes the Wisdom of Solomon (7.26 – ἀπαύγασμα) and proclaims the Son in mythological terms as God's instrument in creation (cf. Prov. 8.27; Sir. 24.9; 1 En. 42; Wis. 7.12, 21; 8.4). This reading is followed by the Johannine Prologue, equally rich in Wisdom motifs – again proclaiming Jesus the revelation of God, and reinforcing this claim with talk of his pre-existence and the instrumentality of the Word in creation. That led later to the doctrinal definition of his divinity and the Triune God – but Wisdom speculation provided only materials to express it. The original impetus for both the New Testament uses of the wisdom myth and the later doctrinal development may be found not there but in Jesus' eschatological self-understanding (as one sent by God) and activity (his healings and exorcisms complementing his preaching God's rule and God's will). The authority of Jesus persuaded his disciples that in following him they were being drawn into what God was now doing. This conviction that in having to do with Jesus we are having to do with God is what all New Testament Christology and subsequent orthodoxy are getting at.

Paul also speaks of the Lord Jesus Christ in the same breath as he speaks of God our Father, and once, at 1 Cor. 8.6, like John and Hebrews and Col. 1, he echoes the wisdom idea in support of that revelational unity. Neither 1 Cor. 8 nor these other passages use the word *sophia* – another warning against its overuse in modern theology – but the idea is present, and if singing to the risen Lord is helped by imagining him in pictorial terms at the right hand of God, even by imagining him as God's Wisdom, begotten before all worlds, and if this helps Christians come to know better the only true God and Jesus Christ whom he sent (Jn 17.3), then this little bit of the symbol-system is doing its job. By showing what the texts mean, and what they ought not to be made to mean, how to read them as a Christian and how not to read them, New Testament theology removes false stumbling-blocks, retrieves intended meanings, and helps the witness of these texts to be heard correctly today.[31]

[31] It is a pleasure to record my debt to colleagues who have discussed these matters with me and persuaded me to modify my views, especially Professors Maurice Wiles and Christopher Rowland.

3. Criteria for a Wise Reading of a Biblical Text

JAMES D. G. DUNN

Since the Renaissance it is possible to distinguish three overlapping phases or emphases in the quest for the appropriate criteria for a wise reading of a biblical text. In what follows I have in mind primarily the NT, but most of what follows could apply also *mutatis mutandis* to the OT.

The givenness of the historical text

The Renaissance gave us two lasting criteria for appropriate handling of historical texts: historical philology and textual criticism.

Historical philology

The Renaissance was characterized, first, by the urge to read the classics in their original tongues. This compulsion gave birth to the new science of *historical philology* – the careful discerning of the meaning of words and sentences in the original language of the text, by reference to the way these words and such sentences were used at the time of writing. Francesco Petrarch (1304–74), the father of the Renaissance, led the way. For Petrarch, 'if classical antiquity was to be understood in its own terms it would be through the speech with which the ancients had communicated

It is a pleasure and honour to be part of this auspicious celebration. I offer these brief reflections in honour of one of the most respected and most loved of the Lady Margaret's Professors, my own Doctor-father Professor C. F. D. (Charlie) Moule.

their thoughts. This meant that the languages of antiquity had to be studied as the ancients had used them and not as vehicles for carrying modern thoughts.'[1]

It would be a mistake to treat this development lightly, or to assume that it is so obvious that it requires no emphasis. On the contrary, its absolutely fundamental character for any and all reading of biblical texts should always provide one of the beginning points for the hermeneutical task. For were it not for the work of our Renaissance forefathers and their successors we would be unable to read these texts as texts; the Hebrew, Aramaic and Greek characters would be indecipherable, little more than strange squiggles on the page. In order to be read, these squiggles must first be identified as the ancient languages they are. And in order to convey meaning they must be read within the context of the language usage of their time. For Schleiermacher, the founder of modern hermeneutics, this was the 'first canon' of interpretation: 'A more precise determination of any point in a given text must be decided on the basis of the use of language common to the author and his original public.'[2] We of the twenty-first century, therefore, dare not forget how indebted we are to the great philologists of earlier centuries, how dependent we are on the fruit of their labour stacked so neatly and so accessibly in our modern lexica. Without such fundamental aids we would hardly know where to start the hermeneutical task.

The corollary of most immediate consequence for us is that the language usage at the time of writing is bound to be determinative in at least substantial degree for our understanding of the language used in the ancient text. The point is perhaps clearer if we put it in terms of translation. The point is simply that there are such things as bad, or even (dare one say it?) *wrong* translations. Presumably even radically postmodern teachers of ancient languages and texts do not dissent from this, and postmodern examiners of such

---

[1] D. Weinstein, 'Renaissance', *Encyclopaedia Britannica* 15.664.

[2] F. D. E. Schleiermacher, *Hermeneutics: The Handwritten Manuscripts by F. D. E. Schleiermacher*, ed. H. Kimmerle, ET Missoula, MT: Scholars Press, 1977, excerpted by K. Mueller-Vollmer, *The Hermeneutics Reader*, New York: Continuum, 1994, p. 86.

translations mark them down like any other teacher. To say this, of course, is not to ignore the fact that there is no such thing as a single correct translation of a foreign-language text, far less a perfect translation. Anyone who has had to engage in translation knows that there is no translation without interpretation, that interpretation is an inescapable part of translation.[3] Individual words in both languages have ranges of meaning, and there is no word in one language whose range and cultural overtones exactly match those of a word in the other language. The abundant diversity of modern translations of the Bible is all the illustration needed.

None of this, however, alters the point that the original-language text is what is to be translated/interpreted, and that each translation has to justify itself as a translation of that text. The historical text cannot determine the exact translation, but unless the text functions as some kind of norm for the translation, unless it is seen to provide a limiting factor on the diversity of acceptable translations, then translation itself becomes irresponsible.

Textual criticism

The second great fruit of Renaissance scholarship was the science of *textual criticism*, the skill of reconstructing from the variant manuscripts available so far as possible the original texts, by identifying and correcting the corruptions caused by centuries of Christian transmission and editing.

Of course we should not deceive ourselves into thinking that textual criticism gives us 'the original text'. At best our Hebrew Bible texts and our Aland Greek texts are eclectic in their readings. And we should be equally cautious about talking of the 'final form' of the text. Alttestamentlers are constantly confronted with the fluidity of the textual form, with Masoretic text, LXX and now Qumran Bible often pulling in different directions. Neutestamentlers too, despite the relative firmness of their text, need

---

[3] The word 'hermeneutics' comes from the Greek *hermêneia*, which can mean both 'translation' and 'interpretation'.

to appreciate more than many do that textual variations are not simply to be counted as scribal errors but often attest the way the text was being read in different communities.[4] Strictly speaking, the text was not fixed but rather bears witness to its character as living tradition, a tradition which grew and developed.

All that said, however, it still remains true for the Neutestamentler that the Greek text (even in its modern, eclectic form) is a *given*, given as a historical text. Which is to say that the text is *normative* in regard to any and every translation and to any and every interpretation made of it. Which also means that the Greek text must inevitably be allowed to determine and limit the range and diversity of translation, and so also the range and diversity of interpretation read from or into the text. Without ceding such control and restriction to the text itself, translator and interpreter are always liable to manipulate the text and to sacrifice that legitimacy which only the text can give to translation and interpretation.

In other words, it is simply important to recognize *the character of historical texts as historical texts*. For the Greek text read as a historical text (interpretations as well as translations taking account of accidence, syntax and idiom of the day) inevitably functions as a norm for legitimacy of modern readings too. Without that basic recognition, the particular text becomes no more than a lump of potter's clay, vulnerable to being shaped entirely by the whim of the interpreter (potter). In short, the very identity of the text is at stake, and historical study and scholarly method are unavoidable if the NT is to be read at all.

The meaning of the text

If the first phase in the modern search for criteria for a wise reading focuses on the givenness of the text, the second phase focuses on the meaning of the text.

---

[4] See particularly B. D. Ehrman, *The Orthodox Corruption of Scripture: The Effect of Early Christological Controversies on the Text of the New Testament*, Oxford: Oxford University Press, 1993; D. C. Parker, *The Living Text of the Gospels*, Cambridge: Cambridge University Press, 1997.

Plain meaning

As the Renaissance introduced the first phase, so we could say that the Reformation introduced the second. For the Reformation was marked precisely by its break with the mediaeval tradition of exegesis in that it gave priority to the *literal sense,* over against the mediaeval openness to the text's polyvalency of meaning, as expressed particularly through allegorical interpretation. Already in 1496, John Colet, in his lectures on the Pauline letters in the University of Oxford, provided the paradigm for the Reformation, by maintaining that the text should be expounded simply in terms of the *sensus literalis* (as understood in its historical context).[5] Martin Luther likewise insisted on the plain or literal or historical sense and dismissed mediaeval allegorizing as so much rubbish.[6] Most influential of all was John Calvin's emphasis on the plain meaning of the text, with his sequence of biblical commentaries providing classic examples of philological-historical interpretation.[7] This in effect was the second principle of biblical interpretation to emerge in the modern period – *the primacy of the plain meaning of the text* – always bearing in mind

[5] J. H. Bentley, *Humanists and Holy Writ: New Testament Scholarship in the Renaissance*, Princeton: Princeton University Press, 1983, sums up Colet's significance thus: 'Though routinely hailed as a harbinger of Reformation exegesis, Colet's real achievement was simply to provide a running literal commentary in the patristic fashion, abandoning the late medieval style of exegesis, which often subordinated the scriptures to the needs of scholastic theology' (pp. 9–10).

[6] See e.g. the extracts in W. G. Kümmel, *The New Testament: The History of the Investigation of its Problems*, London: SCM Press, 1972: 'all error arises out of paying no regard to the plain words'; 'This is the method I now employ, the final and best one: I convey the literal sense of Scripture . . . Other interpretations, however appealing, are the work of fools' (p. 23).

[7] 'Calvin is even less tolerant of allegorical interpretation than Luther' (A. C. Thiselton, *New Horizons in Hermeneutics*, London: Marshall Pickering, 1992, p. 185). Calvin states his attitude most explicitly in his commentary on *The Epistles of Paul to the Galatians, Ephesians, Philippians and Colossians*, Edinburgh: Oliver & Boyd, 1965: 'Let us know, then, that the true meaning of Scripture is the natural and simple one, and let us embrace and hold it resolutely. Let us not merely neglect as doubtful, but boldly set aside as deadly corruptions, those pretended expositions which lead us away from the literal sense' (p. 85).

that the 'plain meaning' may include allegory or symbolism when the particular text is 'plainly' allegorical or symbolical.[8]

Here again immediate qualification is unavoidable. For plain meaning as appealed to by such as Calvin was not always the literal or verbal sense *tout simple*, but a meaning determined in part by Calvin's faith, by the rule of faith – 'plain' to those who shared Calvin's faith. 'Plain meaning' as it has operated in practice is already in some measure a product of the reader's perspective, a negotiated outcome. Kathryn Greene-McCreight concludes from her study of the subject that a 'plain sense' reading 'involves negotiating between the constraints of verbal sense and Ruled reading . . . respecting the verbal and textual data of the text as well as privileging the claims about God and Jesus Christ which cohere with the Rule of faith'. 'The "plain sense" reading will result from a conjunction of verbal sense and prior understanding of the subject matter of the text provided by the conception of the Christian faith supplied by the apostolic tradition.'[9]

Nevertheless, there is a 'bottom line' which needs to be stated and defended here. That is the basic idea of communication, that *communication* is only meaningful if it communicates *meaning*. Of course such a basic model of social relationships has to be endlessly qualified by the reality of irony, deception, misunderstanding, and the like. But these are qualifications of the basic character of language as communication of meaning. Without the conviction that at least the main point and thrust of what we wish to communicate is in fact communicated, no communication could hope to rise above the first stumbling phrases of someone trying to speak in a new foreign language. Without that conviction all lecturers and authors should abandon the pretence that they can inform and persuade. And the same principle

[8] This qualification, if that is what it is, was familiar from the early patristic debates: 'The "literal" may include the use of metaphor or other figures of speech, if this is the meaning which the purpose of the author and the linguistic context suggest' (Thiselton, *New Horizons* p. 173, citing John Chrysostom; also p. 183).

[9] K. E. Greene-McCreight, *Ad Litteram: How Augustine, Calvin, and Barth Read the 'Plain Sense' of Genesis 1–3*, New York: Peter Lang, 1999, pp. ix, 244.

applies to ancient texts and our attempts to understand them. As Hans-Georg Gadamer notes, it 'has always been a principle of all textual interpretation: namely that a text must be understood in its own terms';[10] and that must mean in the first place, in the terms which the text itself most plainly invites.

Intended meaning

In the Romantic revival the focus shifted from 'plain meaning' to *intended meaning*, and to authorial intention. The hermeneutical objective was to enter into the creative experience of inspiration from which the writing was born, and called for a sense of psychological empathy with the author as creator, interpretation being conceived as recreation of the creative act. This was the other side of the art of hermeneutics for Schleiermacher: 'understanding a speech always involves two moments: to understand what is said in the context of the language with its possibilities, and to understand it as a fact in the thinking of the speaker'. Later he distinguishes between 'the historical and divinatory, objective and subjective reconstruction of a given statement'. 'By leading the interpreter to transform himself, so to speak, into the author, the divinatory method seeks to gain an immediate comprehension of the author as an individual.'[11]

In the twentieth century this objective was justifiably criticized, as 'the intentional fallacy'.[12] The interpreter should not be concerned with such issues, or allow speculations about the author's mood or historical context to determine the text's meaning. The intention of the author was a private state of mind, which lay behind the text; to enter into that state of mind is neither possible nor necessary. Instead, the text should be allowed to speak for itself.

---

[10] H.-G. Gadamer, *Truth and Method*, New York: Crossroad, 1989, p. 291.

[11] Quotations from Mueller-Vollmer, *Hermeneutics Reader*, pp. 74, 83–4, 96.

[12] Thiselton, *New Horizons*, pp. 58–9, citing R. Wellek and A. Warren, *Theory of Literature* (1949), and W. K. Wimsatt and M. Beardsley, 'The Intentional Fallacy' (1954).

At the same time, it has proved impossible to dispense with the concept of intended meaning. How far the argument can be pushed in regard to a text consisting in separate oracles or aphorisms is a moot point. But the more substantial, evidently contrived and typically narrative text in effect compels the reader to think in such terms. If it has proved possible to dispense with the 'real author' as inputting the intended meaning, the text itself requires us to speak of what Wolfgang Iser has designated the 'implied author', that is, the author as inferred from the narrative itself, the rationale which has given the text its present structure and content. Similarly Iser's twin concept of the 'implied reader' is another way of speaking of the effect intended by the author, the meaning evidently intended to be conveyed by the text.[13]

In short, it is neither desirable nor necessary to dispense with the concept of authorial intention, but the realistic goal is the authorial intention *as entextualized*. As Francis Watson puts it: authorial intention 'is to be understood not as some subjective occurrence lying behind the text but as the principle of the text's intelligibility', 'is to be seen as primarily embodied in the words the author wrote'.[14] It is the text as embodying that intention, as a communicative act between author and intended readers/ auditors, to which attention is to be given.

The hearing of the text

The third phase can be identified most simply with postmodernism, with its shift from the text itself and the author behind the text to *the reader* of the text, from reading behind the text to reading in front of the text, from text as window to text as mirror. This hermeneutical shift is epitomized in reader-response theory,

[13] See further Thiselton, *New Horizons*, pp. 516–22, referring to W. Iser, *The Implied Reader: Patterns of Communication in Prose Fiction from Bunyan to Beckett,* Baltimore: Johns Hopkins University Press, 1974; also *The Act of Reading: A Theory of Aesthetic Response*, Baltimore: Johns Hopkins University Press, 1978.

[14] F. Watson, *Text and Truth: Redefining Biblical Theology*, Edinburgh: T. & T. Clark, 1997, pp. 112, 118.

which no longer looks for meaning simply 'in' the text, let alone by reference 'behind' the text, but looks for meaning as created by the reader in the act of reading. Texts do not make meaning; readers make meaning. Texts do not dictate to readers; readers dictate to texts. In Stephen Moore's words, 'Prior to the interpretive act, there is nothing definitive in the text to be discovered.'[15]

There is an obvious threat in all this to any ideas of canons for agreed meanings. If all meaning is contingent to each individual act of reading, then it would appear that every man, every woman makes his or her own meaning, and there is no generally acceptable criteria to enable us to judge whether one reading is good or bad, or wise or foolish, or better than another. In postmodernism pluralism is all. However, in the debate over reader-response theory two constraints have been put forward. One is the perception of reader-response as more of a dialogue between text and reader, where the text has to be 'heard', and listened to, lest reader-response deteriorate into the straightforward manipulation of the text to speak to the reader's agenda. In his debate with Stanley Fish, Iser in particular wishes to maintain an objective status for the text, that there is a 'given' to be 'mediated': 'the "something" which is to be mediated exists prior to interpretation, acts as a constraint on interpretation'.[16] George Steiner's exposition of the 'real presence' in a text is attempting to pull the debate in the same direction.[17]

The other constraint is Fish's own recognition that reading is not a wholly isolated, individual experience. In his most influential work, he has emphasized that any reading is conditioned to at least some extent by the reading or interpretive community to which the individual reader belongs.[18] In reference to scriptural

---

[15] S. D. Moore, *Literary Criticism and the Gospels*, New Haven: Yale University Press, 1989, p. 121. See further pp. 71–107.

[16] G. Aichele et al., *The Postmodern Bible*, New Haven: Yale University Press, 1995, p. 41, citing W. Iser, 'Talk Like Whales: A Reply to Stanley Fish', *Diacritics* 11, 1981, pp. 82–7 (here p. 84).

[17] G. Steiner, *Real Presences: Is there anything in what we say?* London: Faber & Faber, 1989.

[18] S. Fish, *Is There a Text in This Class? The Authority of Interpretive Communities*, Cambridge, MA: Harvard University Press, 1980.

texts the emphasis is easily integrateable with an emphasis on the Church, the community of faith, as the context within which the text is heard and its meaning perceived. Here the correlation with the 'plain meaning' as determined by the rule of faith is obvious: the meaning heard within the community of faith will almost unavoidably accord with the *sensus communis*, the *sensus fidelium*.

With similar effect is Hans-Georg Gadamer's more subtle concept of a text's *Wirkungsgeschichte*, the 'history of effect' of the text. The point being that the interpreter and the act of interpretation are themselves caught up in the flow of history, that historical text and interpreter are both part of a historical continuum. Consequently, the interpreter cannot stand above the tradition which links him or her to the past under study, but can only begin to understand adequately as being part of and through that tradition.[19] Gadamer's point is not to be reduced simply to the recognition that the interpreter stands within a history influenced by the text. The key term is actually the more elaborate phrase, *wirkungsgeschichtliches Bewusstsein*, 'historically effected consciousness'; not historically-*affected* but historically-*effected* consciousness. Gadamer's point, then, is that the interpreter's consciousness, or pre-understanding we might say, is not simply influenced by the text; rather, it has in some measure been brought into being by the text, is itself in some degree a product of the text; it is a consciousness of the text to be interpreted. Only because the interpreter's consciousness has been thus 'effected' can it be 'effectual in finding the right questions to ask'.[20]

I have no wish to dispute any of this – far from it. It is important to understand the effective communicative act in terms of reception as well as of delivery. Prophecy is not simply a matter of inspired speech, but of the speech being received as prophecy. The biblical writings are Scripture not simply because they were *theopneustos*, but because they were heard from the first as word

[19] Gadamer, *Truth and Method*, pp. 300–7.
[20] Ibid., pp. 340–1, 301.

of God. Meaning heard in a parable or aphorism depends to a considerable extent on how the parable, the aphorism is heard.[21] No preaching can be effective without a responsive audience. For my own part, faith is an integral part of the critical theological dialogue which is the interpretation of the NT. At this point my hermeneutical agenda overlaps extensively with that of my colleague Walter Moberly.[22]

My only concern in regard to the emphases brought to the fore by Fish and Gadamer is lest it be concluded that the meaningfulness of the biblical tradition can be appreciated only within the interpretive community (that is, the Church), and within the living tradition (that is, the Christian tradition). The concern is twofold. First, lest Scripture be wholly subsumed within tradition, whereas it seems necessary to acknowledge that within the Church and within the flow of Christian tradition, the NT in particular must be accorded some sort of critical role. Precisely by virtue of the NT's pivotal testimony to the incarnation, the NT was bound to function as the *norma normans,* the canon within the canon of Scripture and tradition, otherwise that pivotal testimony would be devalued and its canonical status be effectively lost.[23] It is this readiness for self-criticism in reference to tradition, which marks out the Western Church – its willingness to recognize and acknowledge when it has departed from its norm, whether in the condemnation of a Galileo or in its centuries-long tradition of anti-Semitism[24] – a dialogue of criticism which remains some-

---

[21] See particularly S. I. Wright, *The Voice of Jesus: Studies in the Interpretation of Six Gospel Parables*, Carlisle: Paternoster press, 2000.

[22] R. W. L. Moberly, *The Bible, Theology, and Faith: A Study of Abraham and Jesus*, Cambridge: Cambridge University Press, 2000, ch. 1.

[23] Cf. the criticism of Vatican II's 'Dogmatic Constitution on Divine Revelation' acknowledged by J. Ratzinger in H. Vorgrimler, (ed.), *Commentary on the Documents of Vatican II*, vol. 3, London: Burns & Oates/ New York: Herder & Herder, 1968, pp. 192–3.

[24] It should however also be confessed that the historical method as applied in the nineteenth century did *not* prevent anti-Judaism in Christian presentation of Jesus; the recognition of subjectivity in interpretation did not extend sufficiently to take account of anti-Jewish bias (S. Heschel, *Abraham Geiger and the Jewish Jesus*, Chicago: University of Chicago Press, 1998, pp. 73, 122).

thing of a barrier and bewilderment for the Christianity of East and South.

Second, in the emphases of Fish and Gadamer I perceive a certain risk of locking up the Bible once again within the churches, with a meaning heard clearly enough within the worshipping community, but unable to speak to the world outside, unable to dialogue effectively with other forms of knowledge given to us, and unable to be heard or understood because meaning is thought to reside (only?) in a reading within the continuum and community of meaning. To seek thus to escape postmodernism's pluralism and relativity would significantly diminish the possibility of effective Christian apologetics and evangelism. But Christians belong not only to communities of faith; they also belong to diverse and overlapping communities, of workplace or residence or leisure; and unless they want to live a schizophrenic existence of two disconnected language-worlds, they must learn to speak a common language. A hermeneutic which effectively denies the possibility of the biblical message being heard outside the churches and in the forums of the world's discourses is a hermeneutic of irresponsibility and despair.

Hermeneutical circles

The three phases or emphases in the art of interpretation can be summed up in terms of the hermeneutical circle, or better, in terms of the different forms taken by the hermeneutical circle.

In its initial form the hermeneutical circle was the circularity of part and whole, already noted by Schleiermacher: the parts can only be understood in terms of the whole; but understanding of the whole is built up from the parts. It is called a circle, because the hermeneutical process is unavoidably a movement back and forth round the circle, where understanding is ever provisional and subject to clarification and correction as the whole is illuminated by the parts and the part by the whole.

A second form of the hermeneutical circle sends the interpreter back and forth between the matter of the text and the speech used to convey it, between Word and words, *Sache und Sprache*,[25] between *langue* and *parole*, signified and signifier.[26] This form of the hermeneutical procedure has been played out throughout the period reviewed above, particularly in the way in which again and again a definitive subject-matter perceived through the text has been used to critique the wording of the text itself. One thinks, for example, of the gospel (*was Christum treibet*) serving as the critical scalpel for Luther,[27] or the universal ideals of Jesus indicating for nineteenth-century liberalism an 'essence' from which the merely particular could be stripped, or Bultmann's 'kerygma' providing the key for his demythologizing programme,[28] or 'justification by faith' serving as the 'canon within the canon' for Käsemann.[29]

The third form of the hermeneutical circle is that between reader and text, as already implicit in Schleiermacher's recognition of a 'psychological' dimension to hermeneutics.[30] Bultmann elaborated the point in his insistence that 'there cannot be any such thing as presuppositionless exegesis'.[31] The point is sometimes missed when more conservative biblical scholars deem it sufficient to declare their presuppositions before embarking on what most

---

[25] *Sachkritik* (the English 'content criticism' is not really adequate) builds on the older theological distinction between the Word of God which is heard through the words of Scripture (but is not to be simply identified with them), by distinguishing between the real intention (*die Sache*, the matter or subject) of a text and the language in which it is expressed (*die Sprache*). *Sachkritik* is linked particularly with the name of Bultmann.

[26] Referring to Ferdinand de Saussure's influential distinction between the language system (*langue*) and concrete acts of speech (*parole*) and idea of the text as an encoded sign-system (see Thiselton, *New Horizons*, pp. 80–6).

[27] Luther's famous criticism of the epistle of James: 'What does not teach Christ is not apostolic, even though St. Peter or Paul taught it' (Kümmel, *New Testament*, p. 25).

[28] R. Bultmann, 'New Testament and Mythology' (1941), in H. W. Bartsch, (ed.), *Kerygma and Myth*, London: SPCK, 1957, pp. 1–44.

[29] E.g. E. Käsemann, (ed.), *Das Neue Testament als Kanon*, Göttingen: Vandenhoeck, 1970, p. 405.

[30] Mueller-Vollmer, *Hermeneutics Reader*, pp. 8–11.

[31] Bultmann, 'Is Exegesis Without Presuppositions Possible?' (1961), in *Existence and Faith*, London: Collins, Fontana, 1964, pp. 342–51.

of their fellow-scholars would regard as uncritical exegesis, as though the declaration of presuppositions somehow vindicated the exegesis itself (since 'Everyone has presuppositions'). But the point is not simply that any reading of a text is shaped by the pre-understanding brought to it. The point is rather that as the exegete moves round the hermeneutical circle between pre-understanding and text, the text reacts back upon the pre-understanding, both sharpening it and requiring of it revision at one or other point, and thus enabling a fresh scrutiny of the text, necessitating in turn a further revision of pre-understanding, and so on and on.

The most vicious form of the hermeneutical circle, however, has proved to be that between reader and text as it has been developed within postmodern literary criticism. Indeed, deconstructionist hermeneutics attempt in effect to undermine the whole procedure envisaged in the hermeneutical circle by suggesting that the reality is an infinite series of interlocking circles, where the search for meaning is never ending and the play between signifier and signified goes on *ad infinitum*. The image conjured up is of a computer game without an end; or of an internet search into the infinity of cyberspace as web pages direct to other web pages in an endless sequence. To conceive the hermeneutical process as an infinitely regressive intertextuality is another counsel of despair which quickly reduces all meaningful communication to impossibility and all communication to a game of 'trivial pursuit'.

Perhaps it has been the image of a 'circle' which has misled us, since it invites the picture of an endless 'going round in circles'. In fact, however, from its earliest use, the hermeneutical circles were always perceived as a progressive exercise, in which the circles, as it were, became smaller. Alternatively expressed, the circle was seen more as a spiral, the circle in effect as a three-dimensional cone, so that successive circlings resulted in a spiralling towards a common centre. As readers of biblical texts which are also historical texts, therefore, we need not despair over the hermeneutical circle but can hope to find that the reality of a historical-critical, self-critical, community-critical scrutiny of these texts can and does provide a growing appreciation and understanding of why they were written, what they must have conveyed to their first auditors and readers, and how they may still be expected to function today. The meaning intended by means of and through the text is still a legitimate and viable goal for the biblical exegete and interpreter.

4. Reason, Wisdom and the Implied Disciple of Scripture

MARKUS BOCKMUEHL

It is possible to assert, as twentieth-century scholars often did, that Christian confessional and theological convictions have no place in serious study of the Bible.[1] Until not so very long ago, academic gatherings of biblical scholars witnessed regular recitations of the mantra that biblical exegetes must 'set aside their presuppositions' and read the Bible 'like any other ancient book'. Quite how or why one might achieve either the former or the latter was never made entirely clear.

The mantras, if not perhaps the associated methods, seem less frequently in evidence now. But academic biblical study is in a period of greater flux and change than perhaps at any time in the past couple of centuries. Here I claim no crystal ball with which to prognosticate. I merely wish to acknowledge at the outset my conviction that an interpretation of Scripture wholly outside the historic Christian ecclesial context is sure to misapprehend the nature and purpose of its very object of study.

To read Scripture predominantly as a document of ancient religion, or as an instrument of repression and exclusion, is to commit an elementary category mistake. Such interpretation confuses genesis with meaning, or finds fault with a design for how it is abused and for what it is not. The former reading resembles restricting the study of a Stradivari to the alpine soft-

[1] I am grateful for comments and suggestions on this essay received from Richard C. Beaton, Michael Cain, James Carleton Paget, Richard B. Hays, Aidan Nichols and Benedict T. Viviano.

wood industry of Trentino; the latter, reducing the story of the instrument to who was prevented from playing or hearing it, how it was played badly, or what was *not* played on it. That sort of analysis can be intellectually respectable, and may even have a certain complementary scientific or sociological interest. But it has by definition little light to shed on the instruments actually played by an Itzhak Perlman or a Yo-Yo Ma.

So too the historic significance of the ancient biblical texts is inseparable from the space they have inhabited, and continue to inhabit, as the canonical Scripture of the Christian Church. Critical readings outside that perspective are of course possible and may often provide important historical, literary or ideological insights. Inasmuch as Scripture's affirmations are public and universal rather than private or sectarian, they invite and benefit from open debate. And there are clearly questions that a self-consciously 'secular' or otherwise non-Christian approach may ask rather well; some of them it may even answer well. Universities have often provided fruitful analysis of texts whose implied readers are not critical scholars. Nevertheless, what such external discussions cannot manage is a 'thick' reading of the biblical texts that accounts for the ecclesial dynamics of life and worship in which those texts have in fact had their existence.[2] For that, Christian Scriptures must be read in the context of Christian faith.

In what follows, therefore, I propose to develop such a perspective for the three inter-connected topics before us: reason, wisdom and interpretation.

[2] Compare François Dreyfus's illuminating distinction between scriptural interpretation 'in the Church' (applied) and 'in the Sorbonne' (scientific), as expounded by Aidan Nichols, 'François Dreyfus on Scripture Read in Tradition', in *Scribe of the Kingdom: Essays on Theology and Culture*, London: Sheed & Ward, 1994, pp. 32–77, 215–19 (pp. 35–8), although the nature and historic life of these texts makes it improper to concede, as Dreyfus does, that in their own terms these two approaches are both independently valid.

Reason

The unprepared reader may be perplexed to discover the Bible's lack of explicit interest in critical reason and inquiry. The period of modernity, from its seventeenth-century rationalist beginnings all the way to its logical conclusion in 'late' or 'post'-modernity, has consistently privileged the autonomous rational subject in its approach to both epistemology and hermeneutics. From a biblical perspective, by contrast, one might say this has been an extended story of putting 'Des-cartes' before 'De-rrida'. Of course it is not the case that Scripture has no interest in reasoning subjects; but it remains uncomfortable for any self-consciously modern hermeneutic that critical reason seems here to play quite such an ancillary role as a tool for interpretation and understanding.

For Scripture, reason is indeed an innate and valuable creational gift; but it is fragile and profoundly corruptible. It is what Nebuchadnezzar lost when his arrogance drove him to insanity.[3] In the wisdom literature, human reasoning is seen as largely flawed by its inability to draw close to God. The preacher in Ecclesiastes stresses humanity's failure to find out the meaning of things, despite much searching; human knowledge is partial, fleeting and perishable.[4] The book of Wisdom shares a similar perspective on the nature of reason.[5] Sirach takes a more constructive view of the place of reason in understanding, although he never assumes that the exercise of reason in itself holds a promise of either truth or wisdom.[6]

The New Testament shares this scepticism about autonomous reason. Here the Greek word διαλογισμός, which classically denoted deliberation and reflection, is used more frequently to indicate doubt, anxiety, or evil and cantankerous thoughts. We find here no treatise on the place of reason in human understanding: the perspective seems comparable especially to contemporary

---

[3] Dan. 4.29–37.

[4] Eccl. 7.24; 8.16–17; 9.10.

[5] Wisd. 2.1, 2, 21; 3.10.

[6] Only 4 Maccabees with its clearly Stoic outlook offers a more explicit engagement with the nature of reason (λογισμός) itself. Devout reason rules over the emotions and is the guide to all the virtues.

Jewish apocalyptic literature. The writer of 4 Ezra, for example, reflects on a time of divine judgement when among all manner of ecological disasters both reason (*sensus*) and understanding (*intellectus*) disappear along with the doing of righteousness (5.9–10). In the New Testament, Luke and Paul are perhaps the authors most concerned to demonstrate the rationality and public defensibility of Christian life and faith. But even their most famous statements of 'natural revelation' in Romans 1 or Acts 17 make few claims for the ability of autonomous human reason to discover God's truth. Romans 1, in fact, affirms precisely the opposite: human minds have been darkened by the failure to acknowledge God, who alone reveals truth.[7]

Reason and the skills it entails, therefore, are necessary God-given qualities that we bring to the task of interpretation and understanding. But most of the biblical writers suggest quite clearly that what we bring is insufficient, because it is in significant ways flawed and in need of redemption. The gospel neither affirms nor denies human reason as such, but stresses the need for a Christ-shaped *transformation* of our minds if we are to discern and embrace the will of God (Rom. 12.1–2; Eph. 4.17–24).

Wisdom

Scripture has a good deal more to say about wisdom than about reason, although its perspectives are in some ways analogous. Classic wisdom literature, to be sure, gives considerable encouragement to the pursuit of wisdom, and the quest to understand the moral and scientific workings of the world. In these writings, such understanding is indeed open to patient rational scrutiny, and those who seek wisdom and righteousness will prosper in this life, while the wicked will perish. Wisdom may be found by those who seek her. Even in relatively 'conventional' wisdom texts like Proverbs, Job or Sirach, however, it is already beginning to become clear that reality may be rather more

[7] Rom. 1.21; cf. Acts 17.29–31. See further the discussion in Markus Bockmuehl, *Jewish Law in Gentile Churches: Halakhah and the Beginning of Christian Public Ethics*, Edinburgh: T. & T. Clark, 2000, pp. 129–31.

mysterious. However much one mines it in deep underground shafts, wisdom's true understanding of the ways of the Lord may well elude our human grasp (cf. Job 28).

In post-exilic literature, wisdom is now prayed for rather than independently sought: she is received as a special gift of grace rather than merely 'found'.[8] That gift is increasingly understood as granted by the Holy Spirit, and only to the elect people of God in the Torah.[9] For the Psalmist, the one who meditates on the law of the Lord is as a tree planted by the life-giving water channels, which help it bring its fruit in due season (Ps. 1). In subsequent exegesis this image was increasingly adopted for the teacher of wisdom and Torah.[10] Ben Sira, moreover, distinguishes carefully between two types of scribes, the ordinary and the inspired interpreter.[11] In his work, as in some of the canonical and post-canonical Psalms, wisdom assumes a setting that is as markedly *liturgical* as it is centred on the study of Torah.[12] Wisdom condescends specifically to make her revealed dwelling in Israel[13] – this is a conviction anticipated perhaps as early as Deuteronomy (4.6), but now widely shared in Palestinian and Diaspora Judaism. Its development in Philo's hermeneutics went on to be particularly influential for the Alexandrian fathers.

If this conception of revealed wisdom seems strikingly particular, its formulation is hardly more universalistic in the New Testament. The focus and personification of wisdom is now none other than Christ himself. In the Synoptic Gospels, especially in Matthew and Luke, he is both the teacher and giver of wisdom *par excellence*; and more than once he appears as the personification of the Wisdom of God.[14] For Paul, most explicitly, Christ himself has become the power of God and the wisdom of God, in deliberate contrast to conventional 'secular' definitions

---

8 Wisd. 7.7; 8.21; 9.1–2, 4, 17.

9 E.g. Bar. 3.9—4.4; Sir. 24.8; Wisd. 18.4; *Ep. Arist.* 200; *m. Abot* 1.1ff.

10 Sir. 24.30–31; cf. the Qumran *Hodayot* and see Dan. 9.1–3, 20–27.

11 Sir. 39.1–5, 6–8; cf. Wisd. 9.16–17.

12 E.g. Pss. 1, 19, 119; cf. Sir. 24.10; 39.6–8.

13 See, e.g., Sir. 17.11–14; 24.23; Bar. 3.36—4.1.

14 Mt. 11.19; 12.42; 13.54; Lk. 2.40, 52; 7.35; 11.31, 49; 21.15. Cf. also Rev. 5.12, where wisdom is most properly the attribute of the Lamb.

of wisdom. In Christ all the treasures of wisdom and knowledge are hidden, and it is God's wisdom, secret and hidden in Christ crucified, that has through the Spirit been revealed to those who love God. No other access to that wisdom is possible.[15] And this same Christ, the wisdom of God, is himself the message of the 'God-breathed' Scriptures: in the context of faith in Christ they 'are able to *make you wise* for salvation'.[16]

Biblical interpretation and theology, especially in Britain

How then might a scriptural view of wisdom and reason bear on the task of biblical interpretation and its place in Christian theology? That question seems in some respects singularly difficult to address in the contemporary context. Only a few biblical scholars even bother to ask it;[17] and a number of those who do seem to branch out into hermeneutical meta-discourses that effectively ensure rapid marginalization in a separate sub-discipline. Systematic theology, on the other hand, especially in Britain, has been similarly egregious in its studied avoidance of any formally articulated engagement with Scripture. With painfully few exceptions, it fails to pay so much as lip-service to the idea that Christian theology derives in any palpable sense from Scripture.[18]

Probably the clearest recent statement by a British systematic

---

[15] 1 Cor. 1.24, 30; 2.1–10; Col. 2.3.

[16] 2 Tim. 3.15–16: *τα δυνάμενά σε σοφίσαι εἰς σωτηρίαν διὰ πίστεως τῆς ἐν Χριστῷ Ἰησοῦ.*

[17] In the British scene, the exceptions include Anthony Thiselton, Richard Bauckham and Francis Watson in New Testament studies, or Walter Moberly and Christopher Seitz in Old Testament studies.

[18] Oliver O'Donovan, *The Desire of the Nations: Rediscovering the Roots of Political Theology*, Cambridge: Cambridge University Press, 1996 (cf. idem, *Resurrection and Moral Order: An Outline for Evangelical Ethics*, Leicester: Apollos, 1994) is a marked exception in moral theology. One might also mention Colin Gunton, 'Using and Being Used: Scripture and Systematic Theology', *Theology Today* 47, 1990, pp. 248–59, although his commitment to 'be read by Scripture' does not often surface explicitly in his theological writings. David Ford reflects on Scripture in a number of works, sometimes extensively (e.g. David F. Ford, *Self and Salvation: Being Transformed*, Cambridge: Cambridge University Press, 1999, pp. 107–

theologian is Rowan Williams,[19] with its welcome attempt to reclaim the historical and 'literal' sense of Scripture for theology. Unfortunately, his stated antipathy for integrated canonical readings rather compromises this attempt: branded 'uncritical' and 'totalitarian' (p. 48), they are regarded as summarily refuted by James Barr (pp. 44, 48, ignoring all subsequent discussion since 1983). Williams himself, by contrast, privileges inner-canonical *conflict* to an extent that is sufficiently questionable, both historically and theologically, as to compromise his own subsequent plea for 'limits to pluralism' and his denial of a process-oriented Hegelian developmentalism (pp. 56, 58). His emphasis on an *eschatological* hermeneutic of Scripture and theology is excellent. In fact, however, most of the biblical evidence adduced in support of his conflictual account lends itself more easily to a teleological dialectic of biblical theology, read in the light of a recognizably catholic rule of faith – a process that is no less eschatological in spirit and intent. To brand dissent from relentlessly conflict-driven readings as 'fundamentalist' (*sic*, pp. 48, 58) does little to redeem Williams' lack of a coherent account of Scripture as in any sense the divine word of life (and thus more than 'the production of the meaning of a corporate symbolic life that has some unity and integrity', p. 56). This starting-point still leaves his theologically elegant and laudable effort to engage New Testament ethics (pp. 239–75) mired in moral generalities and lacking in expository vigour. Although prepared elsewhere to speak of a 'grammar of obedience'[20] the

---

65); but he has not thus far offered a considered rationale for its role in theology, beyond the desire 'to explore human flourishing in some of its richest forms' (*Self and Salvation*, p. 107; note, however, David F. Ford, 'Wisdom, Scripture and Learning', in D. F. Ford and C. Cocksworth, (eds.), *Principles for a Principal: Gospel, Scripture and Church*, Cambridge: Ridley Hall, 2001, pp. 1–7, and see n. 22 below).

[19] Rowan Williams, *On Christian Theology*, Oxford: Blackwell, 2000, pp. 44–59, cf. previously idem, 'The Literal Sense of Scripture', *Modern Theology* 7, 1991, pp. 121–34.

[20] Rowan Williams, 'Making Moral Decisions', in R. Gill, (ed.), *The Cambridge Companion to Christian Ethics*, Cambridge: Cambridge University Press, 2001, pp. 3–15 (p. 11).

specific *object* of that obedience seems to be a process rather than a divine person, and notably unfettered by any particularity of revealed truth or positive moral content.[21]

Nor does this state of affairs seem particularly troubling to the majority either of systematicians or of biblical scholars. One extensive recent survey of British theology tellingly confined its comments on biblical studies to a fleeting and patchy list of primarily New Testament practitioners.[22] In a subsequent public exchange with a leading exponent of so-called 'Radical Orthodoxy', the same author did raise the place of Scripture as 'the most radical question' to be asked of that movement. But despite its stated urgency that question did not appear to fall on hearing ears.[23]

To be sure, biblical scholars are hardly in a position to exercise professional one-upmanship. Most of them continue to be content to ignore the question of Scripture's witness to Christian truth. In reading against the grain of catholic faith, moreover, biblical scholarship typically takes for granted a sectarian ecclesi-

---

[21] Williams, 'Making Moral Decisions', pp. 6–7.

[22] David F. Ford, 'British Theology after a Trauma: Divisions and Conversations', *Christian Century* 117.12, 2000, pp. 425–31 (pp. 426–7) (cf. David F. Ford, 'British Theology: Movements and Churches', *Christian Century* 117.13, 2000, pp. 467–73; idem, 'Theological Wisdom, British Style', *Christian Century* 117.11, 2000, pp. 388–91. Francis Watson's omission is particularly surprising in the context, given works such as his 'The Scope of Hermeneutics', in Colin Gunton, (ed.), *The Cambridge Companion to Christian Doctrine*, Cambridge: Cambridge University Press, 1997, pp. 65–80; idem, *Text and Truth: Redefining Biblical Theology*, Edinburgh: T. & T. Clark / Grand Rapids: Eerdmans, 1997; James Dunn, Andrew Lincoln and Craig Bartholomew are among a number of other unmentioned leading players with an arguable interest in Scripture and theology.

[23] David F. Ford, 'Radical Orthodoxy and the Future of British Theology', *Scottish Journal of Theology* 54, 2001, pp. 385–404 (pp. 397–9); see C. Pickstock, 'Reply to David Ford and Guy Collins', *Scottish Journal of Theology* 54, 2001, pp. 405–22, about whose reply to the question David F. Ford, 'A Response to Catherine Pickstock', *Scottish Journal of Theology* 54, 2001, pp. 423–5 (pp. 424–5) is charitable. Cf. similarly, Aidan Nichols, review of John Milbank and Catherine Pickstock, *Truth in Aquinas*, London: Routledge, 2000, *Theology*, 2001, pp. 288–9 (p. 289) on Radical Orthodoxy's neglect of Scripture's importance for Aquinas.

ology, inserting a fundamental chasm between the Church who first believed and the Church who now believes.[24] My thoughts about the current and future state of New Testament studies have been amply developed elsewhere.[25] Here I merely wish to note the seeming contrast between the current state of most British theology, whether biblical or dogmatic, and what used to be a fundamental conviction of Christian theologians: that Scripture's witness to the Triune God is the fountainhead of all Christian theology and worship. Among leading German and American systematicians at least a minority continue to make this point both explicitly and emphatically, in theory if not always in practice. Thus, Michael Welker is among those who follow Karl Barth in understanding dogmatics as 'consistent exegesis' (*konsequente Exegese*),[26] while Robert

---

[24] So rightly R. W. Jenson, 'The Religious Power of Scripture', *Scottish Journal of Theology* 52, 1999, pp. 89–105 (p. 98); cf. Joel B. Green, 'Scripture and Theology: Failed Experiments, Fresh Perspectives', *Interpretation* 56, 2002, pp. 5–20 (p. 10). Jenson insists that 'whatever hermeneutical gaps may need to be dealt with . . . , there is *no* historical distance between the community in which the Bible appeared and the church which now seeks to understand the Bible . . . The text we call the Bible was put together in the first place by the same community that now needs to interpret it.' This sort of 'sectarian' ecclesiology is nicely illustrated in a standard textbook like Bruce J. Malina, *The New Testament World: Insights from Cultural Anthropology*, Louisville: Westminster John Knox Press, 2001, p. 24 (and *passim*), who treats the biblical authors consistently as 'a group of foreigners somehow dropped in our midst'.

[25] Markus Bockmuehl, '"To Be Or Not To Be": The Possible Futures of New Testament Scholarship', *Scottish Journal of Theology* 51, 1998, pp. 271–306.

[26] See Karl Barth, *Kirchliche Dogmatik* I/2, Zurich: Evangelischer Verlag, 1937; also, e.g., I/1, 1932, p. 261; II/1, 1939, pp. 523–98 *passim*; Michael Welker, 'Wort und Geist', in C. Landmesser, H.-J. Eckstein and H. Lichtenberger, (eds.), *Jesus Christus als die Mitte der Schrift: Studien zur Hermeneutik des Evangeliums*, Berlin: de Gruyter, 1997, pp. 159–69; idem, 'Sozio-metaphysische Theologie und Biblische Theologie: Zu Eilert Herms, "Was haben wir an der Bibel?"', *Jahrbuch für Biblische Theologie* 13, 1999, pp. 309–22; Wilfred Härle, *Dogmatik*, De Gruyter Lehrbuch, Berlin/New York: de Gruyter, 1995, pp. 111–39; Friedrich Mildenberger, *Biblische Dogmatik*, Stuttgart: Kohlhammer, 1991–3. Cf. further Werner G. Jeanrond, 'After Hermeneutics: The Relationship between Theology and Biblical

Jenson, Gabriel Fackre and others affirm and practise this discipline in America.[27]

As a Protestant I may perhaps be permitted the observation that I have found no more attractive statement of this sacramental place of Scripture in the Church's faith than that of the 1994 *Catechism of the Catholic Church*:

> Through all the words of Sacred Scripture, God speaks only one single Word, his one Utterance in whom he expresses himself completely . . . For this reason, the Church has always venerated the Scriptures as she venerates the Lord's Body. She never ceases to present to the faithful the bread of life, taken from the one table of God's Word and Christ's Body. In Sacred Scripture, the Church constantly finds her nourishment and her strength, for she welcomes it not as a human word, 'but as what it really is, the word of God' [1 Thess. 2.13]. 'In the sacred books, the Father who is in heaven comes lovingly to meet his children, and talks with them.'[28]

In this 500th anniversary of the Lady Margaret's benefaction, biblical and dogmatic theology at Cambridge might pause to consider in what sense, if any, it would wish to embrace and inhabit that historic conviction. If it does – if we do –, how might

---

Studies', in F. Watson, (ed.), *The Open Text*, London: SCM Press, 1993, pp. 85–102 (p. 99) (also quoted in Watson, 'The Scope of Hermeneutics', p.74). It is also worth recalling Gerhard Ebeling, *Kirchengeschichte als Geschichte der Auslegung der Heiligen Schrift*, Tübingen: Mohr (Siebeck), 1947, on church history as the history of the interpretation of Scripture.

[27] See, e.g., Jenson, 'The Religious Power of Scripture'; Gabriel Fackre, *The Christian Story: A Pastoral Systematics*, Grand Rapids: Eerdmans, 1984–7; L. Gregory Jones and James Joseph Buckley, (eds.), *Theology and Scriptural Imagination*, Oxford: Blackwell, 1998; R. Kendall Soulen, *The God of Israel and Christian Theology*, Minneapolis: Fortress Press, 1996; cf. Kathryn Greene-McCreight, *Ad litteram: How Augustine, Calvin, and Barth Read the 'Plain Sense' of Genesis 1–3*, Issues in Systematic Theology 5, New York: P. Lang, 1999.

[28] *Catechism of the Catholic Church* (§§102–4); the concluding quote is from *Dei Verbum* 21. Note that the context of 1 Thess. 2.13 concerns not Scripture in general but the apostolic proclamation.

we reconceive our work so as to embody this appropriately in our teaching and research?

Dogmatic and biblical theology in Britain may in fact be answerable to a particularly urgent ecclesiological imperative in all this. The demographers tell us that truly, there are some standing here who shall not taste death before they see the light of Christianity extinguished upon these islands.[29] Of course we all have knowledge; and we are well aware of 'lies, damned lies and statistics'. We can decide to sit back and let that prognosis disappear under a thousand qualifications. Nevertheless, it remains the case that for Christian theology in Britain this may be a moment of truth: the question is if it will heed the call to hold forth the witness of Scripture as the word of life for the people of God.

The implied disciple: temptation and discovery

For the biblical and patristic writers, the interpretation of Scripture is itself subject to the hermeneutic of the Spirit: prophetic truth is never just a matter of individual interpretation.[30] So also the meaning of the sacred text is understood not primarily by creative genius or scientific dissection, but by the interplay of divine gift and human delight. In his extensive reflection on divine revelation in Psalm 119, for example, the Psalmist applies to his object of study no transitive verbs of manipulation or deconstruction, but only of discovery – of 'invention' (*invenire*) in its original sense not of a creation *de novo* but of a 'finding' that engages and transforms the 'inventor': 'I rejoice at your word,' he says, 'as one who has found (Vulgate: *invenit*) great spoil' (Ps. 119.162). God's word has become a lamp and a light for this interpreter's path (119.105).

Both testaments of Scripture clearly presuppose such an interpreter. The implied reader of the Christian Scripture is a *disciple*,

---

[29] Peter W. Brierley, *The Tide is Running Out: What the English Church Attendance Survey Reveals*, London: Christian Research, 2000.

[30] E.g. 2 Pet. 2.19–21; 1 Cor. 2.6–10.

just as the implied text of the Christian disciple is Scripture's witness to the Christ.[31] In rabbinic Judaism, the most celebrated Old Testament encapsulation of this posture was Israel's response to the word of God at Sinai: 'We will do and we will heed'.[32] The object of biblical interpretation, in other words, is the interpreter as much as it is the text, and it is *performative* as much as it is hermeneutical.[33]

Part of theology's predicament, of course, has always been that even sincere interpretation of Scripture can be false as well as true; and this hermeneutical contest in turn goes to the very heart of the struggle between good and evil. It is here that transformed reason and Christ-centred wisdom are essential to the interpreter's task.

Permit me to illustrate from Scripture's two pivotal stories of temptation, the temptation of Adam and the temptation of Christ. Both turn on hermeneutics,[34] to wit: a hermeneutic of suspicion, detachment and *Sachkritik*. Interpretation in each case reduces the divine address to an object for an analysis as if from an Archimedean point outside, by staking a pseudo-empirical claim to objectivity.

Step One is to eliminate the ecclesial reception of the word of God and to place interpretation in the hands of the autonomous reasoning subject: the serpent speaks to Eve, not Eve and Adam, let alone to their fellowship with the Lord God himself who walks in the garden. Step Two is to eliminate the *sensus literalis*.

---

[31] Cf. further Bockmuehl, '"To Be Or Not To Be"', pp. 298–301. This is not to deny the complementary insight of those like Green, 'Scripture and Theology', p. 220 who stress the role of Scripture in effecting the interpreter's theological conversion. (Cf. also the remark of Williams, *On Christian Theology*, p. xvi about 'the inescapable place of repentance' in all theology.)

[32] Exod. 24.7; cf. e.g. *b. Shab.* 88a.

[33] This of course is widely acknowledged; cf., e.g., Nicholas Lash, 'Performing the Scriptures', in *Theology on the Way to Emmaus*, London: SCM Press, 1986, pp. 37–46;. Stephen C. Barton, 'New Testament Interpretation as Performance', *Scottish Journal of Theology* 52, 1999, pp. 179–208; Gunton, 'Using and Being Used'.

[34] Cf. also the apposite remarks by E. T. Oakes, 'Stanley Fish's Milton', *First Things* 117, 2001, pp. 23–34, on Stanley Eugene Fish, *How Milton Works*, Cambridge, MA: Harvard University Press, 2001.

The tempter caricatures *what* God said in order to expose it as rationally suspect: he muses provocatively, 'Did God indeed say, "You shall not eat from *any* tree in the garden"?' Eve rises to the bait, responding with a garbled and legalistic interpretation of the divine command that fails to quote God's words accurately, all but eliminates his grace, and greatly exacerbates the severity of his prohibition.[35] Having safely established the external viewpoint from which the divine command is exposed as unreasonable, the serpent now turns to demythologize the judgement. 'Surely you will not die; God himself knows . . . that your eyes will be opened and you will be like God.' Note the substitution of immanent consequentialism for divine judgement, a classic reductionist move in moral hermeneutics ever since: things are wrong not if they violate a sacred principle or mandate, but only inasmuch as their immediate consequences are demonstrably unpleasant. Step Three is simply to move in for the hermeneutical kill. Eliminating the divine command in this fashion allows the deconstruction of the subject along the classic lines of a lust for the forbidden object – material consumption, aesthetic possession, and knowledge as power: 'Seeing that the tree was good for food, and a delight to the eyes, and desirable to make one wise, she took of the fruit and ate.' Adam is simply content to follow the irresistibly footnoted consensus of hermeneutical precedent – and the rest, as they say, is salvation history.

Contrast this with the scriptural interpretation in the temptation story of Matthew 4. The recurring pattern in the tempter's approach is chilling. Step One: challenge the individual interpreter as autonomous reasoning subject. After fasting forty days and nights, Jesus is famished. Then the devil comes to him. Step Two: eliminate the plain sense of the divine word by expropriating it for a seemingly more objective (but in fact only more self-interested) viewpoint. 'If you really are the Son of God . . .' A divine Son surely is and does all that pleases him! Never mind that the baptismal heavenly voice in fact affirmed Jesus to be the

---

[35] The report of what is permitted omits both the 'all' and all reference to divine speech; while the prohibition places the tree in 'the middle of the garden' and forbids even the touching of it.

Son who is and does all that pleases *the Father*. But unlike his foremother in the garden, this Son does *not* rise to the bait, and does *not* produce the invited distortion of the divine command. Instead, the Word himself finds in Scripture the textual icon of the life-giving divine presence: 'man . . . shall live by every word that proceeds from the mouth of God'.

Having failed on that score, the tempter nevertheless raises the stakes. He rolls Steps Two and Three into one, in order to flatter the human craving to know and be like God. First, an attempt to hijack Jesus' own hermeneutics: 'If you are the Son of God, throw yourself down', since Scripture itself promises you the power to do so. Jesus resists this blatant estrangement of the *sensus literalis*, which seeks to make God's word deny itself and malign its author: 'Again it is written, Do not put the Lord your God to the test.' All else having failed, the appeal to Scripture is quietly abandoned in order to indulge the naked lust for power, material and aesthetic possession: 'all the kingdoms of this world and their splendour' I will give you. But just when the tempter's ever grander self-deification dispenses with Scripture altogether, Jesus dismisses him by the simple truth of its most basic affirmation: 'It is written, "You shall worship the Lord your God and serve him only."'[36]

By this hermeneutical reversal of the Fall, faithfully pursued to the cross, the risen Jesus has become the key to Scripture itself. This is recognized by all the New Testament and patristic writers. And it receives its most explicit affirmation on the road to Emmaus, as Walter Moberly has also recently argued.[37] 'Beginning with Moses', the Wisdom of God himself shows 'all that the prophets declared' by the Spirit to speak the one Word of God in Jesus Christ (Luke 24.25–27). Here Scripture and theology cohere in an interpretation that gives life to the people of God, causing their hearts to burn within them (24.32).

---

[36] All three of Jesus' responses are thus quotations from Deuteronomy: 8.3, 6.16 and 6.13.

[37] R. W. L. Moberly, *The Bible, Theology, and Faith: A Study of Abraham and Jesus*, Cambridge Studies in Christian Doctrine, Cambridge: Cambridge University Press, 2000, pp. 45–70.

Aquinas as a disciple of Scripture

Lest all this sound a little remote to exegetes and dogmaticians alike, I wish to close with a picture of one who was both, and who has regained increasing importance in recent theological debate. Here is a Flemish engraving that depicts a scene first mentioned in the early fourteenth-century *Lives* of St Thomas by William Tocco and Bernard Gui:[38]

18.
C. Gia.
Cum pro sensu loci alicuius in Isaia triduo ieiunijs et orationibus institisset, nocte quadam socius
eius Reginaldus duos cum eo loquentes audiuit: quibus abeuntibus, socio ad se vocato, commentaria
in eum locum expeditè admodum dictauit. Quo facto obnixè eum Reginaldus rogauit, vt qui illi
fuissent, cum quibus tanto tempore locutus erat, aperiret: victus Thomas ait fuisse sanctissimos Pe-
trum et Paulum Apostolos, qui eum vnà cum Deipara Virgine in dubijs sæpius edocere soliti erant.

Once when Thomas had wrestled with the meaning of a certain passage in Isaiah for three days of prayer and fasting,

---

[38] Otto Cornelius van Veen, *Vita D. Thomae Aquinatis Othonis Vaeni ingenio et manu delineata*, Antwerp: Sumptibus Othonis Vaeni, 1610, pl. 18; also reproduced in Thomas Aquinas, *Commentary on Saint Paul's Epistle to the Ephesians*, Aquinas Scripture Series 2, Albany: Magi Books, 1966, p. iv.

> one night his friend Reginald heard two men speaking with him. After they left, Thomas called his friend and promptly dictated the commentary on that passage without difficulty. When this was done, Reginald pressed him to explain with whom he had spoken at such length. Thomas conceded that they had been the holy apostles Peter and Paul, who along with the Virgin Mother of God often used to teach him in difficult questions.[39]

For all the evident hagiography of this portrait, it does embody a number of this study's central themes. And it does so in relation to a theological giant whose commitment and towering importance as an interpreter of Scripture has long been virtually ignored on all sides. This picture shows a master of systematicians employing the best of human reason in the demanding and persistent labour of engaging the text of the Old Testament as Christian Scripture. He is prompted and accompanied in this evidently communal, ecclesial task by the twin apostolic witness to the Jews and to the Gentiles – Peter and Paul, who jointly laid the foundation of the Church. Thomas works, in other words, not in splendid critical isolation but as a disciple in the company of the saints.[40] In that work, finally, he is further encouraged and prompted by the testimony of a third fellow disciple – the Mother of God, whose faithful ministry of pointing the world to her Son both illuminates and embodies the Christian interpreter's task.

---

[39] Summary provided on the plate in Veen, *Vita D. Thomae Aquinatis* (my trans.). See the longer accounts in the *Lives* by William Tocco (ch. 31) and Bernard Gui (ch. 16), which date from c. 1319–25 (cf. Kenelm Foster, (ed.), *The Life of Saint Thomas Aquinas: Biographical Documents*, London: Longmans, Green /Baltimore: Helicon, 1959, pp. 6–11). Fr. Aidan Nichols kindly draws my attention to Gui's version in Foster pp. 38–9 (cf. also pp. 70–1, nn. 47–8).

[40] Cf. also Barton, 'New Testament Interpretation as Performance', pp. 199–202 on the saints as fellow 'performers' of Scripture.

5. Reason, Wisdom and the Interpretation of Scripture

DANIEL W. HARDY

Introduction

Presumably, we who join together in a seminar of biblical scholars and theologians have one important thing in common, dedication to the interpretation of Scripture. Despite that, we are probably not so closely related as easily to recognize the different ways in which we show our dedication. No doubt, our different ways are at least partly the outcome of the long-term fragmentation of the 'sciences' of the theological academy. This divided enterprise had particular historical origins, of course, but it has been institutionalized – through agreed curriculums and allotments of personnel – as the state of affairs within which we all exist.

Our common dedication to the interpretation of Scripture puts a question mark over the legitimacy of this fragmentation. So also does the end we all serve. There is a sense in which a university is a 'living encyclopedia' forever advancing and integrating all knowledge needing to be 'read' by the surrounding society for its well-being and advancement. If that is what a university is, we fail it if we do not perform this living integration in such a way as to meet the needs of the society of which we are a part. Furthermore, if the events of 11 September 2001 and their aftermath show anything, it is that societies – in the face of the threats to the meaning of life exemplified in those events – need those capable of interpreting their meaning to them. At their deepest level, the questions of the meaning of life are religious issues, and the interpretation of the meaning of society can only happen if religious people co-operate in attending to this task. So we here have a double responsibility, to the university and to its task of interpreting the meaning of life to the surrounding society.

Between these two, a beginning dedicated to the interpretation of Scripture and the end – with others in the university – of assisting society to rediscover its deeper meaning, lie the really difficult issues of the nature of the deeper meaning of the Scriptures, how to interpret this, and what is the rationality in these matters that we share with others in and beyond the theological academy. *What is it we should be seeking in the Scriptures*, *how are we to approach it through interpretation*, and *how is doing so a rational exercise?*

This combined Seminar presents a remarkable opportunity for addressing these questions. The precondition, of course, is careful attention to our different ways of approaching them, with the intention – even where differences are irreconcilable – of finding ways of holding them within a common project whose end lies beyond all of them. I shall explain what I mean by that later.

So far as we can, however, we should operate from the beginning and ends upon which we may find agreement, and not – at least in the first place – dwell on our different ways. Accordingly, I shall suggest that the questions are best approached through attending to the deeper meaning of the Scriptures themselves, in ways that relocate both biblical criticism and doctrine. My presentation is more programmatic and allusive than I would wish, but there is too little time now to provide the fuller arguments that would be needed to substantiate my case.

Why Scriptures?

We need to begin by asking *why* we attend to these texts. We must not let our common dedication (as I suppose it is) to the interpretation of the Scriptures blind us to the fact that concentrating on texts – and these texts in particular – and on specific ways of interpretive reasoning, is more unusual than it might first appear. As common as it is to engage with the world as if it were textual, or with texts as if they were the most reliable means of access to the world, it is not a foregone conclusion that texts should be regarded as so central. From the early stages of the evolution of 'modernity' – in the philosophy of Francis Bacon, for example – the 'book' of the 'word and oracle of God' was placed alongside the 'book' of nature, in effect separating the meaning of the two and relativizing the former by the latter. And reasoning was also divided by Bacon into the uses to which it was put in special fields, as modes of reasoning varying for history, poetry, nature, natural theology, humanity, bodily arts, ethics, culture, and the like. The effect was to decouple reasoning from its primarily text-connected use, as that was seen in the European Renaissance and Reformation, and to promote the variability of reasoning in different kinds of search for meaning. These two – the isolation and relativizing of the book of the word and the pluralizing of reasoning – present enduring challenges for those who adhere to the primacy of these texts, including the biblical word as found in the living traditions of interpretation. That is something we need to remember as we take part in the 'living encyclopedia' of this University as it addresses the needs of today's society.

Nonetheless, for us who are dedicated to the interpretation of Scripture there is a presumption of the primacy of *texts*, and *these texts* in particular, whether alone or in combination with other sources and reasonings. How is that upheld?

In the wish for external authorization, some jump quickly to the worlds of metaphysics, metahistory, religion or doctrine for claims that are at least notionally distinct from Scripture itself. As Calvin said, for example,

> Therefore, illumined by his power, we believe neither by our own nor by anyone else's judgment that Scripture is from God; but above human judgment we affirm with utter certainty (just as if we were gazing upon the majesty of God himself) that it has flowed to us from the very mouth of God by the ministry of men.[1]

[1] John Calvin, *Institutes of the Christian Religion*, I.vii.5, trans. F. L. Battles, Philadelphia: Westminster Press, 1960, p. 80.

But such claims, it seems to me, unfold an authorization *internal* to the text, *already in the text itself*. In other words, the primacy of the biblical word is justified by the continued impartation by the text of that which justifies the primacy of these texts.

How shall we speak of that? If we consider it in textual terms, we might best speak of it as a *density of meaning* in the Scriptures. In one sense, this is a familiar idea. It underlies the supposition that there are 'multiple meanings, none of them definitive'. 'One of the messages of modern criticism, and of modern literature, [is] that all texts are "ironic": they have multiple meanings, none of them definitive.'[2] If so, biblical criticism and interpretation are sustained by the infinite play of meanings found in Scripture, and rejoice in the extensity of meanings found. But that 'extensity' testifies, paradoxically, to the density of meaning found in the Scriptures.

The depth of meaning of the Scriptures also underlies the familiar claim that there are different levels of textual interpretation: plain sense, the expanding of plain-sense meaning through metaphor or allegory, the use of the text to illuminate the present, and the use of interpretation to show the mystery of Divine speech and words, as well as the inter-textual weaving of texts to convey meaning. But the density of meaning found in the Scriptures further suggests that within and beyond all of these levels, the texts open a new profundity of meaning – and thereby the possibility of an endless finding and renewal of wisdom – that justifies the supposition that texts 'overflow' with meaning in ways beyond other (and nowadays more usual) focuses of attention. Hence, it is the profundity of their meaning that justifies close attention to the texts, and to carefully interpreting them, for thus does the finding and renewal of wisdom – if that word is appropriate – take place.

It seems self-evident, however, that this density of meaning – in the Scriptures to whose interpretation we are dedicated –

---

[2] John Horgan, *The End of Science*, New York: Addison-Wesley, 1996, p. 3, citing Northrop Frye, *Anatomy of Criticism*, Princeton: Princeton University Press, 1957.

conveys more than simply an extensity of meanings to be found there. It suggests an intensity of meaning in which both God and humanity are joined, both heaven and history, not simply by way of assertions about them, but as dynamically interwoven and mutually operative. Not only does this question the assumption that the Scriptures are their sheer extensity of meanings. It also challenges other prevailing suppositions about the availability of that which lies beyond straightforwardly historical matters.

In the first place, it questions the notion that the source for the intensity of meaning found in Scripture is split away from historical truth. For example, since the eighteenth century historical truth has been made the precondition for necessary truths of reason: 'If no historical truth can be demonstrated, then nothing can be demonstrated by means of historical truths. That is: accidental truths of history can never become the proof of necessary truths of reason.'[3] This is but one case of the much more widespread practice of dividing higher and more comprehensive meanings from the more mundane and empirically ascertainable. Other modern assumptions are similar, of which two are notable. One is the separation of Jesus from God; 'the reality and message of Jesus did not support any assent to the existence of God. Nor should an appeal [to him] be made.'[4] The other is the separation of the vitality of life – the human spirit – from the Holy Spirit of God. These dichotomies have begotten a variety of theories, practices and theologies by which they are either perpetuated or overcome. Nonetheless, in the density of their meaning the texts of Scripture include both divine and human, in mutual implication.

In the second place, the Scriptures show the marks of the density of meaning found there. They are not simply a tissue of assertions about God and humanity, respectively, like a textbook recital of facts; they are more like accumulated expressions of passions. Why? In them, God, God's purposes and all the forces of life in the world *actually appear together as associated: the*

---

[3] G. E. Lessing, 'On the Proof of the Spirit and of Power', in H. Chadwick, (ed.), *Lessing's Theological Writings*, London: A. & C. Black, 1956, p. 53.

[4] M. Buckley, *At the Origins of Modern Atheism*, New Haven: Yale University Press, 1987, p. 40.

inner movement of God is intrinsic to the dynamics of human life.

This has comprehensive significance: these are the divine-human-spiritual 'intensity' not only of the 'order' of things – of the intelligibility and value of all things and events – but also of the dynamic movement of the life and practices by which they are fulfilled. In that sense, the wisdom embodied in these texts, if that is what we should call it, is not simply a declaration of the state of affairs of the world and its life, a mixture of the real and the ideal, but also a moving – a motivating and attracting – of all things to their proper end. That amazing combination appears in Proverbs 8, for example.

Their density of meaning imparts remarkable characteristics to the Scriptures. Their indefinability resembles the mystery of God, the most profound form of wisdom, which exceeds, encompasses and guides all other forms of meaning. Secondly, their density of meaning will be the source to which the conventional ways of ascribing meaning in the world (e.g. establishing factuality and value) are ultimately traceable. Thirdly, their intensity calls people to think and act in certain ways, 'call[ing] forth conduct . . . irrespective of any utilitarian calculation of helpful or harmful results';[5] it propels or attracts people to act.

Such characteristics are seen in the familiar – but little understood – view of Scripture stated by S. T. Coleridge:

> With such purposes, with such feelings, my dear Sir! have I perused the Books of the Old and New Testament, each Book, as a Whole and as an integral Part. And need I add that I met every where more or less copious Sources of Truth and Power and purifying Impulse (& that I found) words for my inmost Thoughts, Songs for my Joy, Utterances for my hidden Griefs, pleadings for my Shame and my feebleness? In short, *whatever finds me* bears witness for itself that it had proceeded from a Holy Spirit, even from the same Spirit 'which remaining in

---

[5] Emile Durkheim, *The Elementary Forms of Religious Life*, trans. Karen Fields, New York: The Free Press, 1995, p. 209.

> itself yet regenerateth all other Powers *and in all ages* entering holy Souls maketh them Friends of God and Prophets'.[6]

'Truth and Power and purifying Impulse . . . whatever finds me bears witness for itself that it had proceeded from . . . the same Spirit . . . regenerating all other Powers . . . entering holy Souls making them Friends of God and Prophets': the language is archaic but accurate for a density of meaning actively replenishing all other forms of understanding (cognitive and performative) and impelling and purifying all other life.

The first question of those listed at the outset was: What is it we should be seeking in the Scriptures? The answer, it seems to me, is that we should – and can – agree to seek the density of meaning found there that implicates both God and us. We have also found that we should not suppose an irreducible difference between God and us or translate the density of meaning into assertions about what is knowable. Our task instead is to allow the deep meaning of the Scriptures to find us as 'Truth and Power and purifying Impulse'.

Meaning in texts

Before continuing our exploration of Scripture and interpretation, it will help if we pause to consider what is implied, but often unspoken, in the meaning of texts where they have such density as we have indicated. Long-standing practices of philosophy and theology, and more recent habits of modernity and postmodernity, easily blind us to the full scope of textual meaning. For Christians, the adoption of disputational methods in medieval theology, and later the supposition (by Calvinists, for example) of a straightforward correspondence between Scripture and items of belief, tended to subordinate texts to what is to be believed and lived. Latterly, convictions about the indeterminateness of meaning have undermined the possibility of overarching meanings. Do any of these, earlier or more recent,

---

[6] S. T. Coleridge, 'Confessions of an Inquiring Spirit', in *Shorter Works and Fragments, II, Collected Works*, London: Routledge, 1995, pp. 1122f.

adequately reflect the full scope of the density of meaning found in the texts with which we are concerned?

Whether straightforwardly or by implication, the meaning embodied in such texts incorporates many things:

(1) It configures or maps reality in its spatial and temporal aspects.
(2) It gives human beings both their place in the cosmology of the world and also their place in the continuity of world-history.
(3) It 'plots' actions and events, showing what is done and needs to be done, and establishing the coherence of such actions in events. The correlate of such a 'plotting' is that the meaning of texts is found in performance, through which what has been is then done, and what still needs to be done is actually done.
(4) It provides a calculus for the value to be assigned to reality in its different aspects, to human beings, and to actions, events and situations. In this way, it 'measures' them, and assigns them ethical importance that is then embodied in ethical behaviour.
(5) It 'stirs' appropriate forms of thought and conduct.
(6) Through all these, it brings to light the purposes and activity of the God whose own intensity is found in the density of the meaning of these texts and by behaviour propelled or attracted by it.

These features of the density of meaning give some idea of the range of topics that need to figure in our concerns.

Many of us, and certainly I, struggle for freedom from conceptions of texts that lose such range and richness of meaning. It is too easy to 'objectify' texts as sheer facts, events, narratives, principles or teachings, to coincide with what we already know, or to treat them as interwoven ideas and contexts that need historical confirmation or unravelling by particular kinds of interpretation, or indeed to treat them as artefacts necessary to the identity of a culture. But the richer theological-cosmic-historical-plotting-performative-valuational-attractive texture of meaning is essential if the range and density of meaning embedded in religious texts is fully to be appreciated, with their intrinsic connection to the situation and performance of human beings in the world. Nowadays, that is possible only by struggling with the reductive tendencies of secular and religious alternatives. If we are to make our full contribution to the 'living encyclopedia' of the university, however, we must return to the full scope of the density of meaning to be found in Scripture.

Differing interpretations and reasonings

The concerns with which we should be interpreting these texts are already apparent. We need to be attending to the full scope of their density of meaning. In much study and interpretation of Scripture, it seems that this is lost in other preoccupations.

Part of the reason for this is that we are human beings in specific situations, and led not only by our humanity (with its confusions) but also by the pressures to which we are subject. Human beings – as by nature spatially and temporally extended – can only apprehend density of meaning (at its most intensive where the divine and human meet) *extensively*. That does not imply that they are *confined* to this extensity of meaning, however: even very specific and limited appreciations may contain truthful intimations of the more profound meaning.

And, to be sure, there are some situations of extensity in which there is greater intensity, greater density of meaning. In this respect, there are obvious differences in scriptural texts: they are not all of the same kind, whether in depth, content or purpose; and we are intended to take them differently. We are to focus on texts with greater depth of meaning, and to find their depths.

Such practices are too easily associated with the wish to simplify, however, and with attempts to build simplified frames of reference from which other conclusions can be drawn. In such ventures, the risk of idolatry is great, through which lesser meanings are found within Scripture and made normative. Idolatry is at its most dangerous where 'true meanings' are found.

Amongst all who study Scripture, there is much difference of view as to how the 'intensity' or 'density' of meaning happens in the 'extensity' of meaning in biblical texts and/or in traditional readings, a difference that appears in the variety of interpretations everywhere present. Are we to suppose that this density of meaning should occur simply or straightforwardly?

In academic circles, one set of forms of reasoning weighs most heavily of all, those associated with modern notions of human cognition. Whether these are the sole rightful heirs of the tradition of reasoning that has been important through the centuries is an important matter. Reasoning is implicit in the law, prophets and wisdom of the Old Testament; it is found in the arguments offered by Jesus (e.g. Mk 2.8–10, 17, 19–22, 25–26) and by Paul (e.g. 1 Cor. 7.1–16; 10.23–30); its value in the acknowledgement of God is recognized by Paul (Rom. 1.19–20; Acts 17.23–29); and in varying forms it is employed in scriptural interpretation thereafter. The Church's beliefs and behaviour were often arrived at through rational discernment and argument; pedagogy was central to the implanting of Christian faith and life in Greek, Roman, European and world civilization; engagement with the highest forms of philosophy and humanism was necessary to the life of the Church in the Middle Ages and the Reformation and after. Whether in order to understand what is already believed (from Scripture embraced in tradition), to unveil divine rationality in and for human understanding, or to make faith comprehensible through engagement with others, reason was necessary.

Yet the tendency of modern thought – both secular and religious, both biblical and doctrinal – has been to focus on what is received and construed through the disciplines of human cognition, in our day largely fashioned by rationalism and empiricism, often in the extreme forms of positivism, and latterly by the strictures of postmodernism. Even in their benign form, these are what Coleridge called the 'understanding', the lesser counterpart of the higher reason through which truth is found. But when the disciplines of human cognition are as diverse as they are in our times, the result is inevitably differing and exclusive ways of 'knowing', each often claiming hegemony of truth. No matter how valuable these different ways may prove to be for certain purposes, they are far too partial and limited for fully appreciating the density of divine-human meaning found in Scripture.

We need therefore to relearn the value of such varying, and often harsh, practices, measuring them by their capacity to fathom the density of scriptural meaning. By this standard, we can see that individuals and 'families' of readers find this meaning through differing practices of reading in different situations, as new readings are generated in response to new challenges. If we have a problem, it is that our readings are led by – even confined by – the 'family prejudices' of what is acceptable within our circle, or the wish to appear 'more cognitive – or postmodernist – than thou'. Hence, biblical critics and theologians – as well as others – too easily elevate their theories and practices into ideologies by which to exclude each other, and also others perhaps less skilled in such ways but more wise in the 'house of meaning' that is Scripture. What we must all relearn is the power of this density of meaning to appear in new and different readings. That is to acknowledge the legitimacy of probing and different readings, as distinct from a straightforward singular reading to which all should conform.

To the lovers of narrower versions of truth, whether secular academics and religious dogmatists, such a strategy appears at first dangerously libertarian. For secular academics, by disallowing *a priori* structures of scientific rationality, it would seem to open the way to unrestricted religious or quasi-religious fantasies. For religious dogmatists, it would seem an unwarranted intrusion of pluralistic readings into the 'truth' of the texts as expressed in a singular, frequently doctrinal, form. The dilemma of these opposing camps, each totalitarian in its implications, is too familiar in Christian circles!

Communities of interpretation

There is a twofold answer. In response to the concerns of the secular academics, we should not erect new and exclusive codes of rationality, but instead build a new community of reasoning practice, a community of those who are held and sustained by the task of fathoming the density of meaning of Scripture. Such a community will not be tightly constrained, but will resemble the polyvalence of Scripture itself. It will allow that there are *different forms of reasoning informed and moved by the depth and movement of meaning* in the density of the meaning of Scripture. These different forms will find their place in a community of practice bound together by a 'performative logic' of careful textual reading and by the kind of life called forth by the deeper meaning of texts that are read. That is the community in which biblical scholars and theologians need to join. In effect, this is to advocate a dynamic form of social practice that receives its form and energy of life from the density of meaning found in the texts.

The pursuit of such a community will be particularly important where there are divided views about the meaning of texts, as between rival camps amongst both academics and Christians. What has happened amongst Anglicans in the wake of the 1998 Lambeth Conference illustrates this. Two camps have emerged that differ in the use of biblical texts, in the place accorded to traditions of interpretation, in their conception of reasoning, and even in profound issues about God. For one camp, the meaning of biblical texts is their plain sense, and this is to be found directly (not through traditions of interpretation), in accordance with the content of a religious faith that is not itself subject to reinterpretation. For the other camp, biblical texts are to be approached within traditions of interpretation and with reasoning informed by the struggle to respond to deep human dilemmas and oppressive practices (gender and sexuality, for example). Such a division in the use of biblical texts has proved highly damaging, bringing unending disagreement in matters of faith and life.

Especially where (as they frequently do) the rival camps rationalize the necessity for division from each other in religious terms, or by what is deemed ethically acceptable, the practical, everyday difficulty of maintaining community between them is very great. Here, however, is where the logic found at work in some Jewish 'Textual Reasoning' and Christian–Jewish–Muslim 'Scriptural Reasoning' provides a way forward. On the one hand, what this seeks to do is to identify clearly what is at stake in diverse forms of biblical interpretation. The differences lie not only in diverse forms of reasoning but also in their social counterparts, oppression and exclusion. What is found is that these follow 'the dyadic logic of oppression and exclusion' (Peter Ochs) in which contrasting practices of interpretation are irresolvable, and are used to divide and oppress people. Those engaged in textual and scriptural reasoning seek to find a transcendent possibility of 'repairing' this difference-that-is-oppression.

That possibility resides not in any hitherto knowable state of affairs, but one that is latent in the Scriptures. For Christians this carries the implication that it is beyond the horizons of existing conceptions of biblical and theological truth, laden as they are with notions of what is most fundamental and 'beyond reinterpretation'. Instead, the possibility is a *practical* one: it arises through the establishment of a 'community of dialogue in difference' – a 'tent of meeting' – efficacious because both 'camps' differ and meet through argument, not agreement.

A one-time colleague of mine, a distinguished professor of Christian theology, used to say, 'Why must we assume that we must always be nice, and agree?' This shifts the frame of reference for discussion, from the supposition that universality is found where there is agreement, to the supposition that deeper meaning may be found through argument. Hence, as I would put it, different camps may, through argument, learn more deeply the density of meaning to which their own preferred use of texts, interpretations and reason differently testify. Interestingly, their very difference promotes a more profound intensity of meaning by which they are 'found' and 'held' together.

Yet it can be asked what renders such communal practices of textual reasoning coherent. The answer, it seems, is that a *polity of exploration and expression* emerges in textual and scriptural reasoning, through which certain kinds of search and the finding of meaning emerge as appropriate, where others might be less so. And such a polity 'holds' the activity of the community within the density of meaning of Scripture. In effect, it embodies the movement of the divine in Scripture.

What, then, is the logically transcendental condition for their being 'found' and 'held' together in their difference? For some, following American pragmatic philosophy, this happens when a logical 'third' is achieved. That is a particular kind of philosophical response. But there may also be a theological one, suggesting that community happens as the dynamic of the Trinitarian God in the movement of Wisdom – the Lord conferring favour and life (Prov. 8.35) – calls and stimulates them to meet and embrace. So God is known *a posteriori* in the common engagement in the movement of Wisdom of those who differ in their interpretations of Scripture, not least biblical scholars and theologians.

Scripture and doctrines

There is a second answer. Despite the 'free play' of differing interpretations, a good deal more is at stake, the possibility of truth itself: in that respect, religious 'dogmatists' are right. That recalls us to an issue that was passed over too quickly earlier, the question of how the relative position and actions of God and humanity are discerned in their mutual involvement in the Scriptures. In the density of meaning that finds us – and is found by us – in Scripture, we saw that God and humanity are mutually implicated in who they are and what they do. But how are their roles and actions discerned?[7]

The same divided response as to the roles of Scripture, traditions and reasonings tends also to emerge here. As we saw, one 'camp' suggests that the biblical texts, in their plain sense meaning, simply shows receptive human beings true doctrine, what is truly the work of God and what is the proper kind of human action. Against them are poised those for whom the reading of Scripture is unavoidably plural, in the multiplicity of texts and the situated,

---

[7] When Solomon prays to the Lord God, for example, and in response the Lord God gives him 'a wise and discerning mind' by which to know the wisdom of God, how are we to distinguish the relative positions and responsibilities of God and humanity? (1 Kgs 3.12, NRSV).

contingent, and revisable interpretations that appear in the understanding and interaction of interpreters.

Where they meet (in that transcendental 'third' alluded to before) is in the purpose of interpreting Scripture, the possibility of finding coherent patterns through which what is found of God and humanity can be stated. The result will be the development of focused statements of 'what is the case', which take the form of teaching (doctrine). These will state what is found in Scripture without doing violence to it, and – as organizing principles for reading – will serve the task of further scriptural reading. In that respect, there will need to be a close 'loop' between Scripture, coherent patterns found (teaching), and further reading. It is another matter whether such patterns and teachings should be used as axioms from which further teaching is generated, for then a growing gap between them and Scripture may appear.

Addressing primal truth

Yet this still leaves scriptural interpretation and doctrine in a relatively weak position. Even in combination with the establishment of a 'community of dialogue in difference' – through which exclusion and oppression are repaired – the truth offered by interpretation and doctrine is a *practical* one. What makes it more?

The answer lies in Scripture-and-doctrine as *form of address*, by which the Lord is identified and addressed in worship, in which the very Lordship of this Lord is found through acknowledging it. Hence, it is through the use of Scripture and doctrine as the form by which the Lord is addressed in worship that the intensities (densities) of meaning in Scripture and doctrine emerge.

By comparison, plain sense meanings and the doctrinal statements they sponsor – whether taken as normative or seen as relative in value – do only limited justice to the density of meaning found in the Scriptures. For, it seems, there are *levels of meaning* in the texts, and some approximate more closely to the depth of meaning, while others do less. How do these deeper levels emerge? There are two means by which they seem to.

One is that some levels carry greater *intrinsic* significance, chiefly those that approximate to the identity of the ultimate term of reference, that is the Lord God, and the primary spheres within which the Lord operates, where other levels refer to matters of more transitory significance. Another is that the wish to respond to what is ultimate begets a *passion* to appreciate and think what is most comprehensive, a passion satisfied by the vivid presence of the ultimate. This passion may provide a fundamental basis and motivation for living, under-gird all attempts to explain things and make them intelligible, and serve as motivation for bringing things toward their well being.

These deeper levels of scriptural meaning, both as intrinsically important and as the source of passionate concern, provide a rationale for the locating of 'primal' truths in Scripture. Pursuing such 'primal truths' can readily be co-equal with scriptural study, without displacing either the plain sense interpretation of Scripture or the multiplicity of interpretations. Indeed, it is appropriate to consider this pursuit as co-present with the variety of other kinds of criticism now developed for the study of the Scriptures.

The form of primal truth

If we attend to the Scriptures, the region of primal truth is not a neutral arena like a Platonic universe of the true forms/ideas of things; and it is therefore not an object for cool contemplation. It is intense, with a coherence/identity; and it confers coherence and identity on all else. These characteristics begin to appear in Exodus, where God calls to Moses from out of a burning bush.

> God called to him out of the bush, 'Moses, Moses!' And he said, 'Here I am.' Then he said, 'Come no closer! Remove the sandals from your feet, for the place on which you are standing is holy ground.' He said further, 'I am the God of your father, the God of Abraham, the God of Isaac, and the God of Jacob.' And Moses hid his face, for he was afraid to look at God. (Exod. 3.4–6, NRSV)

From this we learn that the ultimate location of the 'primal truths' is one of sheer *identity* and *intensity* from whose 'call' we learn not only something of what '*it*' is and its extraordinary *vitality*, but also who *we* are as a people and how we are given identity and vitality. It is from this that a continuous *history* and *life* for people arises, as the same intense identity had *moved* and *guided* those who had gone before.

This still leaves a puzzle about the ultimate character of the one who addresses Moses. A little later we hear Moses asking this God who he is:

> God said to Moses, 'I AM WHO I AM.' He said further, 'Thus you shall say to the Israelites, "I AM has sent me to you."' God also said to Moses, 'Thus you shall say to the Israelites, "The LORD, the God of your ancestors, the God of Abraham, the God of Isaac, and the God of Jacob, has sent me to you": This is my name forever, and this my title for all generations.' (Exod. 3.14–15, NRSV)

The word 'God', it seems, only speaks of the ultimate authority this intense identity has over those – for those – who are called; it does not tell us much about who this is. Now that Moses is told the name of God – I AM WHO I AM – this identity is seen as *self-established as an infinite depth of identity*, a *permanently mysterious core of identity that brings identity and coherence to everything*.

By this time we are at the edges of what can be said about this intense and limitless identity that brings coherence to everything. Words themselves derive their meaning from this 'wordless' identity; that is why we need to be very cautious about speaking of this ultimate and intense identity, for by degrees we reduce it to what we can manage, and what fits our thoughts and words. When someone speaks of 'knowing the mind of God', it usually means knowing to what his conceptions lead, and reducing 'the mind of God' to that. But the I AM WHO I AM exceeds all that we can say, both in intensity and identity, and provides a limitless basis and goal for all knowledge, life and words. The word for that is 'holy'.

It is possible to treat all this – the intense identity of the One who is the basis, coherence, and goal of all our striving – as a kind of 'state of affairs' that is the precondition of what we find and do in the world, in effect the rationalization of the accomplishments of the modern era. This One is just 'there', and firm enough to be a foundation for everything else. But that vastly underrates the significance of the infinite and intense identity of the I AM WHO I AM.

For the traces of this Holy One are everywhere, in every serious attempt to make sense of – and explain – things, in every thing with a capacity for life and for making life possible for other people. What draws us to these things, and sustains us in them is the infinite and intense identity of the I AM WHO I AM. The *intensity* of the identity of this One is what leads us to the *extensity* and coherence of our searching. And – to put it the other way around – wherever we are serious about this searching, the identity of this One is latent in what we do.

A fuller conception of this One, a way of understanding what is actually going on between the *intensity* of this One and the *extensity* of our searching and living, is also found in Scripture, in the Gospel of John. Jesus is shown there as one whose life has been lived in the closest affinity to the I AM WHO I AM, and who now prays directly to him before his anticipated death. He has a twofold concern, to be enabled through the intensity of God to live in it and to recognize and fulfil the intensity of God in the world, by giving the intensity of God's full life – 'eternal life' – to all of the people God had entrusted to him. So the issue is how Jesus *fulfills* the intensity of God by *embedding it* in the full range of the lives of those to whom he was sent. And he 'reports' to God that he has done that.

> I have made *your name* known to those whom you gave me from the world. They were yours, and you gave them to me, and they have kept your word. Now they know that everything you have given me is from you . . .
>
> All mine are yours, and yours are mine; and I have been glorified in them. (Jn 17.6–7, 10, NRSV)

Living from the intense identity of God has enabled Jesus to give it to the people entrusted to him: intensity has been fulfilled in extensity, and extensity has been incorporated in intensity. Thereby the people are given the fullest life – eternal life – and given a new, transformed identity.

So at least here in this instance the intensity of the identity and life of God are fulfilled in the transformation of the identity and life of people. What it means is that the intense identity of God is not simply a background *possibility* for life in the world, as it is usually assumed to be. At least here in Jesus, one who fully participates in the intense identity of God, it is *actually* here in the world, fulfilled in these people. The implication is that the intense identity of God is transferred in Jesus to the world. So the oneness of God is 'extendable' without losing its character.

As we recall, what we found in the intense identity of the I AM WHO I AM was not an inert *principle* or *rule* of identity, but One whose identity is *life*, whose life was extended as eternal life to people. So there is a life-fullness in God, there in the intense identity of the I AM WHO I AM. It does not stop there, but amazingly, it is made still more intense as it is extended to others: the 'glorifying' of the Son 'glorified' in the people also 'glorifies' the Father. This 'circling of life' – a surrounding and inter-penetrating life-fullness – does not stop with the death of Jesus; this circling life is far too intense and embracing – both intensive and extensive in my terms. It sponsors the *vigour* with which we *renew* life and understanding by exploring and searching.

So a kind of 'keeping' is needed, for which Jesus appeals to the Father in that reading: 'Holy Father, keep them in your name that you have given me, so that they may be one, as we are one.' From within the intensive identity of the I AM WHO I AM, transferred into the world in one (Jesus) who shares it, there also comes a continuous 'keeping' that keeps people in the *intensive, coherent and full life* that is the primal truth for all life in the world. In one sense, this is not surprising, because the world and its life are marked by integrity and proportion: parts held together in their proper order, and healthy because they are. But the basis for this is more easily overlooked: its basis lies in the 'circling life' of God by which the order and health of the world are 'kept' as they are incorporated in the Jesus through whom the infinite intensity of the I AM WHO I AM is present in the world. The vitality of God is that complex – a Triune vitality, identifying, forming and moving – as it engages with life in the world.

Conclusion

Let me close on a still more hopeful note. It may be that the engagement of those who differ will bring about new and subtler ways of fathoming the density of meaning in the Scriptures. In some ways, our varying strategies of reasoning – especially modern ones – have been much too crude: most have been predicated on harsh ways of reducing the enormous density of meaning in the Scriptures. To use an analogy drawn from information theory, they have all required what is known as 'uniform sampling', what is now used to convert an analogue signal to digital form, on a music CD for example. What this has done, in effect, is to limit what is found to a particular 'band' – in the case of music, a particular range of frequencies – in order to make the sampling accurate. But another possibility – just recently identified in information theory[8] – is to use sampling in a series of mutually-correcting steps to arrive at a fuller and fuller approximation to (interpretation of) the original data. If scriptural interpretation were to be seen in such a way, the variety of ways of scriptural reasoning would, through the ongoing mutual correction of many of us working together, arrive at a fuller approximation to the depth and scope of the meaning of Scripture. By such means, we might make our fuller contribution to the 'living encyclopedia' of the university, and through that to the society around us.

---

[8] 'A New Wave', *The Economist*, 19 January 2002, p. 83.

6. Proverbs 8 in Interpretation (1): Historical Criticism and Beyond

PAUL JOYCE

The exegesis of Proverbs 8 played a key role in the Arian controversy. Over against Arian attempts to use especially 8.22 as a proof-text for the creation of the Son, Fathers such as Athanasius interpreted the text in a way that was compatible with, indeed helped the articulation of, an orthodox understanding of the relation of Father and Son.[1] This provides an excellent example of pre-modern interpretation. (We should not, of course, say pre-critical, for Patristic exegesis was highly critical, albeit on its own terms). Frances Young has explicated the assumptions and demonstrated the coherence of the anti-Arian exegesis of Proverbs 8 very effectively.[2] But it is nevertheless hard to escape the sense that the biblical text is being distorted and even abused in such Patristic exegesis. Proverbs 8 is hijacked and manipulated to suit the demands of the internal conflicts and polemics of developing Christianity. Is this not in fact *eisegesis* of the worst kind? Such a sense played a vital part in the rise of the historical-critical method, in the eighteenth and more especially the nineteenth centuries. Even now, at the start of the twenty-first century, I believe we need the disciplined rigour of the historical-

---

[1] M. Simonetti, *Studi sull'Arianismo*, Rome: Editrice Studium, 1965, ch. 1. For an authoritative discussion of the context in English, see R. D. Williams, *Arius, Heresy and Tradition*, 2nd edn, London: SCM Press, 2001.

[2] See F. M. Young's essay in the present volume, and also *Biblical Exegesis and the Formation of Christian Culture*, Cambridge: Cambridge University Press, 1997, pp. 29–45.

critical method if we are to understand aright an ancient text such as Proverbs 8.

The necessity of the historical-critical method

James Barr has spoken of the 'factuality' of the biblical text.[3] John Barton has referred to 'its givenness, its refusal to say just what we should like it to say'.[4] Confronted by Athanasius' use of Proverbs 8 in the Arian controversy, one longs for the text to be allowed to be itself. Barton's Oxford inaugural lecture of 1993 is an articulate defence of the importance of historical-critical study. 'The best interpreters', he writes, 'are those who are non-acquisitive, who respect the otherness of the text and do not try to turn it into a ventriloquist's dummy for their own opinions and beliefs.'[5] It was this that excited me when, as a cradle Catholic, I arrived in Oxford to be taught biblical studies by John Barton and by Morna Hooker. In so far as the Bible had impinged on me up to that point, it was as presented in the church context. I had encountered the Scriptures in liturgy and in homily, wrapped in the assumptions of Roman Catholic doctrine and practice, but if there was a Bible at home – somewhere – it was not a book I had encountered at first hand. Now the ecclesiastical dust was blown off the text and one was introduced to the exciting business of biblical criticism, seeking the original meaning of texts within their own contexts.

It is with Cambridge that one associates the doyen of British historical-critical study of the Wisdom tradition, at least in the final, most prolific years of his life. I refer to Norman Whybray, resident in Ely until his death in 1998. Whybray pursued tenaciously the original meaning of the Wisdom texts. Here are

---

[3] J. Barr, 'Exegesis as a Theological Discipline Reconsidered and the Shadow of the Jesus of History', in D. G. Miller, (ed.), *The Hermeneutical Quest: Essays in Honor of J. L. Mays*, Allison Park, PA: Pickwick Publications, 1986, pp. 11–45.

[4] J. Barton, *The Future of Old Testament Study*, Inaugural Lecture, Oxford: Clarendon Press, 1993, p. 18.

[5] Barton, *Future of Old Testament Study*, p. 18.

some characteristic words from his discussion of Proverbs 8. Writing of various attempts to understand Prov. 8.22 (RSV: 'The LORD created me at the beginning of his work, the first of his acts of old'), he says, 'some of these translations reflect the presuppositions of the exegetes more than the original meaning of the text. Such exegesis, which has also distorted the meaning of other parts of the poem, began early with the ancient versions.'[6] Note the significant use of words by Whybray: 'presuppositions' – these are apparently bad; 'original meaning' – this is good; 'distorted' – distortion too is obviously bad.

The key word in Prov. 8.22

Let us focus on the key word that is at the centre of the Patristic disputes over the interpretation of Proverbs 8 during the Arian controversy. I refer to the Greek word ἔκτισεν in verse 22. The context of this discussion is provided by the fact that Arius himself, wishing to present Christ as a creature, saw in the use of this word in 8.22 (which was universally understood by Christian theologians to have christological reference) a key proof-text for the creation of the Son. The Hebrew word of which ἔκτισεν is the Greek Septuagint's translation is *qanah*. This is translated 'created' in the Revised Standard Version of Prov. 8.22 (and indeed in its successor, the NRSV): 'The LORD created me at the beginning of his work'. Yes, Proverbs was of course written in Hebrew, not Greek. It has been one of the central emphases of the historical-critical method that we have to go back to the original language in order to get to the original meaning. Eusebius was unusual among the Patristic exegetes of Proverbs 8 in making reference to the Hebrew, whereas the norm was to stay with the Greek of the Septuagint.

The meaning of *qanah* at 8.22 is much debated. The Hebrew verb is common within the Old Testament. There are three main

---

[6] R. N. Whybray, *Proverbs*, New Century Bible, London: Marshall Pickering / Grand Rapids: Eerdmans, 1994, pp. 130–1.

possibilities of meaning here at 8.22, in descending order of probability:

(a) The word almost always means 'acquire' (and so also 'possess'). In Proverbs, outside this verse, it occurs thirteen times: twelve of these speak of acquiring wisdom or similar, and one refers to 'purchasing' in the commercial sense.
(b) Only in a few passages in the Old Testament is the meaning 'create' a possibility. Proverbs 8.22 is one of the cases where such a meaning is possible (an option followed by the RSV). God is almost always the subject of the verb in these cases. But in none, or almost none, does 'create' seem to be the only possibility.
(c) Some modern scholars have proposed a third meaning here in 8.22: 'beget', 'procreate'. This is proposed in view of words used in the following verses 23–25 and also in the light of a motif found in Egyptian Wisdom literature, namely the birth of the girl-goddess Maat.

The meanings attested or proposed for *qanah* overlap to such an extent that in the crucial passages (including 8.22) precision of interpretation is difficult. We should moreover remember (as indeed Athanasius acknowledged) that 8.22–31 is a poem, using figurative language in a context where elusive riddles abound. But, all this said, Whybray judged that the weight of probability lies with 'acquired', 'possessed' as the most likely original meaning of the Hebrew: 'The LORD possessed me at the beginning of his work'. It is interesting to note that Eusebius favoured the same sense, 'acquired', 'possessed', for the key word in 8.22, and no accident either, for, as we have already noted, he alone among the Patristic exegetes in question made reference to the Hebrew. For Eusebius the meaning concerns the operation rather than the origins of divine wisdom. But if 'possessed' is indeed the right sense of the Hebrew of 8.22, we need not assume that Wisdom is seen as having pre-existed before Yahweh acquired her. That would be to read too much into the text, which is much less developed and sophisticated than the Fathers seek to make it. And so we should not allow the doctrinal interests that motivated

Eusebius to intrude, with his reference to the pre-existent cosmic Christ. And still less should we find here in 8.22 the reference to Christ's incarnation found by Athanasius.

Modern critics strive to expose the meaning of Prov. 8.22–31 as a whole within its original setting. The speaker in the passage is the divine wisdom personified. From a historical-critical perspective there is no christological reference here; the passage employs the personified wisdom motif entirely within the ancient Israelite context, in response to factors, known and unknown to us, in the time of the author. It is in this way, according to the historical-critical method, that we shall properly understand the passage, stripped of the meanings foisted upon it by later generations. The sense may be difficult to discern with precision (as we have seen, Whybray himself departed from the RSV translators). But the important thing is that we should strive to find out the original meaning of the Hebrew, with the best tools available and with all the detachment we can muster. There are other important features of the historical-critical method that shed much light on this passage, which we shall next consider briefly.

The ancient context

The contextualizing of material is a distinctive feature of the historical-critical approach. We must attend to the original literary context of our passage, namely Proverbs 1—9. And specifically we should have in view Prov. 3.19–20: 'The LORD by wisdom founded the earth, by understanding he established the heavens . . .'. Prov. 8.22–31 could well be an elaboration (one might even say a 'midrash') of these verses. This should encourage us to read Prov. 8.22–31 in a very theocentric way, very different from the christological emphasis of the Fathers. The reference is to a quality or feature of God, his wisdom, which is here personified. A plain reading suggests that this is simply a literary motif, a vivid way of describing the wisdom exercised by God in his creative activity, rather than a positing of an agent in any sense distinct.

We should look also to the context in the book of Proverbs

as a whole. Proverbs 1—9 constitutes an extensive theological prologue to the rest of the book, quite possibly of later origin than the section that begins at chapter 10. If this is correct, we might posit a development in the later Wisdom tradition towards a more explicit theological discourse. It may be that one way post-exilic Israel responded to a growing sense of the remoteness of her God was to develop the motif of the divine Wisdom as immanent in the world, like a bridge from the transcendent deity. And, beyond the book of Proverbs, we should look to the wider Israelite Wisdom literature, within which Proverbs 8 is so different from, for example, the more sceptical Job and Ecclesiastes.[7] How are these very different faces of post-exilic Wisdom to be related? Could it be that they are divergent, in a sense polarized, responses to the one and the same problem of the remoteness of God, the one response in a sense negative (scepticism) and the other positive (personification)?

And looking still further afield we find in the Apocrypha (the Deuterocanonical Old Testament of Roman Catholic tradition) the book of Ecclesiasticus, otherwise known as the Wisdom of Jesus Ben Sirach, and especially chapter 24, the other great passage presenting the divine wisdom personified. Comparison between Proverbs 8 and Sirach 24 may suggest greater development in the latter, with an equation proposed between Wisdom and Torah (the Law), helping us see Proverbs 8 in clearer historical perspective. And, importantly, beyond Israel we must look to the wider Ancient Near East, and to such potential parallels as the Egyptian girl-goddess figure Maat. This can aid reflection on the female figure of Wisdom in the Israelite tradition, and may help us with the difficult verse 30 of Proverbs 8, where one possible reading of the Hebrew is 'I was beside him, like a little child'.

The historical-critical method helps us see that by thus contextualizing a passage we shall the better understand it. This excited me as an undergraduate and it excites me still.

---

[7] On the book of Proverbs and its relation to other Israelite Wisdom, see K. J. Dell, *'Get Wisdom, Get Insight': An Introduction to Israel's Wisdom Literature*, London: Darton, Longman & Todd, 2000.

The wider benefits of the historical-critical approach

But it is not only for academic reasons that I wish to champion the historical-critical method. There is even a spiritual dimension for me in being confronted by the 'other' of the text as laid bare by historical criticism. The text is not me, it is not my projection or an extension of my own psychology; rather it challenges me from beyond myself in a way that commands humility. Theologically too the historical-critical method can be a very fruitful. The concept of divine wisdom personified and relating to humanity, as highlighted by historical-critical reading, can offer a model for perceiving truth in a whole range of different religious traditions other than one's own, and can indeed provide a basis for a rich natural theology.

There is moreover an ethical dimension to historical-critical reading: firm rooting of a text in its original context may help guard against 'exploitative' reading. The book of Proverbs is a text produced within the Jewish tradition and yet, in the Patristic exegesis, it was usurped for christological reference (the common shared assumption of all the Patristic protagonists, be they Arian or anti-Arian). After the *Shoah* or Holocaust of the twentieth century I believe all Christians should be very self-critical about such Christian appropriation of the Jewish Scriptures. Christian supersessionism, whereby Christian self-definition is developed at the expense of Judaism, played its part in the complex network of influences that fed into the tragedies of the *Shoah*. At the very least this should give Christian exegetes pause for thought, whenever they read those books that were taken over from the Jewish tradition and read within the Christian Bible as the Old Testament.[8]

A historical-critical emphasis acknowledges then the Jewishness of the text. And yet paradoxically it also drags the text and the study of it into the public domain, where scholars of all religious

---

[8] For an important recent attempt to wrestle with these issues, see J. D. Dawson, *Christian Figural Reading and the Fashioning of Identity*, Berkeley: University of California Press, 2002.

traditions and none can work at it together, in marked contrast to the enclosed self-referential world of Patristic exegesis.

The limitations of the historical-critical method

So I am passionately committed to the historical-critical method. And yet some years spent teaching in a theological college brought home powerfully to me the profoundly ambiguous nature of the legacy of historical criticism, when viewed within the context of the reading of Scripture within a faith community. I have highlighted its many strengths, but there is a down side too within this context of theological reading.

In some ways, as the enterprise of historical criticism developed, especially in the nineteenth century, the Bible became just another historical text, a relic of a bygone age. Through being placed within its original setting, it for many lost much of its immediate religious impact. And although the Bible was much illuminated by comparison with the literature of other ancient cultures, such as Egypt, in part this served only to relativize it. The Bible was analysed and dissected (Proverbs 1—9, for example, often treated separately from the rest of the book) and any sense that it constitutes a unified text was eroded. Moreover there developed a widespread sense that only the experts could interpret the Bible, whilst others, including many parish clergy, came to feel deskilled. Within ministerial training, biblical studies often became a process of alienation for students rather than of integration, robbing them of the very Scripture that had played a part in nurturing their vocations. The Bible, which had emerged within the context of the life of God's people, their struggles and their hopes, now often seemed far removed from that life of faith. The functioning of Scripture was undermined and stultified. The Bible meant what the experts told us it had meant originally, and that, it seemed, was the end of the matter.

The dominance of the historical paradigm in biblical studies for much of the past two hundred years has frequently been at the expense of the theological perspective. The insistence on the original meaning has so often failed to take seriously or even to understand the function of Scripture to find new hearers in new situations, to speak anew in new contexts. The cry has been 'But that's not what it meant originally!' and that has been taken as a final answer to the question of what it might mean today. But to give such power to historical criticism is to stultify the life of Scripture. It is to fail to recognize indeed the way that even within the Bible passages are read and re-read in new situations. One has only to think of the sequence of texts represented by Genesis 1, our own passage from Proverbs 8, John 1 and Colossians 1 to be reminded of the rich tradition of biblical interpretation within the Bible itself.

By the 1970s a wide-spread dissatisfaction with the apparently negative effects of historical-critical study had developed. A very influential diagnosis of the problem came from Brevard Childs in his *Biblical Theology in Crisis* in 1970.[9] Furthermore it was gradually being realized that the 'proven' results of historical enquiry were not so assured after all, so that even the positive claims made for it were becoming less persuasive. For example, the historical contextualizing of the Proverbs 8 passage offered above may sound persuasive, but it rests to a great extent on speculation, not least about the relative dating of various parts of the Bible. And is it not a little odd that biblical scholars have devoted so much energy to constructing a narrative *behind* the biblical text, the supposed 'real story' of the history of Israelite ideas? Though few historical critics would welcome the analogy, such a notion of a deeper tale that reveals the real meaning behind the biblical text could even be likened to the allegorical method of pre-modern exegesis, which offered the more profound sense beyond the plain sense of the text.

New approaches

In response to these and similar perceived problems with the historical-critical approach, there followed in the last decades of

---

[9] B. S. Childs, *Biblical Theology in Crisis*, Philadelphia: Westminster, 1970.

the twentieth century an upsurge of new methods and approaches, all of them of course, having earlier roots: literary approaches, canonical approaches, feminist criticism and so forth. The range is vast and it would be a mistake to impose an artificial unity upon such disparate phenomena. Nevertheless many of the newer approaches share some important features, including a renewed concern for contemporary meaning and relevance from the point of view of the modern reader, a move away from a preoccupation with what the text meant originally to a revived interest in what the text can legitimately mean now. In many ways this is refreshingly different from the narrowing down of questions that characterized the heyday of historical criticism.

Study of the book of Proverbs over recent years has reflected the trend to relate the text afresh to modern issues, attempting to read it in the light of the questions posed by our own cultural context. One good example is the highlighting of the place of the feminine in the book of Proverbs, not least in the classic case constituted by our passage, Prov. 8.22–31. Of course in some ways the role of the feminine in this passage has always been obvious, but it is undeniable that in our own age the concern with feminist questions in the reading community has given unprecedented prominence to this theme. One thinks, for example, of Alice Laffey's attempts to study the Wisdom tradition in a way sensitive to feminist perspectives.[10] Another example pertinent to our passage is the concern for nature and the environment that is another item high on the agenda of our age. For example, Katharine Dell has explored the place of 'green' ideas in the Wisdom tradition. Speaking of the Wisdom writings of ancient Israel, she comments: 'I find outlooks and presuppositions in their thought that can be illuminating for our own concerns and even guide us in attitudes we might adopt towards our environment.' Or again: 'Throughout this material God is at the centre, involved in the

[10] A. L. Laffey, *Wives, Harlots and Concubines: The Old Testament in Feminist Perspective*, London: SPCK, 1990, pp. 210–12. See also C. V. Camp, *Wisdom and the Feminine in the Book of Proverbs*, Bible and Literature Series 11, Sheffield: Almond, 1985; J. D. Martin, *Proverbs*, Old Testament Guides, Sheffield Academic Press, 1995, pp. 82–90.

world in a personal way, creating and sustaining in a process that involves human and non-human alike and is forever continuing to nourish and sustain the earth and all its creatures.' With reference to our passage in particular, she writes: 'The world is not static, it is a process, and perhaps the clearest example of this process is the figure of wisdom.'[11]

So why not christological reading?

If there might be a place for reading in the light of modern issues such as feminist criticism or environmentalism, bringing to the text questions and concerns of later ages, should we perhaps reconsider the severe criticisms we made earlier of the Patristic interpretations of Proverbs 8, which made this a central christological text, reading it in the light of the Christian theological agenda? Might it be that having learned lessons both about the value and the excesses of historical criticism we can feel our way to a position that respects the otherness of the original whilst also being open to the power of texts to generate fresh interpretations in later reading situations?

What place then for historical criticism?

We cannot turn the clock back to a pre-modern phase. Historical criticism is here to stay, and I believe that it should be accorded a permanent place of honour. This phrase is carefully chosen however. 'Place of honour' implies a high dignity, but the phrase is meant to convey also a status that is qualified. I wish to propose a dialectical position that defends the role of historical criticism but also puts careful limits upon its authority within the theological context. Historically-informed awareness should always temper our handling of ancient texts, not least when they derive from traditions other than our own immediate tradition. But we must

---

11 K. J. Dell, '"Green Ideas" in the Wisdom Tradition', *Scottish Journal of Theology* 47/4 (1994), pp. 423–51. See also W. P. Brown, *The Ethos of the Cosmos: The Genesis of Moral Imagination in the Bible*, Grand Rapids: Eerdmans, 1999.

keep the historical-critical method well within bounds, lest it be allowed to corrode and undermine the vibrant life of Scripture within the believing community. For the historical-critical approach taken in isolation is of limited value, certainly for the handling of the Bible as Scripture within the faith community.

I look to historical criticism to provide three challenges in such a context:[12]

(a) An intellectual challenge in which the reader is challenged by the probable original meaning, for example, of the word *qanah* in Prov. 8.22. We have acknowledged that this meaning is in fact hard to pin down. And yet we have seen the importance of wrestling for the original meaning. Once this hard work as been done, its fruits may contribute to on-going reflection upon the passage, without constraining interpretation in a narrow way. One might legitimately elect to develop a sense of a word or indeed a passage that seems not to have been the most primitive sense, but one would do this respectfully aware of the probable original sense.

(b) A moral challenge, as for example in the recognition that Christians have so often usurped Proverbs 8 for their own theological purposes and internecine conflicts, forgetting the Jewish origins of the text. Historical study can contribute here both in reminding us of the origins of the text and in reconstructing the story of how it has been handled down the centuries.

(c) An imaginative challenge can be presented by historical criticism too. Within our Proverbs passage I think of that wonderfully tantalizing verse 8.30, in which Wisdom refers to herself as either a 'master workman' or a 'little child': 'Then I was beside him, like a master workman / a little child'. Linguistic study offers us both options as contenders

---

[12] For a fuller development of such an approach, see: P. Joyce, 'First Among Equals? The Historical-Critical Approach in the Marketplace of Methods', in S. E. Porter, P. Joyce, and D. E. Orton, (eds.), *Crossing the Boundaries: Essays in Biblical Interpretation in Honour of Michael D. Goulder*, Leiden: Brill, 1994, pp. 17–27.

> for the original sense. Whilst it is important to seek to define the meaning, the often unresolved nature of this kind of quest can itself pose a challenge. For it can be fruitful to play with the imaginative possibilities of wisdom both as a frolicking child and as a dignified master workman. Even if most of us prefer not to roam far along the road to postmodernism, such influences have at least helped free us up for this kind of imaginative exploration![13]

The neat findings of historical criticism will themselves inform but should never ultimately determine the much broader, more challenging task that is the theological interpretation of the Bible. The input of historical enquiry to theological interpretation should properly be of the more oblique kind represented by our three challenges. Let historical criticism have its place of honour: first allow Proverbs 8 to be itself, in a way that neither Arius nor Athanasius did. But then, respecting the historical but never in thrall to it, let us take seriously the rich capacity of Scripture to find new hearers in new situations, to speak anew in fresh contexts. And so let us respond to the dynamic invitation of God's Wisdom, 'rejoicing in his inhabited world and delighting in the human race' (Prov. 8.31, NRSV).

---

[13] Compare W. Brueggemann, *The Bible and Postmodern Imagination: Texts under Negotiation*, London: SCM Press, 1993.

7. Proverbs 8 in Interpretation (2): Wisdom Personified

Fourth-century Christian Readings: Assumptions and Debates

FRANCES YOUNG

In this essay I propose to focus on fourth-century interpretation of Prov. 8.22–31. I do not start from scratch. The basic research into the interpretation of this passage in the Fathers is provided by Simonetti[1] in the opening chapter of a book of studies in Arianism – for this passage was a significant bone of contention in the Arian struggle. Building on Simonetti's work,[2] my aim is to try and identify the principles at work in the way the passage was interpreted, and hint at parallels to postmodern approaches.

An interpretative community

Postmodern literary criticism has identified the significance of interpretative communities, observing that debates about meaning occur within communities which share assumptions about interpretation. If this is pertinent in a world where people read

---

1 M. Simonetti, *Studi sull' Arianismo*, Rome: Editrice Studium, 1965, ch. 1.

2 In some places I have borrowed paragraphs with little modification from my previous surveys of Simonetti's work, or my previous treatments of, e.g., Athanasius' discussions. These are to be found in Frances Young, 'Exegetical Method and Scriptural Proof: The Bible in Doctrinal Debate', *Studia Patristica* 24, 1989, pp. 291–304; and eadem, *Biblical Exegesis and the Formation of Christian Culture*, Cambridge: Cambridge University Press, 1997.

novels silently to themselves, how much more so when texts were always read aloud, usually as public performance in a gathered community, such as a school or a church! The reality was that no one in the fourth century challenged the fundamental approach to this text which we can already trace in the work of the second-century apologists. The christological reference of personified wisdom was a tradition never questioned. So let's spell this out by reference to texts prior to the fourth century.

Prov. 8.22 consistently appears when the Apologists are explaining their Logos-theology. Let me give you one example from Athenagoras, *Legatio* 10.3–4:

> If in your great wisdom you would like to know what 'Son' means, I will tell you in a few brief words: it means that he is the first begotten of the Father. The term is used not because he came into existence (for God, who is eternal mind, had in himself his Word or Reason from the beginning, since he was eternally rational) but because he came forth to serve as Ideal Form and Energizing Power for everything material . . . The prophetic Spirit also agrees with this account. 'For the Lord', it says, 'made me the beginning of his ways for his works.' (Proverbs 8.22) Further, this same holy Spirit, which is active in those who speak prophetically, we regard as an effluence of God (cf. Wisdom 7.25) which flows forth from him and returns like a ray of the sun.[3]

That final sentence alludes to another passage where wisdom is personified. The conflation and mutual coherence of such wisdom-passages in the LXX was important in developing the Logos-theology, no doubt aided by the fact that Wisdom 7 has clear traces of Stoic influence. But the principal point is clear. The Son of God is both the eternal Logos or Mind of the Father and the first-begotten, and as such identified with the personified Wisdom through whom God created according to Proverbs 8.

This general approach to Proverbs 8 can be further documented

---

[3] ET from the Oxford Early Christian texts edition, *Athenagoras, Legatio and De Resurrectione*, ed. and trans. W. R. Schoedel, Oxford: Oxford University Press, 1972.

by turning to Theophilus of Antioch, *Ad Autolycum* II.10, where the term 'Sophia' is used alongside Logos, and his statement is a collage of biblical phrases:

> Therefore God, having his own Logos innate in his own bowels [cf. Ps. 109.3], generated him together with his own Sophia, *vomiting* him *forth* [Ps. 44.2] before everything else. He used this Logos as his servant in the things created by him, and through him he made all things [cf. John 1.4]. He is called Beginning because he leads and dominates everything fashioned through him. It was he, Spirit of God [Gen. 1.2] and Beginning [Gen.1.1] and Sophia [Prov. 8.22] and power of the Most High [Luke 1.35], who came down into the prophets and spoke about the creation of the world and all the rest. For the prophets did not exist when the world came into existence; there were the Sophia of God which is in him and his holy Logos who is always present with him. For this reason he speaks thus through Solomon the prophet: 'When he prepared the heaven I was with him, and when he made strong the foundations of the earth I was with him, binding them fast [Prov. 8.27–29].[4]

Is Theophilus speaking of both the pre-existent Word and the Holy Spirit, and which is Sophia? Looked at closely the passage quoted from Athenagoras carries the same ambiguity. Despite this fluidity of language, which makes it hard to be sure whether the picture is Binitarian or Trinitarian, the conclusion pertinent to our current concerns is clear. Prov. 8.22–31 is generally read as a passage about the being who was the instrument through whom God created the universe. Irenaeus, building on Logos-theology, notoriously speaks of the Word and the Spirit as God's two-hands, the instruments through which creation was effected. In *Adversus Haereses* IV.20.3, he reckons that he has demonstrated that the Word, namely the Son, was always with the Father, along with the Spirit – in this passage treating the Spirit, rather than the

---

[4] ET from the Oxford Early Christian texts edition, *Theophilus of Antioch, Ad Autolycum*, ed. and trans. Robert M. Grant, Oxford: Oxford University Press, 1970.

Logos, as the Wisdom which is described in Proverbs 8 as being involved with the Father in creation. This clarifies the ambiguity we noted in Theophilus and Athenagoras in a way that did not become the norm, for after Irenaeus it is not the Spirit but the Logos which is taken to be the reference of Proverbs 8.[5]

If the focus did not lie elsewhere, this example could be reinforced by many others. But let me just draw attention to three features important for the future:

(1) It generated intertextuality, collages of texts being built up to create a picture of this pre-existent creating Power of God, with whom God conversed when he said, 'Let *us* make . . .' (cf. Genesis 1).[6]

(2) Prov. 8.22 was construed in such a way that Beginning was regarded as one of the titles of the Logos or Son of God. When exercised about the correct construal of the word 'beginning' in Gen. 1.1, Origen and Tertullian both appeal to Proverbs 8 to settle the issue. Origen takes it (*Commentary on John* I. 17) that 'Beginning' is a title for Christ, confirming this on the basis of Prov. 8.22, where he construes ἔκτισεν (he created) as having a double object, as a verb of appointment would: thus, 'the Lord made me Beginning of his ways'. Tertullian is arguing against Hermogenes, who stated that the Genesis text supported the idea that God created out of pre-existent matter. 'Beginning' Hermogenes had interpreted as something substantial, Matter, in other words. Tertullian (*Adversus Hermogenem* 19) argues that 'in the beginning' is comparable to 'at last', is about order not origin, and simply refers to the inception of the activity. Then appealing to the

[5] See Clement of Alexandria, *Stromateis* vii.2 and Origen, *De principiis* ii.1 and *Commentary on John* i.11 and 39.

[6] See previous note for an example of cross-referencing and intertextuality. For the link with Genesis see Justin, *Dialogue with Trypho* 61–62 where he quotes Proverbs 8 at length and then argues for a correlation with Genesis, raising the question who was God addressing when he said, 'Let us make . . .' and 'Behold, Adam has become as one of us . . .'. For Justin it is clear that God is addressing his Offspring who is to be identified as the one Solomon calls Wisdom.

Greek, ἀρχή (beginning), he adds that the sense is not only priority of order, but of power as well (ἀρχή meaning 'rule' as well as 'beginning'). He goes on to argue that the word must refer to the initial one, that is, the one who says, 'The Lord established me as the beginning of his ways for the creation of his works' – in other words, Wisdom in Proverbs 8. For him Proverbs makes clear that the beginning of God's ways or works was Wisdom. And Wisdom is the Lord's right-hand, the energy that produced creation (cf. *Adversus Hermogenem* 45, which also quotes Proverbs 8).

(3) The doctrinal importance of this interpretative tradition is already clear from Tertullian's repeated references in *Adversus Praxeam*, his principal attack on the Modal approach to Trinitarianism. Arguing for a real distinction between the Logos and the Father he notes (in *Adv. Prax*. vi, for example) that the 'divine intelligence' is also set forth in the Scriptures under the name of Wisdom, and quotes Proverbs 8 at length.

I hope enough has been observed to confirm the fact that we are dealing with an interpretative community with a consistent approach to the basic reference of this text.

Debating the meaning of a key word

This consensus as to the reference of Prov. 8.22–31 was not shattered by the Arian controversy. Debate centred on a particular word and its appropriate synonyms. Commentary has always focused on elucidating the meaning of particular terms in this way. Against a background of shared assumptions, different theological conclusions about the nature of the Logos were drawn from different understandings of the key word.

That word was ἔκτισεν (he created) – Greek, because of course it was the LXX version that was debated. Prior to the controversy, the use of different words in verse 22 and verse 25 was not generally noticed: ἔκτισεν (he created) and γεννᾶ(ι) (he begets) were assumed to be synonyms and to refer to the generation of the Logos from the Father. In a fragment of a work against the Sabellians, preserved for us by Athanasius in the *De Decretis*, Dionysius of Rome stated that he considered it improper to call the Son a *ποίημα* (a creature), for Scripture speaks of his *γέννησις* (genesis/begottenness). So he argued that *κτίζειν* (to create) has various senses – there is a difference between *κτίζειν* (to create) and *ποιεῖν* (to make). He established through cross-references that in Proverbs 8, the *ἔκτισεν* (he created) of verse 22 must be the equivalent of the *γεννᾷ(ι)* (he begets) of verse 25, so making explicit what had been assumed all along.

Arius is notorious for teaching that the Son was a creature, and Prov. 8.22 was for him a prime proof-text. That implies that he took the opposite view, that *γεννᾷ(ι)* (he begets) was to be understood in terms of *ἔκτισεν* (he created). Once a distinction between being created and being begotten was pressed, there was little in principle or in context to establish the superiority of one mode of interpretation over the other.

Eusebius of Caesarea was the one person to discuss the meaning of *ἔκτισεν* (he created) rather than appealing to novel ways of construing the passage as a whole. Simonetti observes that, prior to the Arian controversy, Eusebius had been wrestling with the fact that the generation or creation of the Logos described in Proverbs 8 could not simply imply separation, diminution or division with respect to the Father. On the other hand it could not mean that the Logos was created out of nothing like other created beings. Eusebius was prepared to see the Son as 'the fragrance and splendour of the light of the Father', but observed that the mystery of the generation of the Son is hidden. Consistently with this, in his work against Marcellus, Eusebius refrains from following the Arian interpretation, while also resisting the ploys we shall explore later. He insists on retaining the context with its overall picture of Wisdom pre-existing and assisting in the creation of all else, identifying her with the pre-existent cosmic Christ. He further insists that here there is no description of how this Logos came into being. The passage is about his preceding the creation of the whole world and his ruling over all things because set over them by the Lord, his Father. Thus he reasserts the inherited consensus of the interpretative community.[7] His strategy for establishing this is addressing the philological question concerning the meaning of ἔκτισεν (he created).

Eusebius argues that κτίζειν (to create) is not used here to mean 'create' in the sense 'bring into existence out of nothing', but in the sense 'order' or 'unite'. He turns to the Hebrew and variant translations to show this. The meaning is more like ἐκτήσατο – 'he possessed'. The Father constituted the Logos as the foundation of all things, 'to sum up things in Christ, whether the things of heaven or the things of earth' (Eph. 1.10). Proverbs 8, then, is about the providential functions of the Logos rather than his origin, the manner of which is in any case a mystery beyond description or understanding.

The sequence of thought

By taking this position with respect to the word ἔκτισεν (he created) Eusebius is able to maintain the natural sequence of thought in the passage. This observation is important since most of those opposed to Arius introduced an unnatural sequence into the passage by claiming that ἔκτισεν (he created) referred to the incarnation. The originator of this approach seems to have been Marcellus. Acknowledging that the proper meaning of κτίζειν was 'to create what did not previously exist', he claimed that the 'creature' produced was the human flesh assumed by the Redeemer by means of the Virgin Mary.

Simonetti notes that Marcellus was able to mask the novelty of his interpretation by recourse to traditional typology. Through this technique he contrived to produce a consistent interpretation of verses 22–25 as a prophetic prediction of the new dispensation, in particular the renewal effected by the Saviour, who said 'I am the Way', and was therefore created 'in the beginning of his ways' as the Way of piety for us. The whole passage is made coherent by such moves. Here is one more example: 'before the ages he founded me' is taken to refer to God's providential foreordaining,

[7] Note how he reflects points in Tertullian's discussion, outlined above.

in the light of the text, 'No other foundation can anyone lay except that which is laid, which is Jesus Christ' (1 Cor. 3.11) Whether 'typology' is the best way of describing this procedure might be questionable, but to give a coherent exegesis of this passage as referring to the incarnation rather than the generation of the Son from the Father certainly required exploitation of such typically patristic techniques for shifting reference. To cope with the question how on earth the incarnation might be implied by the apparently unequivocal statements in verse 24, which refer to a time before the earth, the depths or springs existed, he resorted to allegory. The 'earth' is taken to refer to the flesh – for flesh was made of the dust of the earth according to Gen. 2.6, returns to dust according to Gen. 3.19, and is restored by participation in the Logos; 'the depths' is taken to refer to the hearts of the saints, 'which in their depths have the gift of the Spirit'; and the 'springs' are taken to refer to the apostles on the basis of Exod. 15.27, the twelve springs of Elim, a text traditionally associated with the Twelve . . . And so it goes on, though the focus on the incarnation is blurred when the continuation of the passage in verses 27–30 is understood of the immanent Wisdom or Logos of God in the creation.

Undoubtedly Eusebius produces a more satisfactory and less piecemeal approach to the text as he challenges these arbitrary expedients. Another interpretative strategy has clearly enabled this, namely intertextuality: we will explore this further by turning to Athanasius' interpretation. For Athanasius, like Marcellus, adopted the incarnation as the explanation of the awkward word ἔκτισεν (he created).

Genre and intertextuality

That the exegesis of this text was at the heart of the Arian controversy is proved by its high profile in the anti-Arian works of Athanasius, the *De Decretis* and *Contra Arianos*. In the former, discussing the difference between making something external to the maker, like a house, and begetting a son, Athanasius refers to Prov. 8.25, 'Before all the hills he begat me'. But he cannot then escape dealing with the use of 'create' in Prov. 8.22: he does so by asserting that it refers to the incarnation – for then indeed one can say the Son was created. He calls in scriptural cross-references to witness that he became son of man as well as Son of God.

As far as the *Contra Arianos* is concerned, Athanasius devotes the bulk of book II to this text, exploiting a range of exegetical techniques. First he attends to genre: these are proverbs, expressed in the way of proverbs. Enquiry must be made about the reference and the religious sense of each proverb. The sense of what is said must be unfolded and sought as something hidden. This is done by attending to scriptural usage, and intertextuality plays a big role. With cited texts he establishes that the term ἔκτισεν (he created) is elsewhere used of creatures and not where Scripture is speaking of the generation of the Son, and also that there are two scriptural senses of the word, one concerning origin and the other renewal, as in the text 'Create in me a new heart'. So the proverb in question is to be understood not of the generation of the Word, but rather as relating to renewal, and so as referring not to the essence but to the humanity of the Word.

The next tactic is to consider the syntax. He argues (as others had before him) that 'The Lord created me a beginning of his ways' works in the same way as 'My Father prepared for me a body' – the verb has a double object. So the proverb, according to Athanasius, calls the Son a 'beginning of his ways' and he compares this with 'The Word became flesh and dwelt among us'. Neither of these verses speaks of an absolute becoming or creation, but of one relative to 'us' or to 'his works'. Here Athanasius notes that whereas ἔκτισεν (he created) in verse 22 is modified by an expression of purpose, 'for his works', the use of γεννᾶ(ι) (he begets) in verse 25 does not have a similar modifier. So in verse 25, as elsewhere in Scripture, the 'begetting' is stated absolutely, whereas the word 'created' is relative; it is relative to the οἰκονομία – that is, the created order and the incarnation as an expression of God's providential and saving plan.

This distinction between speaking absolutely of the Son's Being and speaking of him relative to the created order (or the 'Economy') is fundamental to Athanasius' discernment of the mind of Scripture. This overarching perspective, coupled with inter-textual references, enables the interpretation in terms of renewal or re-creation to be elaborated: 'We are his workmanship, created in Jesus Christ', he suggests, using Eph. 2.10 among many other passages. Thus he arrives at a classic distinction which he regards as fundamental to Scripture: God's offspring (γέννημα) was *begotten but then made*, made flesh for our salvation in the Economy, whereas creatures (ποιήματα) were *made and then begotten* through Christ, becoming sons by grace. This distinction he thinks applies to this text. He is 'the first-born of all creation' as being the origin of the new creation; he could not be first-born of God, since he is only-begotten of God.

But now the problem of context demands attention. How can this reading of verse 22 be satisfactory in the light of verse 23, where it states: 'before the world, he founded me in the beginning'? Athanasius appeals again to the proverbial character of the material; then (like Marcellus) he calls in the text from 1 Corinthians 'No other foundation can anyone lay . . .', and indicates that Proverbs is speaking of the providential preparation of this grace for us before the foundation of the world. So the essence of Wisdom was not created; what was created was the impress of Wisdom in the works of God as a copy of the divine image. His triumphant conclusion is that thus the whole world will be filled with the knowledge of God. And it must be admitted that he takes a lot longer to get there than my brief survey of his material would suggest!

We can now look back over his handling of the text and see that is raises questions about a number of interpretative strategies. Clearly deductive argument, employing inter-textuality to determine the over-arching 'mind' of Scripture, then determines the sense of particular passages, no matter how implausible! The way Athanasius approaches the questions posed by Arian exploitation of this passage raises issues about genre, not only about the genre of the text in question, which clearly he properly identifies, but also about the 'reading genre' – it is because this text belongs to Scripture, and is to be read as Scripture, that it can be moulded into a meaning that, it is claimed, coheres with the mind of Scripture. This provides a particular reading horizon, and the perspectives which that produces determined what the words may or may not refer to.

The future of the text

From our postmodern perspective it might seem that this kind of interpretation is particularly focussed on the future of the text, as distinct from its original meaning. As noted at the outset, the traditions of an interpretative community had already determined its reference, and the text's future was to generate doctrinal debate about the nature of God's Word. However, this can only be observed through the hindsight shaped by modernity. For the exegetes of the fourth century the issue of distinguishing the 'original' or authorial meaning of the text from other meanings did not arise. This was because the text of Scripture was regarded as fundamentally prophetic. Even proverbs were prophecy – the important point about *παροιμίαι* is that they are figurative, as is evident from the fact that Athanasius appealed to Jn 16.25 to show that there is a difference between proverbs and plain speech. As a prophet, the author *meant* what the exegete discerned in the text; or if maybe the author was unconscious of it, the Holy Spirit certainly meant it. The future of the text was no different from its original meaning. The text and its meaning was regarded as having a timeless quality. There was one horizon not two!

So the 'reading genre', which identified the biblical text as unified and prophetic ensured the primacy of the dogmatic reading. Indeed, orthodoxy, or correct opinion, became a criterion of interpretation. The true meaning was regarded as always there to be uncovered, even if not fully recognized previously. The text had neither a past nor a future. In fact patristic interpretation reveals an assumption that Scripture always addresses its readers (or rather hearers) directly, whatever the time or place. The exegetical techniques of the Fathers were developed and deployed to show what the text meant eternally for the readers of every generation. We might compare this with reader-oriented criticism, but we should be careful. For the

Fathers were convinced they were uncovering the true, eternal meaning, not permitting their own concerns to determine how the text was read, or self-consciously recognizing that the text only comes alive when a reader realizes it, inevitably bringing their own horizon to the process of interpretation. Yet from our perspective that would seem to be exactly what the Fathers were doing.

To sum up then: Let us note that this debate has nothing to do with the standard exegetical questions raised in dealing with patristic exegesis – the issue is not about allegory, typology or literalism. The debate is about particular reference, the general reference already being established by tradition and assumed by the common interpretative dogmatic community. In conducting the debate, verbal sense is subjected to intertextual tests, and the final appeal is to the scriptural over-view – the 'mind' of Scripture which transcends the 'verbal expression' in any given sentence.

So for us these are the questions:

- Is this eisegesis?
- Do Athanasius et al. twist the text to suit their own purposes? Indeed, is not this exactly the kind of thing that justified disciplined attention to the text with philology, with historico-critical acumen?
- Do not the assumptions of this interpretative community distort discussion of the text and cry out for the identification of a neutral, objective reappraisal? Or is the claim to any privileged position, whether dogmatic or scholarly, equally flawed?
- So does this confirm and strengthen the reaction against the historico-critical programme in post-modern interpretation? Or does it rather illustrate the dangers?
- What would be an 'ethical' reading? And would an ethical reading invalidate a Christian doctrinal reading as exploitative?

Towards an ethical reading

In previous work[8] I have developed an approach to ethical reading, stimulated by George Steiner's plea[9] for an ethics of reception, by Wayne Booth's suggestion in *The Company We Keep*[10] that friendship is the best metaphor for reading, and Werner Jeanrond's[11] description of reading as a dynamic process to which both text and reader contribute. Strangely these explorations lead to a remarkable concurrence between their hermeneutics and ancient rhetorical theories.

In brief the conclusion is that readers have a responsibility to the text, but also to themselves. Responsible reading means the articulation of distance. To the extent that the historico-critical method facilitates that distance, it is a vital contributor to a responsible reading. To the extent that it may fail to engage the reader, producing a merely archaeological approach to the text, to the extent that it encourages blindness to the reader's presuppositions by offering an illusory objectivity, to the extent that it does not deliver potential meanings in a plurality of situations, it is inadequate.

Ancient rhetorical theory spelt out the need for a three-way dynamic if an audience (or readership) was to be persuaded – in other words, to achieve *πίστις* (proof, conviction, or in Christian parlance, faith). One point on the triangle was the *λόγος* (the content, the logic or argument), which should be convincing. Another point was the *ἦθος* of the speaker (the character, lifestyle and authority of the author) which confirmed what the text said. The third was the *πάθος* ('suffering' or response) of the audience

---

[8] Frances Young, 'The Pastorals and the Ethics of Reading', *Journal for the Study of the New Testament* 45, 1992, pp. 105–120; and eadem, 'Allegory and the Ethics of Reading', in Francis Watson, (ed.), *The Open Text*, London: SPCK 1993, pp. 103–20.

[9] In George Steiner, *Real Presences*, subtitled *Is there anything in what we say?* London: Faber & Faber, 1989.

[10] Wayne Booth, *The Company We Keep*, Berkeley: University of California Press, 1988.

[11] Werner Jeanrond, *Text and Interpretation as Categories of Theological Thinking*, ET T. J. Wilson; Dublin: Gill & Macmillan, 1988.

or reader, swayed by the convincing character of author and text. The dynamic between these was all important.

I suggest that that remains true. The inspiration of the Holy Spirit the Fathers thought essential not just in the composition of Scripture but in its interpretation. Distance and appropriation are both vital for an ethical reading that does justice to the text. That means there will be a plurality of readings, for readings will take place in many contexts, cultures and communities. There will be justifiable critique of the dubious linguistic and contextual moves Athanasius and others may have made, because being as true as possible to the text matters in an ethical reading. But alongside this there will also be a recognition that a Christian reading of the Bible has to wrestle with issues of its unity and the ways in which it points to a reality beyond itself. For the Fathers, the Rule of Faith provided the crucial criteria, and the creeds were regarded as a summary of the truth of the Bible. A Christian ethical reading has to do justice to 'ourselves', and that includes the tradition of reading in which we stand. The Trinity is not explicit in the New Testament, let alone the Hebrew Bible. But it is implicit in the Christian Bible, and was made explicit through such debates about interpretation as we have sketched. Our hermeneutical theory, while enabling exposure of dubious exegetical moves, surely must also take account of this 'future of the text'.

8. Where is Wisdom to be Found? Colossians 1.15–20 (1)

MORNA D. HOOKER

Trained in the methods of tradition-historical scholarship, the questions I ask when approaching a text are instinctively 'Who?' 'When?' 'Why?' 'What?' In the case of Col. 1.15–20, these are notoriously difficult to answer.

Who? Well – possibly Paul, possibly not – for even if we suppose that the epistle itself was written by Paul – as I tend to do – this section could well have been written by someone else, and so be an early credal composition, used here because it is appropriate for Paul's purpose. If, on the other hand, the epistle is pseudepigraphal, it is possible that the author is here quoting something composed by Paul himself.

Since the question of authorship is so problematical, the questions concerning date and place of composition must also remain unresolved, for they are inextricably linked with that of authorship. Only the question 'To whom?' permits us to give a reasonably confident answer. The letter claims to have been written to Christians in Colossae, and there seems no reason to doubt that it was intended for use by the church there.[1]

But *why* was the letter written – whether by Paul or by a disciple – and *why* was it addressed to Colossae? 'Were there false teachers in Colossae?' I used that question as the title of a paper I wrote some 30 years ago in honour of my predecessor in the Lady Margaret's chair,[2] and it seems appropriate that I should

[1] The only textual variant concerns the spelling of the name.

[2] M. D. Hooker, 'Were there False Teachers in Colossae?', in Barnabas

have been asked to look again at Colossians as my contribution to the celebration of the 500th anniversary of that chair's founding. Since my own answer to that particular question was 'No', and since the great majority of scholars appear to disagree with me[3] – though they are unable to agree among themselves as to what these hypothetical false teachers taught – we are left with yet more unresolved question-marks.

Yet if the epistle *is* by Paul – or is written in the Pauline tradition – we can at least be sure that Col. 1.15–20 has been included in the epistle because it is relevant to the situation in Colossae as the author understands it, and to his insights into the bearing of the gospel *on* that situation. Is its purpose here perhaps to assure the community in Colossae that they need have no fear of astral forces, since Christ is greater than them all (2.8–10, 15)? In a world where pagan deities and superstitions abounded, such assurance would be very necessary.[4] Is it perhaps to remind them that, in Christ, they have already been reconciled to God, and so have no need to adopt the customs of their Jewish neighbours, who believe in the same God, but not in Christ (2.16–23)? Jewish customs and regulations must have seemed to offer an appropriate guide to appropriate behaviour to converted Gentiles wondering what their new faith required of them, and how they might best 'lead lives worthy of the Lord' (1.10). For our author, the answers to these questions are not to be found in abstaining from food or in observing festivals, but in living a life in conformity to Christ's.

Even if we could find the answer to the question concerning

Lindars and Stephen S. Smalley, (eds.), *Christ and Spirit in the New Testament: Studies in honour of Charles Francis Digby Moule*, Cambridge: Cambridge University Press, 1973, pp. 315–31, reprinted in M. D. Hooker, *From Adam to Christ: Essays on Paul*, Cambridge: Cambridge University Press, 1990, pp. 121–36.

[3] Exceptions are N. T. Wright, *The Epistles of Paul to the Colossians and to Philemon*, Leicester: IVP/Grand Rapids: Eerdmans, 1986; and R. Yates, '"The Worship of Angels": (Col 2:18)', *Expository Times* 97, 1985–6, pp. 12–15; idem, *The Epistle to the Colossians*, London: Epworth, 1993.

[4] For an account of these pressures, see Clinton E. Arnold, *The Colossian Syncretism*, WUNT 2:77, Tübingen: Mohr (Siebeck), 1995.

the purpose of this passage in its present context, however, this would not necessarily tell us why it was written in the first place. For if Col. 1.15–20 is a quotation of traditional material, then what we have here may perhaps be a passage that was composed in one context being adapted and expounded for use in another. If that is so, then even though it is not a passage of *Scripture* that is being interpreted here, the process of interpretation is nevertheless similar to that used when expounding Scripture. Certainly the verses that follow build on what is said here and draw out its significance for the Christian community.

The passage itself is relevant to *our* purpose for an even more fundamental reason, however, for there is good reason to believe that Col. 1.15–20 is itself an exegesis of Scripture, drawing out what its author believed to be the true meaning of the text. It was C. F. Burney who suggested that the passage was an exposition of the Hebrew word *berêshith* – 'in the beginning' – the opening word of Gen. 1.1, in the light of Prov. 8.22.[5] Since his time, countless commentators have drawn our attention to the fact that the language of Col. 1.15–20 is reminiscent of passages in the Wisdom literature which describe the wisdom of God.[6] Hence the use of the term 'Wisdom Christology' in relation to this passage.

'Where is wisdom to be found? And where is the place of understanding?' asked Job (28.12) – and the answer he gave was that God alone knows, since it was he who allocated wisdom a place at the creation (28.23–27). But though mortals cannot find it or buy it (vv. 12–19), it is given to those who honour and obey God, for 'the fear of the Lord is wisdom, and to depart from evil is understanding' (v. 28). Many commentators explain this verse as an addition to vv. 1–27, reflecting a traditional approach equating wisdom with 'the fear of the Lord' that is found elsewhere,[7] but the same link is found in Proverbs 8, where wisdom is said to

---

[5] C. F. Burney, 'Christ as the APXH of Creation', *Journal of Theological Studies* 27, 1926, pp. 160ff.

[6] See, e.g., Job 28, Proverbs 8, Wisdom 6—10, Sirach 24. Among those who recognized the relevance of the Wisdom literature for this passage, see Jean-Noël Aletti, *Colossiens 1,15-20*, Analecta Biblica 91, Rome: Biblical Institute Press, 1981.

[7] E.g. Prov. 1.7; 9.10.

have been created 'the beginning of his way' – that is, 'the beginning of his works' (v. 22), and to have been at God's side – like a master craftsman when he created the world (vv. 23–31). Wisdom offers instruction to her children on how to fear God and do what is right. Whoever finds wisdom finds life (v. 35). Psalm 33 (LXX 32), also, links what God did at creation with instructions to fear him, though here it is 'by the word of the Lord' that the world is created (v. 6), and because his word is upright that he should be feared and obeyed.

In the book of Wisdom, wisdom is seen as operating in the world since the beginning, guarding and guiding God's people. She is described as 'the fashioner of all things' (7.22), God's agent at creation (9.1–2), and is understood to be the expression of God's very being, for she is

> a breath of the power of God
> and a pure emanation of the glory of the Almighty . . .
> a reflection of eternal light,
> a spotless mirror of the working of God,
> and an image of his goodness. (7.25–26)

Wisdom demands righteousness, and those who love her keep her laws (6.18), but she condemns those who are unjust and fail to keep the law (6.4).

Similar ideas are expressed in Sirach 24, where wisdom declares that 'before the ages, in the beginning, he created me' (v. 9), and describes how she was commanded to make her dwelling in Israel (v. 8). We are not surprised, therefore, when the gifts she offers are identified with 'the book of the covenant of the Most High God, the law that Moses commanded us' (v. 23).[8]

In these various passages, the word, wisdom or law of God are linked, sometimes identified. All these terms are used in statements that express the conviction that the will or purpose of God that was instrumental in the creation was revealed on Sinai. Once Israel's God had been identified as the creator, that link was inevitable. He had created the world by his word – and had

---

[8] Cf. also Sir. 15.1.

spoken that word again on Sinai, where he revealed his wisdom in the Torah. A similar approach is found in the writings of Paul's contemporary, Philo, who says of this universe that 'its cause is God, by whom it has come into being . . . its instrument the word of God, through whom it was framed' (*De Cherubim* 127). For Philo, the word – or wisdom – of God is also the source of water and manna, symbols of the Torah (*Leg. All.* II.86).

Belief in God as creator, however, had important implications for Israel's future salvation. Yahweh had laid the foundations of the earth and stretched out the heavens (Isa. 51.13–16). It was the God of Israel who is the only God, the creator of the world and the only saviour. The link between creation and redemption is specifically made in Isaiah 40—55. At the Exodus, the power by which God created the world had been demonstrated when he bared his arm and blew with his breath: chaos had overwhelmed Israel's enemies, but she herself had been saved (Exod. 15.1–19). It was because God was the creator of the world that Israel could rely on him to save them again – a theme that is reiterated again and again in these chapters (e.g. Isa. 40.12–31). In these chapters, too, the new 'Exodus' is described in language deliberately reminiscent of the first (Isa. 40.3–5; 43.2). Since Yahweh has already redeemed his people at the Exodus, he will do so again (Isa. 43.11–21).

God's creative word is clearly relevant to this theme. God's salvation is sure because the word of Israel's God will stand for ever (Isa. 40.8). His word has gone out from his mouth and will not return – and that word proclaims him as the only God, to whom every knee will bow (Isa. 45.21–23). His word will go out from his mouth and will accomplish his purpose, which is to restore his people and re-create paradise (Isa. 55.10–13). Wisdom is specifically linked with redemption in the description of the Exodus in Wisd. 10.15–21. Creation and redemption belong together, and both depend on the word of God.[9]

[9] Cf. N. T. Wright, who specifically links both creation and redemption themes in the Old Testament with the wisdom tradition behind Colossians 1 in 'Poetry and Theology in Colossians 1.15–20', *New Testament Studies* 36, 1990, pp. 444–68.

Col. 1.15–20 holds together these two themes of creation and redemption, which are set out in parallel verses (vv. 15–16 and 18b–20), linked by a parallel couplet summing up the same theme (vv.17–18a). The passage is a eulogy of the one *through whom* God has worked, in creation and redemption. If the language used in Colossians 1 echoes the language of the LXX version of the various passages about wisdom which we have mentioned and also the language used by Philo, that is because what had been claimed by Judaism for the Torah – and more – was now being claimed for Christ. *He* was God's word of wisdom, by whom the world had been created and was now being restored.[10]

But Colossians 1 is not the only place in the New Testament where this language and these ideas occur. John 1 and Hebrews 1 are obvious examples. Like Col. 1.15–20, John 1.1–18 appears to be based on an exegesis of Genesis 1. The exposition appears to be entirely Jewish, until we are told that the word through whom all things were created became flesh and dwelt among us, and that what has come to us through him is greater than the law given through Moses. Christ's is the true glory, and he is the one who alone is able to reveal God fully, since – unlike Moses – he has seen God.[11] The familiar link between creation and law is found here, and so, too, is the theme of restoration, for those who receive the word (who is the true light) are enabled to become children of God (v. 12). The same links reappear in 2 Corinthians 3—4 which – like John 1 – expounds both Exodus 33—34 and Genesis 1.[12] Here the glory reflected by Moses on Sinai is compared with the far greater glory of Christ – greater because Christ is the image of God, and the glory revealed in him is nothing less than the glory which shone at creation, when God said 'Let light shine out of darkness'. Those who see this glory in the face of

[10] For a recent detailed defence of the view that Col. 1.15–20 is built on Jewish wisdom traditions, see Christian Stettler, *Der Kolosserhymnus*, WUNT 2.131, Tübingen: Mohr (Siebeck), 2000.

[11] Cf. M. D. Hooker, 'The Johannine Prologue and the Messianic Secret', *New Testament Studies* 21, 1974, pp. 40–5.

[12] Cf. M. D. Hooker, 'Beyond the Things that are Written? St Paul's Use of Scripture', *New Testament Studies* 27, 1981, pp. 295–309, reprinted in Hooker, *From Adam to Christ*, pp. 139–54.

Christ are being conformed to the image of the one who is himself the image of God (2 Cor. 3.18; 4.4, 6): the glory lost by Adam is being restored.

Elsewhere in Paul, in 1 Corinthians, we find the idea of Christ as the agent of creation, 'through whom are all things and through whom we exist' (8.6).[13] In the same epistle he expounds the story of the rock which supplied the Israelites in the wilderness with water. According to the book of Wisdom, wisdom was at work in these events (11.1–4), while Philo identifies the rock with wisdom (*Leg. All.* II.86). For Paul, however, the rock was Christ, and *he* was the source of the water (a symbol of the Torah) supplied to Israel (1 Cor. 10.1–5). Similar ideas are of course expressed in John's Gospel in the miracles and discourses which reveal Jesus to be the source of living water, the true manna, light, life, way, truth – obvious corollaries to the opening declaration that he is the word.

The same understanding appears to have been held by the author of Matthew, in his portrayal of Jesus teaching from the Mount. What Jesus delivers is not a *new* law, but the true understanding of what had been revealed to Moses on Sinai and only partly understood: he does not destroy the old but fulfils it (5.17–20), as he alone is able to do. Only he is able to reveal the Father – because he is the Son of the Father (11.25–27).

For the author of Hebrews, also, the Sonship of Christ is important. Christ is the Son, Moses a servant (3.1–6), who delivered a law which 'has only a shadow of the good things to come' (10.1). Christ is superior not only to him but also to all the angels, for he is the one through whom God has spoken and through whom he created the worlds; he is the reflection of God's glory and the expression of his being (1.1–14), and through him many sons are brought to glory (2.10).

These passages were all written by men who were very much concerned with the problem of relating their growing understanding of the implications of their faith in Jesus with their

---

[13] Like Philo in *De Cherubim* 127, Paul here seems to distinguish between the cause (God the Father) and the agent (Christ).

Jewish roots, and reflect something of the conflict between their previous convictions regarding the Torah and the claims they were now making for Christ. They established their case by identifying Jesus with God's wisdom or word, through which the world had been created, and by which it would be restored.

Col. 1.15–20 sums up these claims: Christ is the image of the invisible God, with him before all things began, the agent of creation, by whom, through whom and for whom all things have been created. In him the fullness of God was pleased to dwell, and was pleased, through him, to reconcile all things to him through his death.[14] Christ, not the Torah, is now understood to be the supreme revelation of God's will or purpose, the fullest expression of his word or wisdom. The parallelism between 1.15–16 and 1.18b–20, and between v. 17 and v. 18a, stresses the link between his work in creation and in redemption.

Colossians 1 is said to express 'Wisdom Christology' rather than 'Logos Christology' – perhaps because Christ is identified with wisdom elsewhere in Paul (1 Cor. 1.24, 30). Interestingly, however, neither the word *σοφία* nor the word *λόγος* is used in this passage! They are not needed, since what was once said about them has been transferred to Christ. But notice the references to *σοφία* in the context, which draws out the significance of the passage for the life of the Christian community.[15]

(1) Col. 1.9: Paul says that he prays unceasingly for the Colossians, that they may be filled with knowledge of God's will, in all spiritual wisdom and understanding.

The language of the whole paragraph (vv. 9–12) is thoroughly Jewish. Knowledge of God's will would, for a Jew, come through the Torah. For Paul, it was now understood to come through Christ, in whom God's purpose for his world is revealed. Observing the law brought wisdom and understanding (*σοφία*

---

[14] The phrase *εἰς αὐτόν* is often translated as thought it were *εἰς ἑαυτόν*, meaning 'to himself', because commentators feel that things should be reconciled to God, rather than to Christ. But the symmetry of the passage (2 × *ἐν . . . διά . . . εἰς*) demands that we should understand the phrase to refer to Christ. As we shall see, this interpretation makes good sense of the passage.

[15] Cf. also 1 Cor. 3.16 and 4.5.

καὶ σύνεσις: Deut. 4.6; Sir. 24.23–26). These gifts are now offered to those who are in Christ, who will thus be enabled to 'lead lives worthy of the Lord' (1.10). The proper response to the revelation of God's will in Christ (as to his revelation on Sinai) is a life that conforms to the divine commands.

(2) Col. 1.28: Paul proclaims Christ, warning everyone and teaching everyone in all wisdom, in order to present everyone mature in Christ.

The phrase *ἐν πάσῃ σοφίᾳ* echoes what was said in 1.9: Paul works to make his prayer a reality. He claims to teach with wisdom, since his aim is to 'present everyone mature in Christ', who is the source of wisdom. The threefold use of 'everyone' in this verse might suggest hyperbole, except that 1.15–20 referred to the reconciliation of *all* things to Christ.[16] The one whom Paul proclaims is 'Christ in you, the hope of glory' (1.27). The glory which had been lost by Adam,[17] which accompanied the giving of the Torah, and which would, so it was said, be restored at the End to those who had kept the law,[18] was in fact to be found in Christ, who is 'the image of the invisible God' (1.15). Maturity in Christ will mean sharing in this glory.

(3) Col. 2.3: God's mystery – a mystery hidden throughout the ages and generations but now revealed to the saints (1.26) – is Christ himself, in whom are hidden all treasures of wisdom and knowledge.

Once again, Paul affirms that his task is to ensure that even those Gentiles who have not seen him face to face (v. 1) should come to the knowledge of God's 'mystery' – that is, Christ himself (v. 2; cf. 1.26, 27). This time Christ is identified as the *source* of wisdom and knowledge – the one 'in whom are hidden all the treasures of wisdom and knowledge'. The verse sums up the implications of 1.15–20. Paul goes on to argue that all other

---

[16] So James D. G. Dunn, *The Epistles to the Colossians and to Philemon: A Commentary on the Greek Text*, Grand Rapids: Eerdmans/Carlisle: Paternoster, 1996, p. 125.

[17] For this idea in later Jewish tradition, see Gen. Rab. 11.2; 12.6; Sanh. 38b. Cf. Rom. 1.23.

[18] 2 Esdras 7.95, 97; 1 Enoch 38.4; 50.1.

claims to possible wisdom and knowledge are simply 'philosophy and empty deceit', whose origins are mere human tradition or the elemental forces of the universe, all of which are inferior to Christ (vv. 8–15).

(4) Col. 2.23: Jewish regulations have a reputation for wisdom, but are of no value.

What had once appeared to be the embodiment of wisdom – God's revelation on Sinai, and the regulations set out in Torah – are now discovered to belong to a partial and temporal revelation. They have the reputation for embodying wisdom, but do not possess the reality. Since the Colossian Christians no longer belong to the world ruled by the elemental spirits of the universe, they do not need regulations that belong to that world: they have been raised with Christ, and should therefore seek the things that belong to the new age, where Christ reigns at God's right hand (3.1).

The mystery hidden throughout the ages and generations – the wisdom sought by men and women in the past and glimpsed by Moses on Sinai – is now revealed to be Christ – or rather, Christ *in you*, the hope of glory (1.27). Why it is expressed in this way? Because he is the εἰκὼν Θεοῦ, not simply the agent of creation but also the *pattern* according to which Adam was created and *to* which men and women (even Gentiles!) are now being restored. 'Christ in you' because Christians have shed 'the old Adam' and have put on the new, which is being renewed *according to the image* of its creator, until it reaches full knowledge (3.10). As εἰκὼν Θεοῦ, Christ is both the agent of creation and the pattern for humanity – the one *by* whom all things were made, and *to* whom all things are reconciled (Col. 1.16, 20).

As we read through Colossians, we see how the implications of this passage for the Christian community are brought out. If Christ is the agent of all creation, then those in him need have no fear of or concern for 'the elemental spirits of the universe' (2.8, 20). If God's 'fullness' dwells in him, then it is he who reveals God's purpose for humanity, and Christian ethics are a matter of living in Christ (2.6; 3.12–17). A passage which is itself an exegesis of Scripture is in turn expounded and applied.

What, then, can we learn from the way in which the author of this passage handles Scripture? Paradoxically, beginning from what he regards as authoritative, he *subverts* the text by pointing to a greater authority *behind* the text. Col. 1.15–20 is not simply an example of exegesis; rather it points us to what its author regards as the fundamental *principle* of exegesis. The word spoken by God at creation and revealed on Sinai was not, after all, encapsulated in the written Torah, but dwells in Christ. In Johannine terminology, that means that the incarnate word reveals God in a way that Moses could not do; the role of the words of Scripture is to witness to the word. In Pauline imagery, it means that the glory displayed in Christ is far greater than the glory glimpsed by Moses on Sinai, and the role of the law and the prophets is to witness *to* him. For Paul, something static – words inscribed on stone tablets – has been replaced by something alive – the Spirit at work in human hearts (2 Cor. 3.1–3). Paul begins from Scripture and appeals to it as authoritative, yet insists that the interpretation of Scripture must not be fossilized. He has no interest in the question which I was trained to ask: 'What did this mean for the original author?' Rather, with the rabbis, he insists '*You* read it this way, but *I* interpret it in this. The text does not mean what you think it means, because it witnesses to the one who is *behind* the text, namely Christ.' For Paul, the 'canon' is not Scripture itself, but Christ, which means that Scripture must be read in the light of Christ. Where is wisdom to be found? Not in the written Torah – not even in the epistles of Paul! – but in the living Christ.

Is Paul's view sustainable? The way in which Christians down the ages have treated the words of Scripture as authoritative and regarded the Bible itself as the word of God – offering clear guidance and hard-and-fast rules – suggests that they have found it difficult to follow him. Tablets of stone are easier to take hold of than the Spirit of Christ. How do we read the mind of Christ? For an answer, we turn back, inevitably, to the written word, though endeavouring to read it with the guidance of the Spirit.

We find ourselves confronted once again, therefore, with the question that has been raised again and again in other essays in this volume: *how* do we interpret Scripture? How do we distinguish between an ethical or unethical reading? Between a reading that is legitimate and one that is illegitimate? Between one that is right and one that is wrong? Between one that is wise and one that is unwise? All those terms have been used by other contributors to this symposium. For Paul, the answer is: look at Christ, and at what *he* reveals to us of the love of God; interpret Scripture in the light of Christ.

In giving that answer, Paul inevitably makes himself vulnerable, for he is in danger both of misunderstanding the text and of being himself misunderstood. But if God revealed himself by what he said to Moses on Sinai, he himself was in danger of being misunderstood; if he revealed himself in Christ and speaks to us through a man born of woman, then it is *God* who has made himself vulnerable. Men and women can so easily reject what is shown them, or simply misunderstand what they hear. If incarnation is at the centre of Christian faith, then we must surely expect the text that bears witness to the incarnate word to be open to the same vulnerability. Vulnerability is built into God's revelation.

Where is wisdom to be found? The answer we are given in Colossians in 'in Christ himself' (2.2–3). Christ, who is the image of the invisible God; Christ, through whose death all things have been reconciled (1.20). It is surely no accident that when, in 1 Cor. 1.24, 30, Paul *identifies* Christ with the wisdom of God, it is in a passage where he is spelling out the significance of the message of *Christ crucified* – to Jews, a stumbling-block, and to Gentiles, folly. There could be no clearer demonstration of the vulnerability of God's revelation than the crucifixion: men and women had refused to listen to his incarnate word and attempted its destruction. Yet it is *here* that God's wisdom is to be found! The gospel message is that God's power is effective even here, and that he has triumphed over death itself in the resurrection.

Because Scripture is the witness to God's revelation, it will be open to the same possibilities of misunderstanding and rejection, for it inevitably reflects the vulnerability of that revelation. But just as God has revealed himself in the crucified and risen Christ, so he has been able to reveal himself through the pages of Scripture. Since Scripture is the witness to God's revelation, it must be understood in the light of the birth, death and resurrection of Christ, in whom all the treasure of wisdom are to be found.

9. Where is Wisdom to be Found? Colossians 1.15–20 (2)

RICHARD BAUCKHAM

Colossians 1.15–20 is one of most remarkable christological passages in the New Testament. It is also one of the most problematic for theological appropriation today. In order to give some indication of the scope of the theological issues involved, I shall begin with the observation that in the theology of the last half century our passage has been prominent in three rather different respects:

First, there is the issue of the pre-existence of Christ. Our passage was an important one for Karl Barth's argument that the pre-existent Christ – the Christ who pre-existed creation and was the one through whom and for whom all things were made, according to this Christ-hymn – should not be thought of as the *Logos asarkos,* the non-incarnate Logos, an abstract principle of cosmic order, but only as the man Jesus, the eternal Son of God already in God's intention the incarnate one.[1] Creation is through and for Jesus Christ. That means: God's covenant with humanity, established in the concrete form of Jesus of Nazareth, the one who is both God and human, is the basis of creation.[2] Barth was

[1] For discussion of this idea in Barth and Hendrikus Berkhof, see Chul Won Suh, *The Creation-Mediatorship of Jesus Christ,* Amsterdam Studies in Theology 4, Amsterdam: Rodopi, 1982.

[2] Karl Barth, *Church Dogmatics*, ed. G. W. Bromiley and T. F. Torrance, Edinburgh: T. & T. Clark, 1956–77, II/2, pp. 94–102; III/1, pp. 50–6. For criticism of this notion in Barth, see W. Pannenberg, *Systematic Theology,* vol. 2, ET G. Bromiley; Edinburgh: T. & T. Clark/Grand Rapids: Eerdmans, 1994, p. 30, who takes Barth to mean only 'that it was a view to the Son

not denying but defining the personal pre-existence of Christ, bringing it arguably closer to the way the Colossian Christ-hymn and similar New Testament passages speak of Jesus Christ himself as the subject of acts prior to his human existence.[3] But if Barth identified the pre-existent subject of the hymn more closely with the man Jesus than traditional theology had done, other discussions of the Christology of this passage, such as those of James Dunn[4] and Karl-Josef Kuschel,[5] have done the opposite, reading the hymn as a poetic expression of the truth that God's action in Christ belongs to the same divine purpose as was expressed also in creation.

Secondly, our passage features prominently in the project of Walter Wink, in his three-volume work, *The Powers*,[6] to interpret and to explore the contemporary relevance of the New Testament, especially Pauline, language about the cosmic powers. Wink takes the powers to be not only angelic powers of the non-human world, but also the inner spiritual dimension of the structures of human power. The Colossian Christ-hymn affirms their creation by God (they are not intrinsically evil), assumes their fall into that condition of hostility to God and to human flourishing that the rest of Colossians evidently assumes, and affirms also

---

that the Father created us humans and our world', thereby neglecting 'the Son's own subjectivity'.

[3] Cf. H. Urs von Balthasar, quoted by W. A. Whitehouse, in A. Loades, (ed.), *The Authority of Grace: Essays in Response to Karl Barth,* Edinburgh: T. & T. Clark, 1981, p. 92: it is 'exegetically impossible to understand [these passages] of an eternal divine Son or Logos *in abstracto*, but solely of him in his unity with the man Jesus'.

[4] J. D. G. Dunn, *Christology in the Making,* London: SCM Press, 1980, pp. 187–94; idem, *The Epistles to the Colossians and to Philemon,* Grand Rapids: Eerdmans/Carlisle: Paternoster, 1996, p. 89.

[5] K.-J. Kuschel, *Born Before All Time?: The Dispute over Christ's Origin,* ET J. Bowden; London: SCM Press, 1992, pp. 327–40, 491–6.

[6] W. Wink, *Naming the Powers: The Language of Power in the New Testament,* Philadelphia: Fortress Press, 1984; idem, *Unmasking the Powers: The Invisible Forces That Determine Human Existence,* Philadelphia: Fortress Press, 1986; idem, *Engaging the Powers: Discernment and Resistance in a World of Domination,* Minneapolis: Fortress Press, 1992.

their reconciliation in Christ.[7] On this interpretation Wink builds an influential contemporary theology of Christian resistance to structural evil in human society which does not despair of the powers but works non-violently, on the model of the cross, for their redemption.

Thirdly, the cosmic Christology of our passage has played an important part in recent attempts to retrieve and develop a theology of creation relevant to the ecological crisis resulting from modern humanity's destructive relationship to the rest of God's creation. In this role the Colossian Christ-hymn already featured centrally in the pioneering ecological theology of Joseph Sittler[8] and remains important in more recent endeavours, such as that of Jürgen Moltmann.[9] Whereas other parts of Scripture affirm the value of all creatures as God's creation, the Colossian Christ-hymn goes further in bringing the whole creation within the central concern of the Christian Gospel: salvation in Christ.[10] It relates Christ himself not only to redemption but also to creation; it relates creation to redemption; and it extends the scope of reconciliation through Christ as far as the whole creation. It seems an appropriate biblical basis for overcoming the anthropological restriction of so much of the theology of the modern period. On the other hand, we might note that Celia Deane-Drummond in a recent book called *Creation through Wisdom*, protests against

---

[7] For criticism of Wink's exegesis of Colossians, see C. E. Arnold, *Power and Magic: The Concept of Power in Ephesians*, Grand Rapids: Baker, 3rd edn, 1997, pp. 47–51; idem, *The Colossian Syncretism: The Interface between Christianity and Folk Belief at Colossae*, Grand Rapids: Baker, 1996, pp. 267–8.

[8] J. Sittler, in S. Bowma-Prediger and Peter Bakken, (eds.), *Evocations of Grace: The Writings of Joseph Sittler on Ecology, Theology, and Ethics*, Grand Rapids: Eerdmans, 2000, especially pp. 30–1, 38–50 (this reflection on Col. 1.15–20 was first published in 1962), 105–12 (first published in 1972).

[9] J. Moltmann, *The Way of Jesus Christ*, ET M. Kohl; London: SCM Press, 1990, pp. 276–86, 304–7, 312. On cosmic Christology in Sittler and Moltmann, see S. Bowma-Prediger, *The Greening of Theology: The Ecological Models of Rosemary Radford Ruether, Joseph Sittler, and Jürgen Moltmann*, Atlanta: Scholars Press, 1995.

[10] Some relationship between redemption by Christ and the whole creation is also suggested by Phil. 2.10 and Rev. 5.13.

the restriction of cosmic Wisdom to Christology that too exclusive a reliance on this passage entails.[11]

These have been the three, rather separate lines of theological interest in our passage in theology from Barth to the present. But do they have any bearing on the question: Where is wisdom to be found? We should recall that the meaning of wisdom, that is, God's wisdom, in the Jewish theological tradition to which our passage belongs has to do with the created order of things and with the divine purpose for creation. It is God's wisdom that orders creation for its well-being, God's wisdom that can be perceived in the good order of the natural creation, God's wisdom that ordains good ways of human living in the world, and God's wisdom that, beyond the disruption of creation's good by evil, purposes the ultimate well-being, the shalom, the peace of the whole creation. According to Colossians, this wisdom of God is all to be found in Jesus Christ. Whatever else we might make of this claim, it is not that Jesus Christ is one among many expressions of the creative and redemptive wisdom of God. It is that Jesus Christ is that wisdom. When we recognize both the scope of wisdom in this passage, encompassing all creation, its origin and goal, and also its christological concentration, such that the reconciliation of all things occurs through the cross of Jesus, it is surely clear that at least all three of the lines of theological interest in this passage I have noted would be needed to do theological justice to it and to answer the question: Where is wisdom to be found? Wisdom is found in the whole creation and it is found in the crucified and risen Jesus and somehow these two are the same.

The following are my own theological reflections on the issue:

(1) The relevance and appeal of the Colossian Christ-hymn today may well lie in the holistic character of its depiction of the wise purposes of God. It clearly surmounts the false dualisms that have too often marred the Christian world view. By false dualisms I mean the privileging of one aspect of reality at the

---

[11] C. E. Deane-Drummond, *Creation through Wisdom: Theology and the New Biology*, Edinburgh: T. & T. Clark, 2000, ch. 4 and pp. 236–41; cf. eadem, 'Futurenatural? A Future of Science through the Lens of Wisdom', *Heythrop Journal* 40, 1999, pp. 47–51.

expense of its correlate – for example, the dualisms of nature and history, the spatial and the temporal, matter and spirit, the non-human and the human, creation and salvation, the order of creation and the eschatological. These dualisms of reality also relate to the contrasts, often set up as exclusive, between such biblical traditions as wisdom and salvation-history or wisdom and apocalyptic, and of course also to such theological polarities as natural theology and theology of the cross. In some sense the Colossian Christ-hymn invites us to see the world whole, and there is much in our cultural climate that makes that congenial.

(2) What may be less culturally congenial is that the holism of our passage is christological. Dualism is overcome or (better) avoided because Jesus Christ is both the firstborn of the whole creation and the firstborn from the dead, because those remarkably significant prepositional phrases 'through him' and 'for him' are so strikingly applied both to the creation of all things and to the reconciliation of all things. This christological coherence of all things is best appreciated, in my view, when we recognize the passage as an expression of what Tom Wright[12] and I have both called the christological monotheism of the New Testament writings. In the terms I have advocated elsewhere,[13] what the passage does is to include Jesus Christ in God's unique relationship to the whole of created reality and thereby to include Jesus in the unique identity of God as Jewish monotheism understood it.

There are two especially strong indications of this. One is the sixfold occurrence of the phrase 'all things' and the twofold reference to the heavens and the earth: these universal references are ubiquitous in the rhetoric of Jewish monotheism. They specify the unique relationship in which God stands to the whole of created reality, as creator of all things and Lord over all things. Especially striking is the inclusion of Jesus in God's relationship as creator to all things. It was creation that most unambiguously marked the absolute distinction between God and all other reality. It was

[12] N. T. Wright, *The Climax of the Covenant: Christ and the Law in Pauline Theology*, Edinburgh: T. & T. Clark, 1991, pp. 114–19.

[13] R. Bauckham, *God Crucified: Monotheism and Christology in the New Testament*, Carlisle: Paternoster, 1998; Grand Rapids: Eerdmans, 1999.

emphatically denied that in the work of creation God was assisted by anyone else, though this was quite compatible with saying that God created by his word or his wisdom, since these were not 'someone else' but God's own word and wisdom, intrinsic to his identity. Secondly, the unique relationship of God to the whole creation was sometimes specified by prepositional phrases indicating three of the forms of causation recognized in ancient philosophy: all things were created by God (efficient causation), through God (instrumental causation) and for God (final causation).[14] It is therefore in God's relationship to the world that the Colossian hymn includes Jesus Christ when it makes him both the instrumental and the final cause of both the creation and reconciliation of all things: 'through him' and 'for him'. Finally, it is important that both these features of monotheistic rhetoric occur, in close parallelism, in both stanzas of the hymn, referring both to creation and to reconciliation. The two stanzas concern the same one God's relationship to his world and include Jesus in this uniquely divine relationship to all things in the same way in both cases.

Thus it is christological monotheism that makes it possible to view the world whole in the way that the Colossian hymn does. The original and restored unity of all things could not be found in Christ if Christ did not share the uniquely divine relationship of the one God to all things.

(3) For all the emphatic universality of the whole hymn, there is also no missing the intense particularity of the man Jesus indicated by the phrase 'the blood of his cross' (1.20). Combination of particularity and universality – the particular identity of Jesus and the universal relevance or effect of his history – is characteristic of New Testament Christology. But whereas in most cases there is a movement from the particularity of Jesus to the eschatological universality of his future, in the Colossian hymn this is also grounded in the prior universality of his relationship to creation. The effect, as far as I can see, is not at all to reduce

---

[14] See the examples in J. D. G. Dunn, *Romans 9–16*, WBC 38B, Dallas: Word, 1988, pp. 701–2.

the significance of the particularity of the man Jesus, relativizing him by reference to a Christ who is bigger than Jesus (a phrase of John Robinson's),[15] but, on the contrary, to reinforce the universal relevance of precisely the man Jesus. To see the world whole we must see it in relationship to the crucified and risen Jesus, for whom all things were created.

(4) What then is the meaning of the hymn's implicit claim that all the wisdom of God is to be found in Christ? The implicit claim is explicit elsewhere in Colossians in the statement that in Christ 'are hidden all the treasuries of wisdom and knowledge' (2.3). The author of one book on Colossians, Richard DeMaris, accuses the writer of denigrating the cosmos, locating 'God's wisdom narrowly, entirely in Christ (Col. 1.26; 2.2–4), to the apparent exclusion of all else (2.8, 20)'.[16] But the cosmic Christ of the Colossian Christ-hymn is not narrow; he is all-encompassing. The effect is not to denigrate wisdom wherever it may be found, but to claim it for Christ, in other words to claim that only from the vantage-point of the crucified and risen Jesus can creation, in all the ways in which it reflects the wisdom of its creator, be seen whole.[17] The reason is the intrusion of evil that takes place implicitly between the first and second stanzas of the hymn (Colossians is as reticent about the origins of evil as most of the Bible is). In this disordered state of God's creation the perception and affirmation of his wise ordering of creation requires faith in his purpose, revealed and established in Jesus Christ, to make it whole. This purpose is hidden because the event that establishes it looks for all the world like a triumph for the forces of violence and disorder

---

[15] J. A. T. Robinson, *The Human Face of God,* London: SCM Press, 1973, p. 10: 'the Christ is bigger than Jesus'.

[16] R. E. DeMaris, *The Colossian Controversy: Wisdom in Dispute at Colossae,* JSNTSS 96, Sheffield: Sheffield Academic Press, 1994, p. 149.

[17] Cf. C. Gunton, 'Christ, the Wisdom of God; A Study in Divine and Human Action', in S. C. Barton, (ed.), *Where Shall Wisdom Be Found?: Wisdom in the Bible, the Church and the Contemporary World,* Edinburgh: T. & T. Clark, 1999, p. 260: 'To say that the crucified Christ is the Wisdom of God is to say that he is the key to the meaning of the whole of the created order, and therefore the source of true wisdom, wherever that is to be found.'

that ravage creation. Hidden in the crucified and risen Christ is the secret of God's purpose for all things that puts in true perspective all traces of his wisdom in the whole creation.

(5) The most difficult aspect of the Christ-hymn for a contemporary hermeneutical appropriation seems to me the notion of cosmic reconciliation. But since this aspect also holds out considerable promise of speaking to our situation of ecological destruction, it may be worth persisting with the difficulty. I am not as troubled as many commentators by the apparent contradiction between the reconciliation of all things, presumably including the powers, in the hymn (1.19–20), and Christ's triumph over the powers, depicted later in 2.15. Both images are of pacification, but since both are *images* I do not see that they need be compatible in literal terms. Since we barely know what the powers are, I do not think we need expect to know, in literal terms, how they are pacified by Christ.

The notion of the reconciliation of all things I find problematic in two other ways. The first is the issue of what there is about the non-human creation that needs reconciliation. Science seems to reveal a world in which the interplay of order and chaos is so intimate that it is very hard to disentangle a good order which would be better for the overcoming of disorder. To put it crudely, the lion that lay down with the lamb would starve. Perhaps we may be content to leave that issue in the mystery of God's purpose and to focus – as surely the most relevant aspect of the matter for our contemporary context – on the disorder wrought by the exercise of human power in creation. This idea of humanly produced disorder in creation is not at all difficult to understand and its evidence is all around us.

The second problem I have is with the apparent anthropocentricity of the picture. The notion of cosmic redemption certainly breaks out of the anthropological restriction of too much Christian theology and encompasses the whole of the creation. But if it takes the blood of the incarnate Christ, of the man Jesus, to redeem the non-human world, does this not presuppose an anthropocentric creation? Perhaps we could say that it presupposes not anthropocentricity in a general sense and certainly not that the rest of creation exists for humanity's sake, but rather the distinctive place that humanity occupies in the world. This distinctiveness is evident in the brute fact of the power we have to affect and to damage the rest of nature. We might connect this also with supposing that it is especially in human society that the powers of evil are able to influence the world for ill. Cosmic reconciliation is focused in the human person of Jesus because it is humanity that constitutes at least the core of the problem for the rest of creation as well as for ourselves. The power of supra-human forces of evil is overcome within human history because it is there that they have gained their most significant hold in creation.

If this makes cosmic redemption anthropocentric, it does so in a very different way from the arrogant progressivism of the modern era, for which human domination of the rest of nature seemed the path of salvation and the humanization of the cosmos its God-given destiny.[18] What prevents the assimilation of the Colossian Christ-hymn to any such progressivist vision of the world is its stubborn reminder of the particularity of Jesus: 'the blood of his cross'. That recognition of the chaos and evil at the heart of human history requires us to relate to the rest of God's creation in humility and trust, with love rather than with mastery, in search

[18] The classic expression of this view in christological form is that of P. Teilhard de Chardin. Cf. Whitehouse, *The Authority of Grace*, pp. 95–6, where, having raised, as an obstacle for the modern mind to belief in the cosmic role of Christ, its 'anthropocentric character', he attempts to remove the obstacle thus:

> The history of nature is coming under man's dominion to an increasing degree; it is being increasingly permeated by man's purposes; and the effect is not wholly detrimental. Is not this a token, however ambiguous or proleptic, that it is already permeated by the mind and will which received historical expression in the man Jesus Christ? The mind and will by which mankind tends to permeate the cosmos independently must of course be transformed if they are to become the mind and will of Christ. But signs of this transformation are not altogether lacking in the changing pattern of man's thought and purposes.

In the light of the ecological crisis, such statements must be subject to a hermeneutic of suspicion. They are theological justifications of the modern project of human domination of nature.

of the peace that is the well-being of all creatures, not the well-being of ourselves at the expense of all others. That is one of the paths along which wisdom is to be found.

10. Remembering Amalek:
A Positive Biblical Model for Dealing with Negative Scriptural Types

DIANA LIPTON

My research and academic teaching (at Newnham College, Cambridge and Leo Baeck College) almost always begins and ends with the question of what Hebrew Bible texts may have meant to their authors, editors and original audiences. In this essay, by contrast, I shall begin and end with a theological challenge that confronts all modern religious communities (or at least, all those with sacred texts): How should we respond to passages from our Scriptures that we find abhorrent or simply unacceptable? In the process of grappling with this theological question, I shall return to the more familiar terrain of pure Scripture as I attempt to show that the Hebrew Bible itself offers a model for addressing, if not solving, the problem of unpalatable sacred texts.[1]

Since attitudes towards sacred texts vary greatly from one religion to another, I must start – with apologies to readers for whom it is self-evident – by outlining why they pose a particular problem from a Jewish perspective (the one from which I am writing). The short answer is that the pre-eminent Jewish sacred text, the Torah, cannot be edited or even selectively ignored, and is likely to be well known among even those Jews whose contact with organized Judaism is limited. In Reform and Liberal synagogues, the Torah is read aloud, in Hebrew and English, in

[1] I am grateful to Davida Charney and Melissa Lane for helpful comments on an earlier version of this essay, and to David Ford and Graham Stanton for inviting me to participate in the conference celebrating the 500th anniversary of the Lady Margaret Chair in Divinity.

three-year cycles, while in Orthodox and Conservative or Masorti synagogues the entire Torah is chanted in Hebrew during the course of each year. Congregants of all Jewish denominations are encouraged to follow the weekly reading from a written text (usually in Hebrew with English translation and a commentary), and sermons are almost invariably based in some measure on the Torah reading.

As well as being bound to be heard, the Torah is integral, indeed indispensable, to Jewish education. Adult study in a synagogue context is likely to focus on Torah itself or on texts that are largely incomprehensible without recourse to Torah, and Torah is central to the concept of Bar and Bat Mitzvah, the age at which a Jewish child becomes responsible for keeping the commandments. The commandments these young adults commit themselves to keeping are, of course, found in Torah, and the Torah features prominently in the ritual that marks the transition. As a minimum requirement, thirteen-year-old boys, and twelve- or thirteen-year-old girls in non-Orthodox congregations, celebrate their Bar or Bat Mitzvah by reciting blessings before and after a section of the weekly Torah reading. Most children do far more than this, reading or chanting all or part of the weekly reading from a hand-written scroll that contains neither vowels nor musical notation. Children who attend synagogue services regularly and undertake the standard commitment for Bar or Bat Mitzvah thus have a great deal of exposure to Torah at a formative time in their lives. All children are taught reverence for the Torah as a ritual object. Prior to being read in synagogue, the scroll – resplendent in garments modelled on the clothing of the biblical High Priest – is removed ceremoniously from the Ark and paraded through the synagogue. Congregants incline to touch it with a prayerbook or the corner of a tallit (prayer shawl) which they kiss. For many children, the Torah will be the starting-point, if not the only source, for most ethical discussions in a Jewish context: Why should we give financial and other kinds of support to refugees? Because we were strangers in the land of Egypt![2]

---

[2] As Head Teacher for the past ten years of the Cheder (Sunday School)

So what can members of a religious community do when faced with a sacred text whose message they cannot condone? I want to use as a case study a text that is both problematic and prominent. As well as being read as part of the regular portion of the week – once a year in Orthodox and Masorti synagogues and once every three years in others – Deut. 25.17–19 has a special shabbat of its own. The shabbat immediately preceding the festival of Purim is named for its opening word, *zakhor* (remember):

> Remember what Amalek did to you on your journey, after you left Egypt – how, undeterred by fear of God, he surprised you on the march, when you were famished and weary, and cut down all the stragglers in your rear. Therefore, when LORD God grants you safety from all your enemies around you, in the land that the LORD is giving you as a hereditary portion, you shall blot out the memory of Amalek from under heaven. Do not forget. (Deut. 25.17–19)[3]

For Jewish readers, this passage amounts to far more than a record of a distant skirmish with an extinct enemy. Just as the Passover *Haggadah* asks us to recall the Exodus as if we ourselves were in Egypt, so the Amalek text requires more than a passive remembrance of things past. It is hardly surprising that many Jews find *Shabbat Zakhor* the most ethically and theologically challenging of the year.

The renewal in each generation of the struggle with Amalek is traditionally enacted through typological links with Israel's later enemies. The earliest example occurs in the Bible itself; Haman, the villain of the book of Esther, is a descendant of Agag, the Amalekite king whose life was spared by Saul (at the cost of his kingdom), and Mordecai, Esther's male hero, is a descendant of Saul.[4] Well aware of the potency of archetypal enemies, Josephus

---

of Beth Shalom Reform Synagogue, and the mother of two boys who have quite recently become Bar Mitzvah, I have many reasons to reflect on the role of Torah in the moral and ethical development of children.

[3] English translations from *Tanakh, The Holy Scriptures*, Philadelphia: Jewish Publication Society, 1985.

[4] Esther 3.1 and 2.5 (cf. 1 Sam. 15.8 and 9.1–2).

worked hard to distance Amalek from Edom, the biblical nation identified in Jewish texts with Rome. Though hardly positive, the typological link between Rome and Edom was less damaging to Josephus's hoped-for peaceful co-existence with Rome than an association with Amalek, Israel's eternal enemy.[5] Notorious enemies of Israel, from Titus to Hitler, have since been depicted as types of Amalek.[6] Does remembering Amalek amount to an everlasting incitement to hatred of the other, undermining attempts at reconciliation even where they might succeed? Is violent nationalism the inevitable, unacceptable face of Judaism's distinctive approach to historical memory?

Jewish commentators through the ages, sensitive to these very issues, introduced shades of grey into the Bible's apparently black-and-white representation of Amalek and our obligation to blot him out. A midrash on 1 Samuel 15 has Joab playing, rabbinic-style, with alternative meanings of *zcr* (memory and male) in order to persuade Saul that only *male* Amalekites need be blotted out (bad enough, but not as bad as the entire people).[7] Joab's interpretation thus distances the biblical injunction from Amalek's crime of killing women and children alongside men capable of self-defence. In a similar example, Rashi depicts Saul's inner debate about how the command to kill Agag can be reconciled with the Torah's concern for human life.[8] Another midrash on Amalek's place in the genealogy in Gen. 36.12 ('Timna was a concubine of Esau's son Eliphaz; she bore Amalek to Eliphaz') claims that Timna had hoped to convert to Judaism

---

[5] J. Maier, 'Amalek in the Writings of Josephus', in F. Parente and J. Sievers, (eds.), *Josephus and the History of the Greco-Roman Period*, Leiden: Brill, 1994, pp. 109–26.

[6] J. Cohen, 'The Remembrance of Amalek: Tainted Greatness and the Bible' in N. Harrowitz, (ed.), *Tainted Greatness: anti-Semitism and Cultural Heroes*, Philadelphia: Temple University Press, 1994, p. 291. For a discussion of Esau as a typological enemy, see G. D. Cohen, 'Esau as a Symbol in Early Medieval Thought', in A. Altman, *Jewish Medieval and Renaissance Studies*, Cambridge, MA: Harvard University Press, 1967, pp. 14–98.

[7] L. Ginzberg, *Legends of the Jews*, Baltimore: Johns Hopkins University Press, 1998, orig. publ. Philadelphia: Jewish Publication Society, 1909–38, 6:259 n.77.

[8] Rashi's commentary on 1 Sam. 15.5.

but, rejected by Abraham, Isaac and Jacob, became a concubine instead and gave birth to Amalek.[9] This midrash diminishes Amalek's guilt by hinting that the attack was provoked by Israelite wrongdoing.[10] Equally important for our purposes, it also indicates that this is not a straightforward ethnic issue; had events taken a different turn, Amalek's mother would have been an Israelite and, as it was, his father was Jacob's nephew. This certainly undermines the notion of an eternal war with a symbolic agent of evil.

Yet while many commentators have tried to address moral difficulties arising from the command to blot out the memory of Amalek, none has been able to neutralize it. By one route or another, we come back to the classic opposition of Israel and *the other*. Where can we turn? I propose we examine the Torah itself, where we find that the very proof-text for the commandment to blot out Amalek's memory (Deut. 25.17–19) may in fact have been intended to turn on its head the original biblical invective against Amalek in Exod. 17.8–16. In this essay I shall attempt to demonstrate – not via a midrashic response like those mentioned above, but through textual analysis of the biblical text – that the Deuteronomic authors were as uneasy as the rabbis with the idea of an eternal war with Amalek. Far from promoting genocide, they sought to shift the focus from Amalek's crimes in the wilderness to Israelite social injustice in their own generation. I hope to show here that the Torah itself provides us with a successful model for dealing with unacceptable sacred texts. The authors of Deut. 25.17–19 retain the authoritative account of the encounter with Amalek in Exod. 17.8–16, even implicitly directing readers to it with their command to 'remember'. At the same time, they encourage us to read it through their eyes. It is a measure of their success that, asked to identify the crime of Amalek, most Jewish readers refer to Deuteronomy's weak and sick at the back of the line leaving Egypt and are very surprised indeed to find it absent from Exodus.

---

[9] Babylonian Talmud, Sanhedrin 99b.

[10] Cohen, 'The Remembrance of Amalek', p. 298.

I have noted that a particular challenge for Jews in relation to unacceptable scriptural passages is that they cannot be excised or even sidelined. In advocating Deuteronomy as a model for dealing with difficult texts I am thus assuming that its authors did not intend to displace altogether their Exodus source. This, however, is a controversial assumption, and I cannot proceed without defending the notion that these ancient writers shared some constraints with the modern faith community that inherits a sacred text it can neither excise nor condone.

Bernard Levinson's excellent *Deuteronomy and the Hermeneutics of Legal Innovation*[11] demonstrates the far-reaching nature of the Deuteronomic transformation of Israelite religion and society, together with the hermeneutic means by which the authors of this legal corpus accomplished their programme. Levinson characterizes Deuteronomy as the manifesto of a seventh-century BCE movement whose principal aim was the centralization of worship in Jerusalem. Centralization affected sacrificial and judicial procedures, the festival calendar, and public administration, including the monarchy; power relations were reorganized in the central sphere – the Jerusalem Temple – and conventional structures of clan piety were disrupted as local shrines were abolished. He argues that Deuteronomy's influence extended even into the home; the original blood rite of Passover is wrested from the hands of the paterfamilias and repackaged as a national holiday, and the family is scrutinized for apostasy. If the Deuteronomists are beginning to sound like Big Brother, it should come as no surprise that Levinson credits them with a desire to silence all competing voices, prophetic and legal:

> There is no prophecy, not even that performed by a prophet whose oracles are fulfilled, but that which conforms to the norms of the Deuteronomic Torah . . . They disenfranchised conventional norms of prophecy while asserting the authority of their own authorial voice.

---

[11] Bernard Levinson, *Deuteronomy and the Hermeneutics of Legal Innovation*, Oxford: Oxford University Press, 1997.

> The absence of precedence – of legal and textual justification for their departure from convention – forced the authors of Deuteronomy paradoxically to seek sanction for their new composition from the very literary corpus that they simultaneously displaced.[12]

To be sure, the silencing of competing voices is compatible with other Deuteronomic recommendations – the elimination of alien altars, gods and sacred trees, not to mention peoples – but is it plausible that Deuteronomy's authors sought simultaneously to sanction *and* displace earlier texts? What fate did they envisage for the texts they plundered – the Exodus Law Code, for instance? Why were new documents written when old ones could have been reworked? What explains the apparently Deuteronomic textual amendments to earlier material? (Why edit a source you expect posterity to discard?) Does it make sense to claim authority from a text you hope to displace? Levinson has two primary responses to questions of this sort: Deuteronomy's desired changes were too radical to be effected by embedding new material into a pre-existing text, and a new literary form was required to replace the political treaty that had made Judah the vassal of the neo-Assyrian empire. On Levinson's account, the Deuteronomists were eventually hoist with their own petard. The Chroniclers pre-empted the Deuteronomistic historian by assuming an identical voice, that of an anonymous, authoritative historiographer, while the authors of the Samaritan Pentateuch and the Qumran Temple Scroll marshalled Deuteronomy's arsenal of textual strategies (pseudepigraphy, exegesis, resequencing) to sanction their own sectarian laws.[13]

Marc Brettler's work on Chronicles offers another way of understanding the relationship between Deuteronomy and its sources.[14] He suggests that the books on which Chronicles was based (Samuel and Kings) would have been well known to contemporaries of the Chroniclers and probably in some sense

[12] Levinson, *Deuteronomy*, pp. 144–5, 146. [13] Ibid., p. 155.

[14] Marc Brettler, *The Creation of History in Ancient Israel*, London: Routledge, 1995.

authoritative. The Chroniclers thus aimed not to displace, but rather to *supplement* earlier material, a possible reason why so many passages demand to be read alongside their sources. 1 Chronicles 10, for instance, narrates the death of Saul and notes the impact of his encounter with necromancy, but it fails to introduce Saul and does not repeat the long story of the necromancer told in 1 Samuel 28. It seems unlikely that it was intended to stand alone.

In some respects, Brettler's supplemental theory works well for Deuteronomy. It may explain why its authors chose Moses as the mouthpiece for their programme of reforms, yet did little to underline the source of his authority. (Deuteronomy omits the burning bush and the details of Moses' encounters with Pharaoh). In other ways, though, the supplemental theory is inadequate; in particular, it fails to address the Deuteronomic passion for editing. It is certainly possible that the Deuteronomists, unlike the Chroniclers on the whole, were belt-and-braces men; not content with writing a supplement, they made slight 'improvements' to the original. Though possible, this suggestion seems to me to underestimate Deuteronomy's immense sophistication – rhetorical, political and theological. More plausibly, I believe, the authors of Deuteronomy aimed neither to displace nor merely to supplement, but were rather the first seriously self-conscious intertextual writers.

Daniel Boyarin has established that there is a sense in which every text is intertextual:

> Now if the term 'intertextuality' has any value at all, it is precisely in the way that it claims that no texts, including the classic single-authored works of Shakespeare or Dostoyevsky are organic, self-contained unities ... [but rather that] every text is constrained by the literary system of which it is a part and that every text is ultimately dialogical in that it cannot but record the traces of its contentions and doubling of earlier discourses.[15]

[15] Daniel Boyarin, *Intertextuality and the Reading of Midrash*, Bloomington and Indianapolis: Indiana University Press, 1994, p. 14.

Following Gerald Bruns, Brevard Childs and others, however, Boyarin attributes to the Bible a special kind of intertextuality. For in biblical texts, 'the parts are made to relate to one another reflexively, with later texts . . . throwing light on the earlier, even as they themselves always stand in the light of what precedes and follows them'.[16] This seems to me an excellent account of the Deuteronomic authors' understanding of the relationship between their own texts and their sources which, if correct, justifies an appeal to Deuteronomy for a model of how to deal with problematic yet authoritative texts.

Having now at least made a case for the view that the authors of Deuteronomy intended their work to be read intertextually with its sources, we can now turn to the Exodus source for Deut. 25.17–19:

> Amalek came and fought with Israel at Rephidim. Moses said to Joshua, 'Pick some men for us and go out and do battle with Amalek. Tomorrow I will station myself on the top of a hill, with the rod of God in my hand.' Joshua did as Moses told him and fought with Amalek, while Moses, Aaron and Hur went up to the top of the hill. Then, whenever Moses held up his hand, Israel prevailed; but whenever he let down his hand, Amalek prevailed. But Moses' hand grew heavy; so they took a stone and put it under him and he sat on it, while Aaron and Hur, one on each side, supported his hands; thus his hands remained steady until the sun set. And Joshua overwhelmed the people of Amalek with the sword. The LORD said to Moses, 'Inscribe this in a document as a reminder, and read it aloud to Joshua: I will utterly blot out the memory of Amalek from under the heaven!' And Moses built an altar and named it Adonai-nissi. He said, 'It means, "Hand upon the throne of the LORD!" The LORD will be at war with Amalek throughout the ages.' (Exod. 17.8–16)

---

[16] Boyarin, *Intertextuality*, p. 16, citing G. Bruns, 'Midrash and Allegory', in R. Alter and F. Kermode, (eds.), *The Literary Guide to the Bible*, London: Collins, 1987.

Deut. 25.17–19 differs from the Exodus account in several ways,[17] but most interesting from our perspective is its expansion of Amalek's crime. Exodus reports simply that 'Amalek came and fought with Israel at Refidim'. Exegetes claim it must have been a gratuitous attack, motivated by desire neither to defend nor to expand territory.[18] Yet this seems wholly inadequate as a justification for eternal war, especially since the Bible neglects to confirm the location of Amalek's territory.[19] Deuteronomy, by contrast, is explicit about Amalek's crime: 'he surprised you on the march, when you were famished and weary, and cut down all the stragglers in your rear'. What did the Deuteronomic authors have in mind when they levelled this particular charge?

Many commentators assume a war crime here, the contravention, perhaps, of an ancient Israelite Geneva convention, such as M. Walzer sees behind Amos' oracles against the nations.[20] Yet Deuteronomy shows little interest in warfare, omitting the battle scene that dominates the Exodus account. More importantly, no mention is made of a cosmic war between the LORD and Amalek; it is now Israel, not God, who must blot out the memory of Amalek. To be sure, this does not rule out physical violence, but a call for the defeat of an external foe sits uneasily in a passage that evokes a time of peace, when God will give Israel rest from surrounding enemies and the land will be inherited, not conquered.

---

[17] It is impossible to prove that the author of Deut. 25.17–19 knew Exod. 17.8–16, but its opening exhortation – '*remember* what Amalek did to you' – makes it likely. This command could refer to a past event rather than an earlier account, but we are dealing with a period when written texts offered the best hope of historical longevity. Exodus 17 itself commands that the story of Amalek be inscribed *in a document* and read aloud *as a reminder* for Joshua (v. 14).

[18] Mekhilta d'Rabbi Ishmael 10, cited by A. Sagi, 'The Punishment of Amalek in Jewish Tradition: Coping with the Moral Problem', *Harvard Theological Review* 87.3, 1994, pp. 323–46 (p. 325).

[19] D. Edelman, 'Saul's Battle against Amaleq (1 Samuel 15)', *Journal for the Study of the Old Testament* 35, 1987, pp. 71–84, offers a detailed discussion of Amalek's location.

[20] M. Walzer, 'The Prophet as Social Critic', in *Interpretation and Social Criticism*, Cambridge MA: Harvard University Press, 1987, pp. 69–94.

An important indication of the hermeneutic thrust of Deut. 25.17–19 lies in its context. Had the authors of Deuteronomy wished to present the Amalekites as an archetypal enemy, they might have been expected to include them with the Amorites, Edomites and Moabites in the opening catalogue of wilderness encounters with hostile outsiders (Deut.1—4). Instead, and significantly, Amalek is first mentioned in a legal code for use by Israelites.[21] An equally important indication of the authors' intention is their emphasis on the victims: 'the famished and weary . . . the stragglers in [the] . . . rear'. Now Israel is settled in the land, it is the socially deprived who correspond to the weak and sick at the back of the line that left Egypt. Amalek's victims surely allude to the group that so commanded Deuteronomic attention: the poor, widows and orphans. This identification accounts for the transferral from God to Israel of the obligation to blot out Amalek's memory. Deuteronomy hammers home the point that the poor, widows and orphans are the people's responsibility, not God's (15.7–8; 16.9–12). And since the poor will always be in the land (15.11), the obligation to care for them – like the obligation to blot out Amalek's memory – is eternal. External enemies are not a natural focus at a time of national security, but this is precisely the occasion for Israel to confront the social problems not easily addressed by a nation fighting for survival.[22] Deuteronomy's reference to Amalek thus implies no interest at all in the Amalekites or any other nation, but draws attention to crimes God abhors *in Israel*, the very crimes, indeed, associated in Deuteronomy with expulsion from the land.[23]

The reinforcement of laws by promise and threat (blessing

[21] I am extremely grateful to Meira Polliack for this point and for many other valuable observations and suggestions.

[22] Amos 2.6–11 offers an interesting parallel. God's main complaint against Israel is her failure to develop a heightened sense of social justice despite his intervention to release her from the endless cycle of territorial violence that drained the resources of other nations. Israel 'sold the needy for a pair of sandals' even after God 'destroyed the Amorite before them'.

[23] This is a standard Deuteronomic device; ostensible hostility towards *Canaanite* religion (e.g. 7.5) functions as an attack on the corruption of the *Israelite* cult in the seventh century BCE.

and curse) is a common Deuteronomic strategy. The book closes with curses for those who break the laws and blessings for those who keep them and – significantly for us – smaller legal units often end with thematically related justifications drawn from Israel's wilderness experience. Laws about proper treatment of skin affections are thus coupled with a reminder of what God did to Miriam (24.8–9), while laws concerning gleaning rights for strangers, widows and orphans conclude with a reminder of slavery in Egypt, when Israelites depended on the kindness of strangers (24.19–22). Negative episodes from Israel's past are thus recalled to encourage *current* obedience to the laws.[24] I believe the reference to Amalek in Deut. 25.17–19 functions in precisely this way with regard to the laws preceding it.[25]

Deuteronomy 25.5–10 deals with levirate marriage:

> When brothers dwell together and one of them dies and leaves no son, the wife of the deceased shall not be married to a stranger, outside the family. Her husband's brother shall unite with her: he shall take her as a wife and perform the levir's duty. The first son that she bears shall be accounted to the dead brother, that his name may not be blotted out in Israel. (Deut. 25.5–6)

The levirate law serves two purposes: it protects the childless widow, a vulnerable figure in the ancient world, and guarantees the survival of a family line (albeit through a type of legal fiction). Yet levirate marriages could not be enforced:

> But if the man does not want to marry his brother's widow, his brother's widow shall . . . go up to him in the presence of the elders, pull the sandal from his foot, spit in his face, and make this declaration: Thus shall be done to the man who will not

---

[24] It is worth noting here that the preoccupation of 1 Samuel 15 is Saul's disobedience, not Amalek's wickedness.

[25] C. Carmichael, *Law and Narrative in the Bible: The Evidence of the Deuteronomic Laws and the Decalogue,* Ithaca: Cornell University Press, 1984, sees various connections between Deuteronomy 25 and narratives (such as Gen. 38) on the theme of levirate marriage.

> build up his brother's house! And he shall go in Israel by the name of 'the family of the unsandalled one'. (Deut. 25.7–10)

Just as Miriam is recalled to underline laws about skin diseases, so Amalek underscores the seriousness of the recalcitrant brother's crime. In failing to meet his (legally unenforceable) obligations as a levir, he consigns his brother's name to the fate of Amalek's. (The verb *mch*, to blot out, applies both to the brother's name [v. 6] and to Amalek's memory [v. 19].) He also loses his own name into the bargain (v. 10). Indeed, since 'foot' is a euphemism for penis (cf. Ruth 3.4), he may have received the double blow of losing his name and *gaining* a humiliating nickname. What, though, of the two laws that intervene between the levirate law and the command to remember Amalek?

Another law featuring two men and a woman follows the levirate law. This law specifies the punishment for a woman who intervenes to free her husband from the hand (*yad*) of an assailant by stretching out her hand to grab his opponent's genitals: 'You shall cut off her hand' (25.12). After this comes a law about fair weights and measures: 'You shall not have in your pouch alternate weights [lit. stones], larger and smaller . . .' (v. 13). Stones are a euphemism for genitals, which thus feature, obliquely or otherwise, in all three laws (see vv. 9, 11). But what connects these three laws with Amalek?

Exod. 17.8–16 shares two important words with these two laws, *yad* (hand) and *even* (stone). *Yad* is a key word in the Exodus text. It occurs seven times (a significant number in biblical terms) in these verses, and the victory over Amalek is, in every sense, in Moses' hands. Though mentioned only once, the stone too plays a pivotal role. It supports Moses when his hands are growing weak, and may be linked to the altar mentioned in 17.15. As well as playing a crucial role in Exodus 17, *yad* and *even* share a secondary meaning that binds them together and creates a strong thematic link to Amalek. Both words signify a memorial,[26]

---

[26] F. Brown, S. R. Driver and C. A. Briggs, *Hebrew and English Lexicon of the Old Testament*, Oxford: Clarendon Press, 1906/1951, p. 390 (*yad*)

precisely what Amalek is denied if we blot out his memory, and exactly what a levirate marriage is intended to secure.

In Exodus 17, the hands of Moses are used in combination with a stone to overcome an external enemy. Although Joshua is fighting, the real battle is between the sword of Amalek and the justice of Moses.[27] Deuteronomy relocates this battle from the wilderness to the land of Israel, where its opponents are no longer sword and justice (external and internal), but injustice and justice (both internal). Deuteronomy, as I interpret it, has transformed the eternal war with Amalek from a battle with an external enemy to the battle with injustice perpetrated by insiders. It this injustice that functions as a memorial (*yad, even*) to Amalek and must be blotted out.

So to return now to the question with which I began: How can members of a religious community deal with sacred texts they find abhorrent or unacceptable? I have focused here on a biblical text that has traditionally been read as a commandment to obliterate external enemies, a text we might be tempted to blot from the Scriptures if we saw that as an option (which, Jewishly speaking, it is not). I have suggested, though, that the very text that seems to us unacceptable for its violent hostility towards outsiders may in fact have been intended to address precisely this form of violent hostility in an earlier text. The Deuteronomic authors could not excise the Exodus text, but they could affect the way it was read; in their hands, a traumatic encounter with an external enemy was simultaneously memorialized and transformed into a vehicle for constructive self-criticism. This is not at all to say that Deuteronomy has presented us with a mechanism for purging sacred texts of their problematic elements. On the contrary, the instruction to remember Amalek points back to the promise of an eternal war between God and an enemy of Israel, and no amount of interpretation or allegorizing can (or should) rob a text of the meaning its authors intended. Deuteronomy's achievement is

and p. 60 (*even*). Saul raises a *yad* (memorial) after his defeat of Amalek in 1 Samuel 15.

27 Moses even had the visual appearance of justice as he sat on a stone with his hands raised, looking for all the world like a pair of weighing scales.

rather to superimpose a constructive message on a text whose moral teaching would otherwise be unremittingly negative.

Unlike the Deuteronomists, we cannot write our own versions of problematic biblical texts, to be read alongside them or at least as part of the same canon. We can, however, affect the way these texts are read, through written and spoken commentaries and, the essential precursor to both, by reading them with the right intentions. A *sofer* (Torah scribe) begins each working day by fulfilling the commandment to blot out the name of Amalek. He writes the Hebrew letters *ayin mem lamed kuf* (Amalek) on a scrap of parchment and quickly excises them with several strong lines. Only the inclinations of the scribe's heart as he performs this ritual will determine whether it signifies for him a violent rejection of 'the other' or an ethical rejection of social injustice.[28] The authors of Deuteronomy made both alternatives available, but choice must remain with the scribe himself. The same choice faces readers of difficult sacred texts. We must surely hope that those of us who read from within a faith tradition are at once sufficiently brave to confront the plain meaning of 'unacceptable' passages, and strong enough to turn them to good, not bad. This seems like a tall order but, as we see in an eminently acceptable passage from Deuteronomy, the ability to make such distinctions and choices is no more than is expected of us:

> . . . I have put before you life and death, blessing and curse. Choose life – if you and your offspring would live – by loving the LORD your God, obeying Him and holding fast to Him, for He is your life and the measure of your days . . . (Deut. 30.19–20)

---

[28] I am grateful to Prof. Klaus Hofman for his valuable suggestions. In particular, he clarified my thoughts on the difference between allegorical readings that may attempt, usually unsuccessfully and in a sense dishonestly, to rid a text of its problematic elements, and what I see as Deuteronomy's introduction of a new significance *alongside* the original meaning.

11. Jonah, God's Objectionable Mercy, and the Way of Wisdom

WALTER MOBERLY

Introduction: wisdom and biblical interpretation

We have been invited to consider the relationship between Scripture and theology with special reference to wisdom. The significance of wisdom in relation to biblical study can be conceived in at least two quite different ways. On the one hand, there is the familiar agenda of wisdom as an aspect of biblical religion, to be studied like any aspect of biblical religion. Familiar issues here include: the history and development of wisdom within Israel; the nature and extent of wisdom literature; the relationship between wisdom in Israel and wisdom in the Ancient Near East; Jewish and early Christian developments and reworkings of wisdom, especially, in a Christian context, in relation to Christ; and so on.

On the other hand, there is wisdom as an existential reality, less the object which one studies than that light and enablement whereby one's study is (one hopes) carried out. Here, of course, the familiar debates are those about the relationship between *faith* and biblical study, where the context is set by the fact that it was only by disentangling the Bible from certain kinds of faith-defined contexts and assumptions in the eighteenth and nineteenth centuries that biblical study could become a subject in its own right. Thankfully, the intense hermeneutical debates of recent decades have put an end (at least in principle) to the kinds of implicit positivism that could sometimes characterize biblical study in formal detachment from faith and theology. I hope that an emphasis on wisdom, rather than faith as such, may be one way of helping us to rethink what is, and is not, appropriate to our continuing responsibility to relate Scripture and theology in imaginative, faithful, searching and life-enhancing ways.

Although all these issues could usefully be discussed as issues of principle, my preference is to work with the text of Scripture itself. For I take it that one element in the renewal of interaction between Scripture and theology is to show how theological thinking can be enhanced by attention to scriptural exegesis and interpretation; and if that is so, then it is more fruitful not just to talk about it but to try to do it.

Introduction to Jonah

My chosen text is the book of Jonah (which, remarkably, has become one of the most intensively studied books of the Old Testament in recent years). I propose a perspective, or interpretative strategy, whose justification lies in its ability to make good sense of the book in terms of its explicit concerns and its scriptural preservation. This perspective is compatible with, and construable in terms of, a number of possible historical scenarios, but is not dependent upon any one such scenario (such as the post-exilic self-definition of Judah as a religious community, or the demise of prophecy in its classical form; additionally there are possible scenarios to do with canonical reception and compilation within the Book of the Twelve). This strategy is not, however, ahistorical and could be invalidated if one could show either that it were not compatible with what may plausibly be surmised about the nature and function of religious texts in Jewish antiquity, or that it did not do justice to what the book of Jonah actually says.

My proposal – which, as far as I can tell from the history of interpretation,[1] has, for better or worse, not previously been

---

[1] A succinct guide to the major interpretative options down the ages can be found in Elias Bickerman, 'Jonah *or* The Unfulfilled Prophecy', in his *Four Strange Books of the Bible*, New York: Schocken, 1967, pp. 1–49 (available with full annotation as 'Les deux erreurs du prophète Jonas', *Revue d'Histoire et de Philosophie Religieuses* 45, 1965, pp. 232–64). A fuller

expressed in quite this form[2] – is that the book of Jonah revolves around a basic, perennial problem: How is revelation (or fundamental theological confession) rightly to be understood and appropriated? For it is a recurrent phenomenon in both Jewish and Christian faiths that religious language which on one level appears simple and straightforward is in fact harder to understand and appropriate than initially appears. Numerous major movements in Christian history can be read as attempts genuinely to penetrate and grasp the meaning of certain fundamental biblical terms and categories, and to propose remedies for failures in so doing. It is therefore *prima facie* plausible to look heuristically for comparable engagement with the nature and meaning of theological confessions already within a biblical context.

The book of Jonah revolves around Jonah's memorable complaint to YHWH (4.2).[3] What is going on here? The storyline to this point is a drily humorous and larger-than-life portrayal (one should note the repeated use of the adjective *gādôl*: things in this story are 'big'). Jonah is given the hardest conceivable assignment, to go to the capital of Assyria, the greatest earthly power in his world, a power that has no reason to heed Hebrew prophets. Jonah is the most unlikely prophet; although it is common for prophets to respond to God's call with an expression of inadequacy and diffidence, Jonah excels them all by saying nothing but acting – when told to go East he catches a boat to the West. When Jonah's

---

and lively (but tendentious) account is Yvonne Sherwood, *A Biblical Text and its Afterlives: The Survival of Jonah in Western Culture*, Cambridge: Cambridge University Press: 2000.

[2] Phyllis Trible, in her initial doctoral work on Jonah, proposed a reading of the book as a midrash on Exod. 34.6f. ('Studies in the Book of Jonah', PhD diss., Columbia University, 1963; University Microfilms, pp. 162ff.). Although it is not uncommon for scholars to designate Jonah as a 'midrash' (see recently R. B. Salters, *Jonah & Lamentations*, OT Guides, Sheffield: JSOT Press, 1994, pp. 47, 49), the term tends to be used imprecisely, and Trible herself has come to express reservations as to its appropriateness ('The Book of Jonah' in Leander E. Keck et al., [eds.], *The New Interpreter's Bible*, vol. VII, Nashville: Abingdon, 1996, pp. 472–4).

[3] To see the interpretation of 4.2 as crucial to an understanding of the nature and purpose of the book as a whole would, I think, command a wide consensus.

flight proves futile he receives God's mercy in a most remarkable way. When Jonah finally does reach Nineveh he has only to preach a short and half-hearted message[4] in order to achieve the most complete success imaginable – *everyone* in Nineveh turns to God, so much so that even their cattle are to be included in the acts of repentance, and in response to this God relents of executing judgement upon the Ninevites. At this point the storyline turns from its narrative exposition to a parley between Jonah and God about the meaning of what has happened, and such further narrative developments as there are in furtherance of this parley. This larger-than-life storyline, presenting an extreme scenario, has a 'Let's imagine; what would it be like if . . . ?' feel to it.[5] It is a story of grace that is amazing. So what follows from amazing grace? When Jonah has achieved a response that should be the heart's desire of any prophet, how does he respond? Is he pleased? Is he grateful? He is neither, but rather complains to God that he is too merciful and sparing (4.2b). Indeed he infers (*w*ᵉ*'attâ*, 4.3a) from this merciful and sparing nature of God that God should now kill him. Since the consistent OT association of YHWH's mercy is with life, not death, Jonah's inference is clearly as mistaken as it could be. So what is happening? And what is to be done about it?

What is Jonah's problem?

First, we need to establish the precise nature of Jonah's complaint, that to which he appeals in justification of his initial flight: 'for I knew that you are a gracious and merciful God, slow to anger and rich in steadfast love, and one who relents of inflicting disaster'. When this is read as part of the OT as a canonical collection, it constitutes an appeal to two of the most fundamental theological

---

[4] See R. W. L. Moberly, 'Preaching for a Response? Jonah's Message to the Ninevites Reconsidered', forthcoming in *Vetus Testamentum*.

[5] It is thus comparable to Job 1—2, where also a fundamental theological issue is explored in an imaginatively engaging narrative that envisages extreme scenarios (see R. W. L. Moberly, *The Bible, Theology, and Faith*, Cambridge: Cambridge University Press, 2000, pp. 84–8, 75).

axioms of the whole OT.[6] First comes part of those words in which God speaks his name, YHWH,[7] and thereby reveals his gracious and steadfastly loving nature, in what is the fullest depiction of the nature of God in the whole biblical canon – Exod. 34.6–7 (whose language is, unsurprisingly, regularly used elsewhere in the OT, especially the Psalms, where the gracious and merciful nature of YHWH is a regular warrant for Israel's prayers to YHWH).[8] This is conjoined, however, with another fundamental axiom about the nature of YHWH, an axiom formally set out in Jer. 18.7–10 which sums up a basic and recurrent characteristic of God in the Old Testament, that is divine responsiveness (*niham*) to human attitude and action (especially repentance, *šûb*); a characteristic which is intrinsically complementary to the affirmation of YHWH's merciful nature, for the sparing of the repentant is a prime outworking of mercy.[9]

But *why* does Jonah have a problem with God's mercy and responsiveness? It is here that our problems begin. For while there is no doubt that Jonah is complaining, the precise nature of his complaint can be read in more than one way, as the history of interpretation readily shows. Broadly speaking, there are two main directions in which Jonah's problem can be understood to

---

[6] In traditio-historical and compositional terms it is almost impossible to be sure which passages are earlier or later than others. How Exod. 34.6–7 relates in these terms to other expressions within the OT of YHWH's merciful and compassionate nature is unclear, and similarly for Jeremiah's axiom with reference to other texts which speak of YHWH's relenting. My point relates to reading the OT in the light of the shaping processes which have made it the textual collection it now is.

[7] Although in terms of the Hebrew of Exod. 34.5, 6 either YHWH or Moses could be speaker of the key words, the citation of this passage in Num. 14.17–18 regards YHWH as the speaker and I see no reason to dissent from this.

[8] Num. 14.18; Neh. 9.17, 31; Pss. 86.6, 15; 103.8; 145.8, etc.

[9] The combination of Exod. 34.6 with Jer. 18.8 is also found in Joel 2.13b. Since the 'who knows whether He may turn and relent . . . ?' of Jonah 3.9 also appears in Joel 2.14a, there is clearly an interrelationship between these two passages, though the nature of that interrelationship is not our present concern. See T. B. Dozeman, 'Inner-Biblical Interpretation of Yahweh's Gracious and Compassionate Character', *Journal of Biblical Literature* 108, 1989, pp. 207–23.

lie. The first (and in my judgement less likely) is to do with some aspect of Jonah's prophecy as an apparently unfulfilled prophecy (an issue which can take many forms).[10] Probably the most sophisticated recent exposition is an influential essay by Elias Bickerman,[11] which I will take as representative of this kind of construal.

According to Bickerman, Jonah knows of Jeremiah's axiom about divine responsiveness but objects to the 'almost mechanical reciprocity between man's repentance and God's changing His mind' (p. 41). Jonah protests against the popular post-exilic view that 'penitence reinstates the sinner in divine favour' (p. 43). Jonah is seen instead to uphold a distinction between two different types of prophecy – 'conditional fate' (*fata conditionala*) which 'gives man an alternative' and 'declaratory destiny' (*fata denunciativa*) which 'works like a spell' (p. 31) – and to be an advocate of the latter. Commending Augustine's terse 'Jonah announced not mercy but the coming anger' Bickerman presents Jonah thus: 'Jonah was not a missionary preacher threatening divine punishment as *fata conditionala*. Herald of God's wrath, Jonah declared the immutable and inevitable *fata denunciativa*: "Yet forty days, and Nineveh shall be overthrown"' (p. 32). Thus Jonah's protest is against a theological view represented by major canonical prophets. 'The author of Jonah's story makes a confrontation between the thesis of Jeremiah, Ezekiel, Joel, and Malachi that if you repent God will also change His mind, and the antithesis, of Jonah, that God's word once spoken must be steadfast' (p. 43). What then is the purpose of the book? 'The thesis of Jeremiah and the antithesis of the prophet Jonah are

---

[10] Cf. Brevard Childs, *Introduction to the Old Testament as Scripture*, London: SCM Press, 1979, pp. 417–27 (419–20): 'The main issue is described either as Jonah's effort not to be a false prophet, or as analysing the relation of conditional to unconditional prophecy, or as dealing with the lack of fulfilment of the prophecy against the nations. This position has generally been advocated by Jewish interpreters . . . , but also by an impressive number of non-Jewish exegetes.'

[11] See n.1. A valuable summary of Bickerman's interpretation is provided by Michael Fishbane, *Biblical Interpretation in Ancient Israel*, Oxford: Clarendon Press, 1985, p. 346.

reconciled and surmounted in a so-to-say Hegelian synthesis by the author of the book, who, as the ancient Jewish commentators noted, wrote a parable for Jerusalem . . . To the restored [sc. post-exilic] and still sinful city [sc. Jerusalem], the author tells his parable. If God once did spare Nineveh, would He not save Jerusalem by His sovereign decision?' (pp. 44–5). The mystery of divine omnipotence – that YHWH spares for his own reasons – is the message of the book (pp. 47–8).

Fascinating though Bickerman's construal is, it faces serious difficulties. First, Bickerman does not properly establish that the category of 'declaratory destiny' is a genuine OT category; a couple of quick allusions to Amos 1.4 and Nahum's saying to Nineveh 'I will make thy grave' (pp. 31–2) do not suffice to establish the category, let alone to give it the kind of status necessary for Jonah to be able to appeal to it.[12] Secondly, Bickerman in effect makes Jonah the mouthpiece for a characteristic modern scholarly difficulty with Jer. 18.7–10. When, however, the language about divine reciprocity is read in its context of God as the potter whose power is absolute and unlimited (18.6), it becomes one strong formulation to be held in tension with another strong formulation, whose point is that YHWH's sovereignty is not exercised arbitrarily but responsibly and responsively – '*where God is most free to act, God is most bound in that acting*'.[13] Thirdly, Jeremiah's axiom is seamlessly woven into the Mosaic axiom about YHWH's mercy, and it is implausible to see a critique of the one without a simultaneous critique of the other.[14] Fourthly, Bickerman objects to characteristic modern

---

[12] Bickerman appeals to the idiom of 'cry against' (*qārā' 'al*) as demonstrating declaratory destiny (p. 32). But even on the understanding that prophecy is intrinsically conditional, a message of judgement is a genuine message of judgement unless and until it evokes repentance.

[13] See R. W. L. Moberly, '"God is Not a Human That He Should Repent" (Numbers 23:19 and 1 Samuel 15:29)', in Tod Linafelt and Timothy K. Beal, (eds.), *God in the Fray: A Tribute to Walter Brueggemann*, Minneapolis: Fortress Press, 1998, pp. 112–23, esp. pp. 112–15 (p. 114).

[14] Bickerman could perhaps argue that the Mosaic axiom is in effect interpreted by Jeremiah's axiom – mercy entails relenting – but such a focussing of the Mosaic axiom is not self-evident in context, and is not supported by the concluding divine question (4.10–11).

Christian tendencies to find opposition between Israel and the Gentiles, because this introduces into the book 'more than is really there' because 'the morality play of Jonah has a cast of three characters: God, the prophet, and the Ninevites' and 'there is nothing about Israel' (p. 28). Yet his introducing of Jerusalem as necessary for understanding the book's concern transgresses his own principle of respecting the book's silence.

The other general approach is to see Jonah's problem as in some way specifically with divine mercy as such. Here it is worthwhile to set out a number of proposals.

First, Jonah's problem could be that divine mercy is morally and spiritually debilitating, in that it undercuts the cost of living before God with faithfulness and integrity and can induce cynicism. Wolff, for example, says:

> This exposes the essential reason for Jonah's despair . . . God does not abide by his word of judgment. On the contrary, through his mercy he puts himself on the side of Israel's merciless enemies. In this way Jonah chimes in with the voices of the people with whom Malachi quarrels: 'It is pointless to serve God' (3.14f.). What difference is there 'between the person who serves God and the person who does not serve him' (3.18)?[15]

Such a difficulty with the potential moral problematic of mercy is undoubtedly a real and recurrent issue (though the explicit articulation of the point is only in Malachi, and its transference to Jonah may in fact skew Jonah's own concern, as it resonates with nothing else in the book). One contemporary outworking might be welfare dependence. The policy of social compassion, realized through the provision of benefits to try to ensure that the hard-up are not deprived of a position within society, all too readily engenders a frame of mind in which it is not worth going to

[15] Hans Walter Wolff, *Obadiah and Jonah: A Commentary*, Minneapolis: Augsburg, 1986 (ET by M. Kohl from German of 1977), p. 168, cf. p. 176. Similarly, Terence E. Fretheim, *The Message of Jonah: A Theological Commentary*, Minneapolis: Augsburg, 1977, p. 121 (and pp. 31–7).

work or trying to better oneself if the financial and social benefits of work are not greatly different from those of social security. Compassion undercuts moral effort.

A second reading of Jonah's complaint is that it is a protest against unfairness: the Ninevites do not *deserve* mercy and sparing, presumably either because they are notorious sinners (1.2, though the text lays no special emphasis upon their sin) or because they are gentiles (though the text never makes a point of this), or both. It is common for commentators to cite the older brother of the prodigal son as a good parallel, for his angry resentment at his father's generosity to his undeserving younger brother (Lk. 15.28) parallels Jonah's angry resentment at YHWH's generosity to the Ninevites. The point of Jonah's objection is then not mercy as such, but *disproportionate* mercy: some people are so undeserving that to be merciful and spare them becomes a moral outrage.

A contemporary example would be the difficulty many have with forgiveness in extreme cases of suffering and evil. The refusal of some who suffered in German concentration camps or Japanese prison camps to forgive their erstwhile tormentors, or the attitude of Jamie Bulger's mother towards those who tortured and murdered her son, would be cases in point.

Another construal of Jonah's complaint sees it as a complaint against the risk to Israel of mercy to the Ninevites. This depends upon two considerations (neither of which are specified in the Jonah narrative); first, the role of Assyria elsewhere in the OT as the great enemy of Israel; secondly, the likelihood that the book is written from a perspective when the Assyrian destruction of Israel had already taken place. To be an agent in the sparing of Nineveh could mean helping Nineveh towards the destruction of Israel. Jonah 'was being asked in effect to sign his own people's death warrant'.[16] The recognition that the bestowal of mercy may be costly, even sometimes fatal, for the human bestower (or agent of divine bestowal) arises from the fact that even a repentant

[16] John F. A. Sawyer, *Prophecy and the Prophets of the Old Testament*, Oxford Bible Series, Oxford: Oxford University Press, 1987, p. 114.

recipient of mercy may only be repentant in the short term and may turn against a benefactor in the longer term.

A good recent example is the major subplot in Steven Spielberg's film *Saving Private Ryan*. In the aftermath of D-Day Captain Miller (Tom Hanks) leads a group of soldiers to recover Private Ryan who has parachuted into occupied France, because Ryan's three brothers have already been killed. Miller takes as an interpreter Corporal Upham, who is naïve and thoroughly unmilitary (whenever there is fighting he shrinks and cowers). En route they capture a German soldier. When most of Miller's soldiers want to shoot him, Upham protests 'This is not right', and Miller eventually releases him with instructions to hand himself in to an Allied patrol. When Ryan is found at the town of Ramelle, Ryan insists on staying at his post, and so Miller and his soldiers prepare to defend Ramelle against a German attack. When the Germans do attack Ramelle, the released German soldier is among them. He kills one of Miller's men in a knife fight, but ignores and spares Upham who had been friendly towards him during his earlier capture. But Upham sees the German shoot Captain Miller and contribute to Miller's death. When Allied reinforcements arrive and the German soldiers surrender, Upham, who hitherto has not used his gun, shoots the German in cold blood. For Corporal Upham mercy has become too costly.

Finally, Jonah's complaint may be an attempt to limit divine mercy for no reason other than simple selfishness. Here the point depends upon contrasting Jonah's own receipt of divine mercy, which he celebrates within the big fish (with the resounding conclusion 'deliverance is of YHWH', 2.10b), with his unwillingness to see this extended to the Ninevites – an unwillingness without moral rationalizing. A biblical parallel here would be the teaching of Jesus in Matthew's Gospel where the receipt of forgiveness from God must be accompanied by the extension of forgiveness to others. This issue, which features in the Lord's Prayer (Mt. 6.12) and is underlined in the comments immediately following the Lord's Prayer (6.14–15) is illustrated in the parable of the unforgiving servant (18.23–35) which concludes the discourse on church discipline (18.1–35): to refuse to extend to another that mercy which oneself has received is by that very token to nullify the mercy. Jesus' definitional analysis of divine mercy could be developing the kind of concern already felt by the author of Jonah: to receive divine mercy oneself, yet selfishly to begrudge it to others, is to contradict and nullify the very nature of that mercy.

Which, if any, of the above represents Jonah's problem? Although my own inclination is towards the last mentioned (it develops a contrast clearly present within the text, and imports no reason from another text), it is probably not possible to specify any one version in such a way as to rule out the others. Although this could be construed as an interpretative failure, it may rather be the case that the lack of specificity as to the precise nature of Jonah's problem is intrinsic to the story. For the story's openness to a variety of construals, construals suggested especially by the book's rich canonical context, is a standing invitation to consider the variety of ways in which divine mercy can be considered objectionable and so be more or less misunderstood.

God's response to Jonah

Given that, for whatever precise reason, the divine compassion towards, and sparing of, Nineveh, constitutes a problem for Jonah, what then happens? We should first note possibilities that the book does not adopt. First, if Jonah's problem is with the understanding of central affirmations within Scripture, one possibility would be to respond with scriptural argument of some kind or other. Yet of this there is nothing. Secondly, although the book repeatedly portrays God's sovereignty (over sea, fish, plant, worm, wind), a sovereignty that can engender responsiveness among sailors and Ninevites and accommodate it accordingly, there is no exercise of this sovereignty upon Jonah in such a way as to 'compel' his response. Jonah outside Nineveh is left to decide how he will respond.

So what approach does God take? Here we need to recollect a commonplace of the study of OT wisdom: wisdom literature characteristically eschews themes peculiar to Israel's identity and vocation (election, covenant, prophecy, priesthood, holiness – or, indeed, the citation of Scripture) and appeals rather to regular characteristics of the created order; in schematic terms, instead of the authoritative voice 'from above', that is, 'thus says YHWH', we have theology 'from below', for example, 'Go to the ant, you sluggard; consider its ways, and be wise' (Prov. 6.6). As Trible puts it, 'YHWH develops the argument through natural rather than revealed theology.'[17]

YHWH's argument, an analogical appeal to the bush which grows and withers,[18] may at first sight appear strange, as Jonah's concern is not the withering of the plant as such but rather the loss of his shelter and his consequent discomfort; that is, his concern is not for the plant but for himself. But the point would appear to be a persuasive redescription of Jonah's situation, thereby allowing Jonah to see himself as not merely selfish. Jonah at any rate does not resist the suggestion that his misery may not be merely selfish (4.8) but may in some sense be altruistic (4.9, with an implicit 'Why yes, my misery is because of my concern for that poor plant'), even though this opens the way for a final riposte.

Two aspects of YHWH's final words are striking. First, the Ninevites are characterized as profoundly ignorant. The precise nature of this ignorance is not specified. Although it is easy on the basis of other OT texts to give moral and religious content to that ignorance (e.g. Isa. 10.5–15, arrogance; Nah. 3.19, cruelty), our text simply stresses ignorance *tout court*. YHWH's redescription of Jonah's selfish misery as care for the plant is minor compared to this redescription of the most powerful culture of Jonah's world as marked by the ignorance characteristic of infants. It is a stark case of a religious evaluation being at odds with an evaluation by conventional criteria. Despite the form of YHWH's words as

---

17 Phyllis Trible, 'Divine Incongruities in the Book of Jonah', in Linafelt and Beal, *God in the Fray*, pp. 198–208 (p. 207).

18 The relationship between Jonah's booth (4.5) and the plant (4.6), the purpose of each of which is to give shade, is not entirely clear. The situation can, of course, be rationalized without difficulty – 'Anyone who has sat in a tent for a day in the Near East understands that additional shade is always welcome!' (Fretheim, *Message of Jonah*, p. 123).

natural theology, one should not overlook that the evaluation presupposes the wisdom of revelation represented for Israel by *torah* and prophecy (cf. Deut. 4.5–8). The point is that the wisdom which comes from *torah* should engender towards those who lack it not arrogance or disdain but rather pity.

Secondly, YHWH's keyword is *ḥûs* ('pity', 'care about'). This is perhaps initially surprising, as one might have expected a repetition of one of the terms characterizing YHWH in 4.2, either *ḥānan* ('be gracious') or *riḥam* ('have compassion'). But maybe the point is precisely that this is a term that does not have the resonances of association with the character of God that mark the other terms. The most common usage of *ḥûs* is with the eye as subject,[19] so that its primary resonances are with the human phenomenon of a tear coming to the eye, the spontaneous and unpredictable bodily response to other creatures in need. One needs no special intelligence, never mind special revelation, to recognize and understand the tear that shows the care of the heart. How much more then should something so basic to human experience be recognized as characterizing humanity's creator – and, by extension, any who might claim in some way to know this creator.

Conclusions

What should we make of the book's presentation of Jonah's complaint and its strategy for seeking to resolve it? First, in our contemporary theological pedagogy we should never lose sight of that issue around which the book of Jonah (so I have argued) revolves, the problem of defective understanding of confessions which are foundational within Scripture and for faith. The ease with which truths that should inspire worship and service can become slogans to be bandied around in point-scoring or self-

[19] As Wolff succinctly says about *ḥûs*, 'The word occurs 24 times in the Old Testament. On 15 of these occasions the eye is the subject' (*Obadiah and Jonah*, p. 173). For general discussion see S. Wagner, '*chûs*', *Theological Dictionary of the Old Testament*, vol. IV, ed. G. J. Botterweck et al., Grand Rapids: Eerdmans, 1980, pp. 271–7.

justification should be a permanent critical concern for what we as theologians do. For many today, both within and outside the Church, the theological confession which plays a role comparable to those of Exod. 34.6–7 and Jer. 18.7–8 is 1 Jn 4.8, 16, 'God is love'. This is regularly taken as a freestanding axiom that hardly needs the particularity of the death and resurrection of Jesus to give it content, and that can readily be used to undercut a greater or lesser number of other moral and theological elements of historic Christian faith. It too rarely plays the role of enabling critical discernment of true knowledge of God in Christ that it plays in its Johannine context. But there is little or nothing in either Scripture or the creeds which is not misunderstood by someone somewhere. Theological education, like spiritual growth, must be an unending process.

Secondly, when Jonah's problem is that he knows the scriptural words but cannot grasp their true meaning, the book moves the issue onto a different level – appealing not to Scripture but to reason, not to revelation but to natural theology, not to a divine imperative but to analogical wisdom. Although we are familiar with this mode of argument in the teaching of Jesus in the Synoptic Gospels, we perhaps less readily recognize it in an OT context. The book of Jonah does not question the foundational role of Israel's particular knowledge of God or of the corresponding task of prophecy, nor does it suggest that appeal to natural theology could dispense with the word of YHWH to Moses or Jeremiah. Rather natural theology plays a subordinate and critical role, to enable fresh re-engagement with the given content of revelation when that content has for some reason become problematic.

Finally, the book of Jonah reminds us that theological understanding is exemplified in a person's attitudes and actions. 'Theology is a practical, not a merely theoretical discipline: it aims at wisdom, in the broad sense of light for the human path. Our theological enterprises must therefore be judged at least in part by their fruit.'[20] But this is something that is increasingly

[20] Colin E. Gunton, *The One, The Three and the Many: God, Creation and the Culture of Modernity*, Cambridge: Cambridge University Press, 1993, p. 7.

difficult to aim for in the contemporary academy with its concern for measurable learning outcomes, measurable by immediate tests according to specific academic criteria. This represents a narrowing of the nature and purpose of higher education that will increasingly impoverish us the longer it holds sway. It is no doubt too much to ask for that practical implementation of qualities such as compassion should be able to hold any formal place in a university's assessment of a student's learning of theology. Yet if we do not recognize that practical implementation of appropriate qualities over the long term is in fact integral to our work, we may lose sight of what makes theology the discipline that it truly is. We may find ourselves intellectualizing and institutionalizing Jonah's problem in the kind of way that makes progress beyond the problem ever harder to come by.[21]

---

[21] I am grateful to David Day for comments on a draft, also to those who responded when the paper was read in Cambridge and at a meeting of the Durham OT research seminar.

12. The Law of Christ: A Neglected Theological Gem?

GRAHAM STANTON

There are some neglected gems hidden in early Christian writings which are worth careful examination. The phrase 'the law of Christ' is one such: it teases exegetes, it raises central questions of method and it can still stimulate theological reflection. Although it is used only once in the New Testament (Gal. 6.2), there are a handful of related passages. As we shall see, in several early-second-century writings the phrase is more prominent. From time to time in later centuries this gem has been dusted down and polished, and sometimes partly re-cut, but it has captured theological imaginations all too rarely.[1]

John Fisher, the first holder of the Lady Margaret's Professorship of Divinity at Cambridge, is a notable exception. When King Henry VIII began to seek a divorce from Catherine of Aragon in 1527, Fisher soon became the Queen's foremost defender. In 1531 he wrote the mitigating words by which the clergy in Convocation qualified their earlier acceptance of Henry as their Supreme Head on earth: *quantum per legem Christi licet*, 'as far as the law of Christ allows'. Those words raise several intriguing questions. Why did Fisher appeal to the phrase 'the law of Christ'

---

[1] Bernard Häring's *The Law of Christ*, 3 vols., Cork: Mercier, 1963 is only a partial exception. In this very traditional Roman Catholic moral theology, the phrase 'the law of Christ' is not discussed until pp. 252–63 where it seems to refer to the ethical teaching of the NT as a whole and to be synonymous with Thomas Aquinas's frequently used phrase, 'the new law'. I am grateful to my colleague Dr Markus Bockmuehl for this reference and for a number of helpful comments on an earlier draft of this chapter.

at such a tense time? What did he understand by 'the law of Christ'?

The phrase was not part of Thomas Aquinas's vocabulary; he preferred 'the new law'. And John Fisher does not seem to have been influenced by Erasmus in his choice of this phrase. For in none of the five editions of his *Annotationes* does Erasmus say a single word about 'the law of Christ' in his comments on Gal. 6.2.[2] Perhaps Fisher chose the phrase because it was vague and ill-defined, but sounded good.[3] Or perhaps Fisher picked up the phrase quite deliberately from Gal. 6.2. If the latter, then I would love to know how he interpreted Paul's baffling phrase!

Martin Luther commented powerfully on the phrase in his 1519 and 1535 commentaries on Gal. 6.2, but it played no more than a very minor role in his expositions of the two uses of the law or in the later controversies over the *tertium usus legis*. Neither John Calvin nor Karl Barth found any theological use for the phrase. And since very few contemporary systematic theologians bother to wrestle with exegesis, we shall be surprised to find much interest in the phrase in their writings.

The phrase 'the law of Christ' is still used from time to time today, as, for example, in the simple intercessory prayer based on Gal. 6.2: 'Help us so to bear the burdens of others that we may fulfil the law of Christ.' But more often than not this gem has been allowed to gather theological dust in a corner.

As we shall see, over the centuries 'the law of Christ' has been understood in several different ways. Paul was the first to use the phrase. What was his intention? Should his understanding determine any continuing theological use today? Do the second-century uses of the phrase help us theologically? I shall start with Gal. 6.2 before turning to its closest relatives elsewhere in the NT and in early Christian writings. I hope to show that 'the law

---

[2] See Anne Reeve, (ed.), *Erasmus's Annotations on the NT: Galatians to the Apocalypse:. Facsimile of the final Latin Text with all earlier variants*, Leiden: Brill, 1993.

[3] So my colleague Dr Richard Rex in a written communication dated 30 January 2002. See his fine *The Theology of John Fisher*, Cambridge: Cambridge University Press, 1991.

of Christ' raises perennial questions for biblical scholars and for theologians, and for those who want to wear both hats.

Galatians 6.2

Gal. 6.2 is the thirty-first of Paul's references in Galatians to *νόμος*, law. In nearly all the preceding instances the reference is to '*the* Law', that is, the law of Moses.[4] So it is most unlikely that without alerting his listeners Paul changes tack and refers to the teaching of Jesus as 'law', or to 'showing love for others' (i.e. bearing the burdens of others) as 'law'.

Ever since Gal. 2.16 'law' has been pounding relentlessly in the Galatians' ears with a negative beat. However in 4.21b, 5.14 and 6.2 Paul's tone changes dramatically: *νόμος* is used in a positive sense in all three verses. The reference in 5.14 to fulfilling the law in loving one's neighbour is particularly striking; it paves the way for 6.2, for verbs from the same root are used. Although 'Christ' and 'law' have regularly stood in stark contrast earlier in the letter, in 6.2 they are brought together in an ear-catching but baffling phrase. Since 'fulfilling the law' in 5.14 clearly refers to the law of Moses, the use of the similar verb in 6.2 strongly suggests that 'law' here also refers to the law of Moses, and not to a norm or principle.

'Carry one another's burdens', urges Paul, 'and in this way you will fulfil the law of Christ.'[5] The careful listener to Galatians being read aloud can hardly have failed to miss Paul's insistence that Christ himself 'bore the burdens of others' and so provided an example for the Galatian Christians. Paul's expansions of his opening 'grace and peace' formula in his letters often foreshadow several of the letters' main theological themes. This is certainly the case in Galatians. In Gal. 1.4 Paul notes that Christ 'gave himself for our sins'. Christ's self-giving love forms the climax

---

[4] J. L. Martyn, *Galatians*, Anchor Bible Commentary, New York: Doubleday, 1997, p. 555.

[5] Dr Michael Thompson has drawn my attention to the partial parallel at Rom. 15.1–3, where encouragement to bear (*βαστάζειν*) the failings of the weak is linked to the example of Christ.

of the richest section of the letter, Gal. 2.15–20: 'the Son of God loved me and gave himself for me'. Christ has fulfilled the law himself in his self-giving in love for others.

So in Galatians we have *one* answer to the question, What is the law of Christ? In Gal. 6.2 it is the law of Moses interpreted by Christ, with the 'love commandment' and 'carrying the burdens of others' as its essence; it is fulfilled by Christ in his own self-giving love.[6]

Several further comments are in order. (1) With their positive references to law, Gal. 4.21b; 5.14 and 6.2 stand in counterpoise to Paul's other references to the law of Moses in Galatians. Taken together these verses confirm that in spite of the numerous negative comments on the law elsewhere in this letter, Paul did not repudiate the law of Moses, as some of his later followers (most notably Marcion) and some of his opponents (see Acts 21.28) wrongly supposed.

(2) The immediate context emphasizes that those who live by the Spirit are not free to gratify the desires of the flesh (5.16). However Paul does not spell out the precise ways in which the law of Moses is to be retained now that believers in Christ have been set free from the present evil age (Gal. 1.4). No one will be right-wised by God on the basis of carrying out the law of Moses (2.16), but the law is not to be ignored or discarded, for it is not opposed to the promises of God (3.21).

Paul continued to mull over this antinomy. The apostle takes a further step in Rom. 13.8–10. 'Love is the fulfilling of the law' to be sure, but this axiom does not mean that the commandments concerning adultery, murder, theft and covetousness may be ignored. This passage seems to have encouraged the later strong Christian conviction that the ten commandments are the core of the Mosaic law; they (and for some, they alone) have abiding significance for Christians.

(3) The encouragement to 'bear one another's burdens' is

---

[6] Cf. John Barclay's explanation, *Obeying the Truth*, Edinburgh: T. & T. Clark, 1988, p. 134: the law of Christ is 'the redefined and fulfilled by Christ in love'; and also Martyn's comment on the phrase (see n. 4 above): 'the law as it has fallen into the hands of Christ'.

almost certainly taken from the Socratic tradition and the Greek doctrines about 'friendship'.[7] A well-known maxim is transposed by Paul into a new key. We should welcome Paul's appropriation of the conventional ethical teaching of his day at several points in Galatians 5 and 6, and especially in the lists of virtues and vices in Gal. 5.19–23. For in so doing Paul has given us an example to follow. Why should we not appropriate some of the insights of the moral philosophers of our day and set them in a firmly drawn theological framework, as Paul himself does?

I do not think that Paul is picking up a slogan used by the agitators in Galatia and throwing it back in their face. Nor do I think that Paul is being merely playful, as has been suggested. In the preceding argument of the letter Paul has carefully prepared his listeners and readers for his dramatic use of the phrase in 6.2. Paul's failure to spell out more fully its meaning may mean that the Galatian house churches had already been well drilled by Paul in its meaning. This is an interesting possibility which has been overlooked in the voluminous literature. In his letters Paul does use a series of key 'short-hand' phrases whose content his recipients could readily fill out for themselves. 'The law of Christ' may be one such phrase.

Not long after writing Galatians, Paul wrote 1 Corinthians. In a highly rhetorical paragraph Paul comments on his missionary strategy. In 1 Cor. 9.20 he explains that when preaching to Jews he was prepared to exercise a measure of self-renunciation. In 9.21 he comments on his strategy when preaching to Gentiles: I identified as one outside Mosaic jurisdiction with those outside it. A rider is added immediately: 'Of course I am not outside God's law (*ἄνομος Θεοῦ*), but I am *ἔννομος Χριστοῦ*.' The latter phrase is often translated 'I am under the law of Christ', which is adequate, though it suggests that the Greek here is the same as in Gal. 6.2. Given the subtle play on words in 1 Cor. 9.20 and 21, it was hardly an option for Paul to repeat the phrase used in Galatians, *ὁ νόμος τοῦ Χριστοῦ*. In fact, as far as we know, the apostle never reused that phrase.

---

[7] H. D. Betz, *Galatians*, Hermeneia, Philadelphia: Fortress Press, 1979.

What did Paul mean by ἔννομος Χριστοῦ? 'I am under Christ's jurisdiction' catches the sense. The preceding chapters of 1 Corinthians suggest that the phrase may include commitment to sayings of Jesus, but to limit it in that way would miss its christological thrust.

Paul's use of the phrase 'the law of faith' in Rom. 3.27 has teased many a commentator. Although many claim that Paul here uses νόμος to mean 'principle' or 'rule', it is most unlikely that Paul jumps without warning from using νόμος to refer to the law of Moses to the more general sense of 'principle', and in any case the context will not allow this reading. We must take our cue from v. 31, the final step in Paul's argument. 'Do we overthrow the Torah on the basis of faith in Jesus?' By no means: we uphold the law. So 'the law of faith' is the law discerned and obeyed on the basis of faith in Jesus. In other words, this phrase is a first cousin of ὁ νόμος τοῦ Χριστοῦ.[8]

Similar NT phrases outside the Pauline corpus

In Jas. 1.25; 2.8 and 12 the writer qualifies νόμος three times. His other uses of νόμος refer to the law of Moses or to one of its specific commandments. So it is probable that 'the perfect law of freedom', 'the royal law' and 'the law of liberty' are almost synonymous references to the law understood from a Christian perspective; in the context of this letter that means the teaching of Jesus.[9] In other words we are not far from 'the law of Christ'. This is especially clear in Jas. 2.8: 'You are doing well if you are carrying out the royal law according to the Scripture, "Love your neighbour as yourself".' There is a clear implication that the love commandment lies at the heart of the law (cf. Mt. 22.34–40).

---

[8] Perhaps Rom. 8.2 is also a first cousin of Gal. 6.2: in Christ Jesus the law (of Moses) becomes life-giving (cf. 7.10 and 14a) and of the Spirit.

[9] So also Sophie Laws, *The Epistle of James*, Black's NT Commentaries, London: A. & C. Black, 1980, p. 110: 'It is probable that when James quotes Lev 19.18 as *scripture* he does so in the knowledge that this scripture has received the added authority of Jesus' use.'

What is implicit in James is much more explicit in Matthew's Gospel. The evangelist has taken great care over the composition of his five discourses because he values the sayings of Jesus so highly. The sayings of Jesus are to be prominent in the missionary proclamation and catechetical instruction of the 'new people' (28.18–20). The closing verses of the Sermon on the Mount emphasize strongly the importance of hearing and acting on the words of Jesus (7.24–27). For Matthew 'the will of the heavenly Father' is equated with carrying out *the sayings of Jesus* (7.21; cf. Lk. 6.46).

Matthew's Gospel provided the 'new people' with a set of authoritative traditions to be set alongside the law and the prophets. The evangelist does not spell out as clearly as his modern interpreters would like the precise relationship of 'new' and 'old'. Matthew's Jesus does not repudiate the law: its continuing importance is affirmed very strongly (5.17–19). The love commandment is singled out by Jesus as expressing the very essence of Scripture (7.12; 22.37–39), but in no way does this contradict the law, any more than do the so-called antitheses in 5.21–48. Matthew hints – but no more – that the sayings of Jesus are the criterion for the interpretation of the law, but his primary emphasis is on the ways the sayings of Jesus strengthen and fulfil the law and the prophets.

In Matthew, as elsewhere in the NT, Christology and ethics are linked inextricably. The full significance of the teaching of Jesus can only be discerned in the light of the conviction that Jesus is 'God with us' (Mt. 1.23). With his coming, in fulfilment of Isa. 9.1, 'light has dawned' (4.16). The Sermon on the Mount is proclamation of the good news of God's kingly rule (4.17, 22). It is both gift and demand; it is not a new set of rules and regulations.

Matthew does not use the phrase 'the law of Christ', but he would not have been unhappy with this term. For Matthew the person and words of Jesus are the criterion by which the law is to be interpreted. Although some exegetes argue that the teaching of Jesus is also in view in Gal. 6.2, in my opinion they are mistaken. However, in spite of differences, Matthew and Paul agree that 'the law of Christ' has as its focal point the love commandment and has a christological reference. Both notions were to be important in later theological exposition of our phrase.

The writer of 1 John insists at 2.3 that we know God if we keep God's commandments. The phraseology recalls Sir. 29.1 and Mt. 19.17, and we are only one step from Tob. 14.9, Acts 15.5 and Jas. 2.10 where the verb *τηρεῖν* is used of keeping the law of Moses.

Three verses later the writer's train of thought turns to Christ: whoever says, 'I abide in him' ought to walk just as Christ walked (1 Jn 2.6). He then refers to the old commandment which his readers have had from the beginning, the 'word' that they have heard. What is it? It is of course Christ's command, 'love one another'. In short, the writer implies that the love commandment is the focal point of God's commandments, that is, the law of Moses. There is certainly no suggestion that the commandment to love is not found in the OT, for in 3.11–12 Cain is attacked for failing to love his brother Abel.

Although *νόμος* is not used in the Johannine letters, we are not far from the thought that 'the law of Christ' and in particular the commandment to love one another is the lens through which God's commandments should be read and obeyed.

A similar pattern of thought is found in 2 Jn 6–10. God's commandments and Christ's command to love one another are juxtaposed and all but fused together. But this letter adds a note not found explicitly in 1 John: Christ's teaching is referred to twice over (vv. 9 and 10) and it is fairly clear that this teaching extends beyond the love commandment.

The preceding paragraphs have confirmed that there is a strikingly similar pattern to be observed in several NT writings – a generally overlooked show of unity amidst diversity. There are almost certainly no direct literary relationships between Paul, James, Matthew and the writers of the Johannine letters. Yet in all four strands of earliest Christianity we find a continuing commitment to the law of Moses alongside an insistence that it should be understood from a new perspective. That new perspective is not sketched out fully, but in every case it includes a christological element, and either the sayings of Jesus or the love commandment, or both.

This theological pattern can be traced down through the centuries whenever our theological gem 'the law of Christ' is dusted down. Sometimes Christology is more prominent, sometimes the teaching of Jesus, sometimes the love commandment. I shall now give the merest sketch to back up that contention.

Second-century writers

In the early decades of the second century the *Shepherd of Hermas* takes an interesting step beyond the NT writers. The Son of God is the lawgiver: he has given to the people the law given to him by the Father (*Sim.* 5.6, 3; ch. 59). The Son of God is himself 'the law of God' given to the whole world (*Sim.* 8.3, 2–3).

Christ is also called 'the law' three times in the *Kerygma Petri* which dates from the same period. Alas, all we have from this treatise are a handful of quotations in later writers, especially Clement of Alexandria. Christians worship God neither in the manner of the Greeks nor the Jews. 'We worship God through Christ in a new way.' 'For we have found in the Scriptures, how the Lord says: "Behold, I make with you a new covenant, not as I made (one) with your fathers in Mt Horeb." A new one he made with us. For what has reference to the Greeks and Jews is old. But we are Christians, who as a third race worship him in a new way.'[10] Here we have early evidence for a very radical sense of self-understanding on the part of Christians. Scripture is not abandoned, but Christ himself has become 'the Law'.

A fuller exposition of the same theme is found in Justin Martyr's *Dialogue with Trypho*, written *c.* AD 160, possibly in dependence on the *Kerygma Petri*.[11] For Justin, Christ is himself given by

[10] For the texts and bibliography, see J. K. Elliott, *The Apocryphal New Testament*, Oxford: Clarendon Press, 1993, pp. 20–3; more fully, W. Schneemelcher, (ed.), *New Testament Apocrypha*, vol. 2, Cambridge: James Clarke, 1992, pp. 34–41.

[11] So O. Skarsaune, *The Proof from Prophecy*, Leiden: Brill, 1987, pp. 72–3.

God as the final and eternal law (*Dialogue* 11.2, twice), and the new law (11.4, *ὁ καινὸς νόμος*).[12] Justin elaborates his point in a striking credal passage in 43.1: by the will of the Father Christ was born Son of God by means of the Virgin; he was proclaimed by the prophets as about to come 'as an everlasting law and a new covenant for the whole world'. Justin insists that the law given by God to Moses at Mt Horeb is antiquated and belongs to Trypho and his fellow-Jews alone, whereas Christ, the new law, was given to all people (11.2). Justin does not believe for one moment that the law of Moses has been abolished, though he does have difficulty spelling out precisely how Christians should use it, as, of course, did Paul himself.

Justin also understands 'the law of Christ' in a different sense. His Jewish opponent Trypho issues a strong challenge: Justin and his fellow-Christians claim to worship God, but fail to make their lives different from Gentiles in that they keep neither the feasts nor the sabbaths, nor have circumcision, nor carry out God's commandments (10.3). In short, Christians are law-less. As a key part of his extended response Justin refers to Christ as *the new lawgiver* (*ὁ καινὸς νομοθέτης*, 12.2 and 14.3), through whom 'the poor have the Gospel preached to them, and the blind receive their sight' (cf. Mt. 11.6 = Lk. 7.22). The sayings of Jesus are understood here as the gift of the new lawgiver. For Justin the teaching of Jesus embedded in the Gospels is 'the law of Christ'.[13]

So for Hermas and for Justin, Christ is himself both the new law and the new lawgiver, but without the implication that the law of Moses is to be abandoned. The Epistle of Barnabas comes perilously close to the latter notion: the Lord has abolished sacrifices, new moons and sabbaths so that 'the new law of our

---

[12] The most accessible translation is by A. Lukyn Williams, *Justin Martyr, the Dialogue with Trypho*, London: SPCK, 1930.

[13] For a fuller discussion, see G. N. Stanton, 'Jesus Traditions and Gospels in Justin Martyr and Irenaeus', in J.-M. Auwers and H. J. de Jonge, (eds.), *The Biblical Canons*, Leuven: Peeters, 2002, pp. 351–68. Although Justin does not refer explicitly to Paul or to his letters, at numerous points he betrays knowledge of them. So it is possible that his understanding of Christ as the new lawgiver has been influenced by Gal. 6.2.

Lord Jesus Christ which is free from the yoke of compulsion might have its offering, one not made by man' (Barn. 2.6). For Barnabas the Mosaic law has mistakenly been interpreted literally rather than spiritually as intended (10.2, 9).

The teaching of Jesus as 'the law of Christ'

Justin Martyr's notion of Christ as the 'new lawgiver' became all pervasive on the later tradition of the Church. I shall now refer briefly to a handful of examples. First of all, the magnificent thirteenth-century statue of Christ the lawgiver from the south side of Chartres Cathedral in France. Here Christ is depicted holding up one arm in blessing. His other hand is offering a beautifully bound codex which I take to be the Gospels. In other words, Christ is offering his own teaching as a 'new law'. Protestants probably underestimate the powerful influence a statue such as this had on the on-going Christian tradition.

In many parish churches in England to this day two panels painted with Scripture texts hang behind the altar: the ten commandments on the left, and the Lord's prayer on the right. This practice goes back to the late sixteenth century, with even deeper roots in the medieval period. The setting up of these panels is related to the catechism in the 1552 Book of Common Prayer. Every person brought before the bishop for confirmation was expected to be able to recite the ten commandments and the Lord's prayer, as well as the brief explanations of both texts in the catechism. Perhaps the panels often acted as a crib for those with short memories!

The impact of this practice on the life of the Church is clear. The ten commandments are singled out as the essence of the law of Moses, while the Lord's prayer is assumed to provide the essence of the 'law of Christ'. The theological instincts which lie behind the erection of those two panels of texts are profound, and in my view profoundly correct.

Given the strength of the tradition I have just sketched, it is no surprise to discover that Gal. 6.2 has often been taken as a reference by Paul to the importance he attached to the teaching of

Jesus. There have been several influential modern supporters of this interpretation. In his ICC commentary on Galatians (1921, p. 329) E. C. Burton wrote: ' this is one of the few passages in which the apostle refers to teaching of Jesus transmitted to him through the Twelve or their companions'. Burton, however, failed to list the Jesus traditions which might have been in the apostle's mind.

C. H. Dodd was more specific, arguing in 1951 and 1953 that Gal. 6.1–5 was an adaptation of Jesus' teaching in Mt. 23.4 and 18.15–16.[14] At about the same time Dodd's pupil W. D. Davies was equally adamant. 'When he (Paul) used the phrase *νόμος τοῦ Χριστοῦ* (the law of Christ) he meant that the actual words of Jesus were for him a New Torah.'[15] More recently R. N. Longenecker has defended a more sophisticated version of the same interpretation. He takes 'the law of Christ' to refer to those 'prescriptive principles stemming from the heart of the gospel (usually embodied in the example and teachings of Jesus), which are meant to be applied to specific situations by the direction and enablement of the Holy Spirit, being always motivated and conditioned by love'.[16]

The difficulty with this general line of interpretation is that

[14] Barclay, *Obeying the Truth*, p. 129 n. 70, astutely notes that in 1935 Dodd had denied that Gal. 6.2 could mean the 'Torah of Jesus', but had changed his position by 1951 in his *Gospel and Law*, Cambridge: Cambridge University Press, pp. 64–83. See also Dodd's important article '*Ἔννομος Χριστοῦ*' reprinted in his *More New Testament Studies*, Manchester: Manchester University Press, 1968, pp. 134–8.

[15] In his *Paul and Rabbinic Judaism*, London: SPCK, 1948, p. 144, Davies went somewhat further than Dodd in claiming that there was rabbinic evidence (albeit somewhat limited) to suggest that in the new age there would be a new 'law of the Messiah'. See especially W. D. Davies, *The Setting of the Sermon on the Mount*, Cambridge: Cambridge University Press, 1963, pp. 109–90. H. Schlier also insisted that the 'law of Christ' is 'die Tora des Messias Jesus'. *Die Brief an die Galater*, KEK, 12th edn., 1961, p. 272. As there are major problems over the dating and interpretation of the handful of rabbinic passages Davies and Schlier cite, their case has won little scholarly support. See especially R. J. Banks, *Jesus and the Law in the Synoptic Tradition*, Cambridge: Cambridge University Press, 1975, pp. 65–81.

[16] See especially R. N. Longenecker's Word commentary on Galatians, Dallas: Word, 1990, pp. 275–6.

Paul alludes very rarely to sayings of Jesus, and refers explicitly to them even less often.[17] There is limited evidence in 1 Corinthians and in Romans 12—14, but even less evidence in Galatians.[18] When the phraseology of Gal. 6.1–5 is compared closely with the synoptic tradition, there are only two words in common, *βάρη* (burdens) and *φορτίον* (load), and even they are not used in similar contexts.

In my view interpreters of Gal. 6.2 who claim that the words of Jesus are 'the law of Christ' are reading Paul through Matthean eyes. Their reading may not do justice to Paul, but it does resonate with a long and strong tradition which should not be rejected without further ado. We turn now to a further interpretation of 'the law of Christ' with an equally impressive pedigree, even though it too does not do full justice to Paul's intention in Gal. 6.2.

Love is the law of Christ: *Lex Christi, lex amoris*

In his first commentary on Galatians (1519) Luther wrote several powerful and perceptive paragraphs on Gal. 6.2, which he describes as 'a very beautiful and thoroughly golden maxim: Love is the law of Christ'. In his 1535 commentary on Gal. 6.2 Luther goes even further. 'The Law of Christ is the law of love' he writes three times over. 'After redeeming and regenerating us and constituting us as His church, Christ did not give us any new law except the law of mutual love (John 13.34–5).' 'To love does not mean, as the sophists imagine, to wish someone else well, but to bear someone else's burdens, that is, to bear what is burdensome to you and what you would rather not bear.'

Two centuries after Luther, J. A. Bengel echoed Luther's interpretation in a typically pithy comment on Gal. 6.2 in his

---

[17] For a recent cautious assessment, see D. C. Allison, 'The Pauline Epistles and the Synoptic Gospels: the Pattern of the Parallels', *New Testament Studies* 28, 1962, pp. 1–32.

[18] For Romans see especially M. B. Thompson, *Clothed with Christ: The Example and Teaching of Jesus in Romans 12.1–15.3*, Sheffield: Sheffield Academic Press, 1991.

influential *Gnomon Novi Testamenti* (1742): *Lex Christi, lex amoris*, 'the law of Christ is the law of love'.

The same interpretation is set out much more fully in V. P. Furnish's standard textbook (*The Love Command in the New Testament*, London: SCM Press, 1968, pp. 59–65) and supported by many other writers. It is probably the consensus interpretation of Gal. 6.2 at present.

Who would want to deny the importance of love in Paul's ethical thinking? In Gal. 5.14 love is said to sum up the whole law. Love heads the list of the fruits of the Spirit in Gal. 5.22, a list which ends with the ironic comment, 'there is no law against such things'. Nonetheless I am not convinced that this interpretation does full justice to Paul's intention in Gal. 6.2, for if the 'law of Christ' is taken to mean no more than 'the law of love', Paul's careful counterpoise with 'the law of Moses' is missed, as is his emphasis on Christ's own example of self-giving love.

Concluding reflections

In Gal. 6.2 and 1 Cor. 9.21 Paul's christological emphasis is clear, as is the love commandment, but there is little or no trace of the teachings of Jesus as constituting the law of Christ. If we are reflecting on the current value of our neglected gem, 'the law of Christ', why should we privilege Paul's usage?

Quite independently of Paul, we find James, Matthew and the writer of the Johannine letters using *the concept*, even if they do not use the actual phrase. As with Paul, there is a continuing commitment to the law of Moses as interpreted by Christ. But there is also the addition of a much clearer emphasis on the teaching of Jesus and a less explicit christological note.

Early in the second century notable theological steps were taken. In the writings of Hermas, the *Kerygma Petri* and Justin Martyr, there is a strong emphasis on Christ himself as the new law. Arguably one of Paul's notions is taken much further, even though it is difficult to trace direct use of Paul's letters. In Hermas and Justin, Christ is not only the new law, he is the new lawgiver.

The later Christian tradition develops one or other of the strands of thought found in the NT and in early Christian writings, but without adding significant or new understandings. As far as I am aware, the phrase 'the law of Christ' is suffering benign neglect in contemporary theological writing. However I hope I have shown that if we consider Christian writings up to the middle of the second century and do not confine ourselves to Paul or to canonical writings, we are not going to be bereft of matters for on-going theological reflection. Indeed we have an agenda:

(1) Christology and ethics must not be separated.
(2) The 'law of Christ' or whatever alternative or synonymous phrase we choose must not be allowed to imply abandonment of the law of Moses. In particular if we use the phrase 'new law', we must do so with care, for 'new' can easily imply that we are discarding the 'old'. The terms 'new covenant' or 'new testament' are analogies. They may be used, but there are lurking dangers. In saying this, I am well aware that there are unresolved issues concerning Christian theological interpretation of the Old Testament or the Hebrew Scriptures, if you prefer. But I am heartened by the number of biblical scholars who are now wrestling with these very issues.
(3) The radical, disturbing teaching of Jesus recorded by the evangelists is of continuing importance, with the love commandment as its focal point.
(4) In Galatians (and elsewhere) Paul juxtaposes the wisdom of Scripture (the love commandment of Lev. 19.18 at Gal. 5.14) and the conventional ethical wisdom of the day baptized into Christ (bear one another's burdens at Gal. 6.2). Why should not we do likewise?
(5) Our explorations have warned us yet again not to allow the strength of particular strands of the later Christian tradition to determine our biblical exegesis. On the other hand, we have seen that later interpretation and development of a biblical tradition may stimulate theological reflection in unexpected directions.

All this seems to me to be a useful starting agenda for a theological ethics in which Scripture is taken seriously. I am not advocating a return to the old model whereby the biblical scholar hands over to the systematic theologian his or her results to be used according to whim. Rather, I am urging that there should be an on-going dialogue between close attention to biblical text, the effects of the text (for good or ill) through the centuries, and contemporary theological reflection.

13. The Books of Solomon in Ancient Mysticism

WILLIAM HORBURY

Dean Inge famously judged the influence exerted on mysticism by the Song of Solomon to be 'simply deplorable'.[1] In this respect he has been called typically Victorian, but a not dissimilar view of Christian mystical tendencies was later taken by Gershom Scholem, in line with his own characteristic contrast between Jewish and Christian mysticism;[2] and Inge's reservations could already be found in the Church well before the Victorian age. Something related to them can in fact be suspected behind the withholding of the Song of Solomon from the immature which is recommended by Origen to Christians and noted by him as a laudable Jewish custom.[3] In the earliest period of Christian mysticism, however, by contrast with its whole history since the time of Origen, the influence of the Song of Solomon is by no means obvious.

The biblical books in general, transmitted within a tradition of interpretation which is itself partly mystical, have formed a great link between ancient and medieval mysticism, and also between the mysticism of Jews and Christians. In both the ancient and the medieval periods both communities exhibit a mystical ardour which is focused through attention to biblical texts, and in both

[1] W. R. Inge, *Christian Mysticism*, London: Methuen, 1899, pp. 43, 272n; see also pp. 369–72, where praise is found as well as blame.

[2] G. Scholem, *Major Trends in Jewish Mysticism*, ET London: Thames & Hudson, 1955, vol. 2, pp. 25–6, cf. 55–6.

[3] Origen, *Prol. Cant.*, in Rufinus's translation; PG 13.634, GCS 8 (ed. W. A. Baehrens, 1925), pp. 62–3.

periods some at least of those texts are common to Jews and Christians. In the ancient period this is true already of the time of Christian origins, as attested in the New Testament and in the non-Christian Jewish literature of the Herodian age.

Yet this biblical link with mysticism has itself been changeable. One notable sign of discontinuity appears in mystical use of the biblical books traditionally classed as Solomonic. These are Proverbs, Ecclesiastes, and the Song or Canticle of Solomon, among the books now found within a Hebrew Bible, and the Wisdom of Solomon and the Wisdom of Jesus son of Sirach, commonly called Ecclesiasticus, among the books which form the Old Testament Apocrypha in the English Bible of 1611. Ecclesiasticus was often quoted by ancient Christian authors as Solomonic, and in its Latin text it ends with the prayer of Solomon from 2 Chron. 6.13–21. The first three Solomonic books are older than the last two, and Ecclesiasticus and Wisdom respectively represent the second and (probably) the first century BC; but all five books originated in the Jewish community, and they were all transmitted within the Old Testament of the Church as read in Greek and Latin, notably in the Septuagint and the Vulgate. In antiquity texts of importance for mysticism were supplied by the Wisdom of Solomon and Ecclesiasticus, themselves developing Proverbs, on the one hand, and by the Song of Solomon, on the other; but mystical attention was not evenly shared between the wisdom books and the Canticle.

This point emerges when literature of the Second Temple period, including the New Testament, is viewed together with later rabbinic and patristic texts. After the Second Temple period the principal mystical focus then seems to shift within the Solomonic books from Wisdom and Ecclesiasticus towards Solomon's Song. A related and partly comparable variation, between Christian use of all three of these books and Jewish concentration on the Song of Solomon and Proverbs, appears when the Solomonic biblical foci of medieval Jewish and Christian mysticism are compared with one another.

The discontinuity which emerges in these ways from mystical use of the Solomonic books is explored below, with special reference to the early period, as an instance of interrelationship between biblical interpretation and mystical theology. It is suggested that an emotional and intellectual mysticism was focused before and during the time of Christian origins on the figure of wisdom as presented within the Solomonic corpus in the Wisdom of Solomon and Ecclesiasticus, both of them being viewed together with Proverbs; but that from the second Christian century onwards the mystical focus tended to shift within the Solomonic books towards the Song of Solomon, not least because of emphasis on the Hebrew canon. This shift was reflected successively in Jewish and in Christian teaching, and the mystical importance of the Song of Solomon became particularly clear in the work of Origen.

Now in section I below the Solomonic books are viewed together with other biblical texts of importance for Jewish and Christian mysticism in antiquity and the Middle Ages. Section II considers what seems to be the limited influence of the Canticle in the Herodian age, and the increasing later importance of its mystical interpretation. In section III I suggest that the other side of this coin was a movement at the end of the Herodian age away from what had been a comparable and widely influential focus of mysticism, the figure of wisdom as presented in Ecclesiasticus and the Wisdom of Solomon. Finally in section IV there is brief comment on the aftermath in Christianity of this development, and on implications of the point that it was a development in biblical interpretation as well as mysticism and theology.

I

The changing fortunes of the Solomonic books in the period before Origen form part of a broader interrelationship between biblical texts and mysticism. The classical Jewish biblical texts of mysticism in late antiquity became the creation narrative in Genesis and the vision of the chariot of the cherubim in the first chapter of Ezekiel. These passages, dealing respectively with Ma'aseh Bereshith 'the work of the Beginning' and Ma'aseh

Merkabah 'the work of the Chariot', are mentioned in this connection in the Mishnah (Hag. ii 1) as texts which may not be expounded even to the smallest auditory: 'they may not expound the Work of the Beginning before two persons, nor the Chariot before one alone, unless he be a Sage and one that understands of his own knowledge'. To these two mystical foci others can be added, including the narrative of Moses, Isaiah's temple vision, and also the Song of Solomon, with reference to their exposition in Targum and midrash and the Hekhaloth and Shiur Qomah texts. Origen, as cited above, says correspondingly that Jews keep back from the immature the opening of Genesis and the opening and the close of Ezekiel, as well as the Canticle. The additions to Genesis and Ezekiel, especially the Canticle, offer glimpses of the tendency towards envisaging mystical union which Scholem, as cited above, thought atypical of ancient Jewish mysticism, but which has been detected for instance in the 'transformational mysticism' of the Hekhaloth texts,[4] wherein Enoch becomes the godlike angel Metatron.[5] Lastly, there is what can be called a Torah mysticism, although it is not always discussed under the heading of mysticism, and this is focused on the figure of wisdom in Proverbs, wisdom being identified with Torah, as in Ecclus 24.23 and Baruch 4.1 (section III, below). A famous instance of this view of Torah is the interpretation of Gen. 1.1 by wisdom's sayings in Prov. 8.30 and 8.22 in the Midrash Rabbah on Genesis, to show that God, using the Torah like an architect's plan, 'was looking into the Torah and creating the world' (Ber. R. 1.1); compare the rendering of Gen. 1.1 in the Fragment Targum, 'By wisdom the Lord created'.

The Christian mystical tradition in antiquity inevitably offers some contrast with the Jewish in its biblical foci; but if the New Testament is left aside, the narrative of Moses and the

---

[4] M. Idel, *Kabbalah: New Perspectives,* New Haven: Yale University Press, 1988, p. 60.

[5] 3 Enoch 9.1; 12.1–5, 15.1–2, discussed by C. R. A. Morray-Jones, 'Transformational Mysticism in the Apocalyptic-Merkabah Tradition', *Journal of Jewish Studies* 43, 1992, pp. 1–32 (pp. 10–26).

Song of Solomon, both important among Jews, can perhaps be called the two classical mystical foci in both Eastern and Western Christianity, as exemplified by Origen, Gregory of Nyssa and Augustine. The Canticle is especially related to the characteristically Christian Christ-mysticism, and by the early Middle Ages this book had come to be important for the cult of our Lady as well as the cult of Christ; but Christ-mysticism had been fed from the beginning by meditation on the figure of wisdom, and especially on wisdom as presented in two other Solomonic books, the Wisdom of Solomon and Ecclesiasticus. Both books were important in this christological mystical interpretation from the patristic to the mediaeval period, and, like the Canticle, they came in time to be linked with our Lady as well as Christ.

In the medieval West, the degree of difference as well as overlap between Jewish and Christian mystical use of biblical books reappears precisely because the Solomonic books were especially dear to Christian mystics, for that applies not only to the Song of Solomon but also still to the two books which are in the Christian but not the Hebrew Scriptures, namely the Wisdom of Solomon and Ecclesiasticus – witness the centrality of these books in the Christ-mysticism of Meister Eckhart, Henry Suso and others in the thirteenth and fourteenth centuries. On the other hand, the figure of wisdom in Proverbs could continue to supply a related focal point for Jewish mysticism.

Thus, even when the New Testament is left aside, there is still some contrast as well as overlap between the biblical foci of Jewish and of Christian mysticism, a contrast arising partly from the special importance of Genesis and Ezekiel in rabbinic tradition, and partly from Christian use of Solomonic books found in the Septuagint but not the Hebrew Bible. This contrast is related to the earlier contrast which forms the main topic here, the contrast between attention to the wisdom books and the Canticle, respectively, in the years between the Maccabaean revolt and the compilation of the Mishnah. Towards the end of the Second Temple period and for some time afterwards the figure of wisdom portrayed in Wisdom and Ecclesiasticus is prominent, and traces of mystical use of the Song of Solomon are rare; from the later Roman period onwards, however, although the figure of wisdom does not disappear, mystical understandings of the Canticle become prevalent among both Jews and Christians.

II

A fuller outline of these trends can now be sketched, beginning with the Canticle. Towards the end of the Second Temple period its mystical interpretation is no more than sparsely attested. 'Mystical' is being used broadly here, to cover the interpretation of the Shulamite in the Canticle in a communal as well as individual sense, as Israel or the Church as well as the soul, in search of a beloved who is understood as God or Christ. On the other hand, some antecedents of rabbinic visionary concern with the beginning and the chariot and of the transformational mysticism noted above can be traced in apocalypses like Enoch or hymnody like the Songs of the Sabbath Sacrifice known from Qumran texts. Moreover, the importance of the figure of wisdom for mysticism is abundantly represented in poetry by the presentation of wisdom in Ecclesiasticus in the second century BC, and then later in the Wisdom of Solomon and in other compositions which can be compared with the wisdom poems of Ecclesiasticus; in prose the mystical interpretation of wisdom emerges in Philo's wisdom-linked treatment of the patriarchs.

In the literature of the Herodian age, however, there are no more than hints of the importance of a mystical interpretation of the Song of Solomon. In late Herodian times traces of such interpretation of Solomon's Song can be detected occasionally among both Jews and Christians. The clearest examples are found in the Christian apocalypse of John the Divine and the Jewish apocalypse of Ezra; see Rev. 3.20, 'I stand at the door and knock' (cf. Cant. 2.9; 5.2) and 2 Esdras 5.24, 26 'thou hast chosen thee one lily, . . . thou hast named thee one dove' (cf. Cant. 2.1–2, 14; 5.2; 6.9). There are perhaps traces elsewhere in the New Testament Johannine literature, for example 2 John 1 on the 'elect lady' as interpreted by M. Hengel with reference to Cant. 6.9–10 LXX (and Vulgate), where 'my dove, my perfect one' is 'elect to her that bare her' and 'elect as the sun'.[6] Again, the Qumran copies of the Song of Solomon discussed by E. Tov, as noted below, may constitute a further and earlier hint.

Yet these hints and traces are remarkably slight. It is true that traces of the Song of Solomon might perhaps not be expected in Philo, with his overwhelmingly Pentateuchal emphasis, or in Josephus, who was writing as an historian and apologist. What is striking, however, is the absence from the Qumran literature and the New Testament, with their broad range of biblical citation and their concern with mystical themes, of signs that mystical interpretation of the Canticle had the clear prominence which it later enjoyed.

This absence is also striking from the point of view of the history of the biblical canon, for by the time of Josephus the Song of Solomon probably had an established place in the series of books regarded as authoritative by Jews.[7] This series then broadly corresponded to the books of the Hebrew canon, as Josephus shows (*Ap.* i 37–41), and already it was customarily reckoned up to a fixed number, twenty-two according to Josephus, twenty-four according to the roughly contemporary 2 Esdr. 14.44–45; the two totals probably refer to the same series of books counted with slight differences in combination or disjunction, as in respect of Jeremiah and Lamentations, Judges and Ruth. The discovery in the Qumran caves 4 and 6 of four fragmentary copies of the Song of Solomon,[8] including instances of what is probably

---

[6] M. Hengel, 'Die "auserwählte Herrin", die "Braut", die "Mutter" und die "Gottesstadt" ', in M. Hengel, S. Mittmann, and A. M. Schwemer, (eds.), *La Cité de Dieu / Die Stadt Gottes,* WUNT 129, Tübingen: Mohr Siebeck, 2000) pp. 245–85 (pp. 248–53).

[7] A. van der Kooij, 'The Canonization of Ancient Books Kept in the Temple of Jerusalem', in A. van der Kooij and K. van der Toorn, (eds.), *Canonization and Decanonization,* Studies in the History of Religions 82, Leiden: Brill, 1998, pp. 17–40 (pp. 17–23, 37–8).

[8] M. Baillet, 'Textes des Grottes 2Q, 3Q, 6Q, 7Q à 10Q', in M. Baillet, J. T. Milik and R. de Vaux, OP, *Les 'Petites Grottes' de Qumrân*, DJD 3, Oxford: Clarendon Press, 1962, pp. 45–164 (pp. 112–14); E. Tov, 'Three Manuscripts (Abbreviated Texts?) of Canticles from Qumran Cave 4', *Journal of Jewish Studies* 46, 1995, pp. 88–111.

deliberate abbreviation,[9] independently suggests that the book was revered before the time of Josephus. Pre-Mishnaic rabbinic assertion that the Canticle is indeed holy and inspired, an instance of which is quoted below, is then likely to reflect dispute over a book which tradition already presented as authoritative, rather than questions raised by a wholly new suggestion that the book should be revered.

From rabbinic traditions which probably reflect second-century biblical interpretation it is in fact clear that after the time of Josephus non-mystical understanding of the Song of Solomon still overlapped with mystical exegesis, and that the Song's status as holy, like that of Ecclesiastes, had been correspondingly questioned. R. Akiba, who died in Hadrian's repression of the Bar Kokhba uprising, is represented as unwilling to admit the accuracy of his brother-in-law's recollection that the status of both books had been confirmed after dispute; the Song could never have been doubted, 'for all the Writings are holy, but the Song of Songs is the Holy of Holies' (M. Yad. iii 5). The possibility of non-mystical understanding of the Song of Solomon is however recognized when it is condemned, again in a saying ascribed to R. Akiba: 'whoever trills the Song of Songs in the banqueting house . . . has no share in the world to come' (Tos. Sanh. xii 10); and such interpretation is envisaged again when in the Mishnah the daughters of Jerusalem dancing in the vineyards after the fast-days are said to have twitted the young men with biblical verses including Cant. 3.11, 'Go forth, O ye daughters of Zion, and behold king Solomon with the crown wherewith his mother crowned him in the day of his espousals, and in the day of the gladness of his heart' (M. Taan. iv 8).

It seems to signify a trend, however, when the Mishnah then adds (Taan. iv 8) what is probably a secondary mystical interpretation: the day of his espousals – this is the giving of the law; the day of the gladness of his heart – this is the building of the house of the sanctuary. The comment on this Mishnaic text in the Babylonian Talmud (Taan. 31a) likewise speaks mystically

---

9 Tov, 'Three Manuscripts', pp. 88–90, 96–7, 107.

of the round-dance of the righteous around the Holy One in the time to come. These passages touch the communal or liturgical aspect of mysticism, whereby the Song of Solomon is associated with the Sinai narrative and the sanctuary, as in the Targum, and speaks of the mystical vision and union vouchsafed to Israel as a whole. The conception of the dance has its Christian second-century parallel in the round-dance of the disciples around the Saviour as he sings and dances before his arrest in the Acts of John (94—6). Here, however, perhaps significantly, the hymn of Christ echoes the Wisdom of Solomon rather than the Song; compare Acts of John 96 on 'holy souls' and 'word of wisdom' with Wisd. 7.27.

The complement of this picture derived from the Mishnah is the striking absence of reference to the Song of Solomon and its mystical interpretation in surviving literature of the Hasmonaean and Herodian age, including the Qumran texts and, for the most part, the New Testament. In later Christian writing it is not yet quoted to support the unity and sanctity of the Church in Justin Martyr or Irenaeus, but it finally emerges as a source of such proof-texts and a commented book at the beginning of the third century, in Tertullian and the Hippolytean corpus. Then, as M. W. Elliott put it, the Canticle like its heroine seems to come 'out of a wilderness of neglect'.[10]

Thus in the East Clement of Alexandria, a lover of the book of Wisdom, had not dwelt on Solomon's Song, but Origen construed it as the wise king's contemplation and the soul's quest;[11] and in the West, where Tertullian had just once quoted it among proof-texts on Christ and the Church (*Marc.* iv 11, 8), Cyprian cited it freely in this sense in epistles as well as treatises. This gradual Christian adoption of a mystical interpretation of the Song of Solomon like that which had found favour among Jews is perhaps comparable with the gradual contemporaneous Christian adoption of Jewish

---

[10] M. W. Elliott, *The Song of Songs and Christology in the Early Church 381–451*, STAC 7, Tübingen: Mohr Siebeck, 2000, p. 3.

[11] See R. B. Tollinton, *Clement of Alexandria: A Study in Christian Liberalism*, London: Williams & Norgate, 1914, vol. 2, pp. 169–71.

revision of the Septuagint; the revised Greek versions formed a tampering with the text for Justin Martyr, but an instrument of study, for Origen.

Hence, roughly between the time of Philo and the time of Origen, there appears to be a shift in the biblical foci of mysticism within the Solomonic corpus, from Ecclesiasticus and Wisdom towards the Song of Solomon. At the same time there was debate among Jews, reflected later among Christians, over the authority of the Solomonic books in general. Ecclesiasticus was current in Hebrew and continued to be read and quoted by Jews as well as Christians, but its status among Jews was doubtful; and Wisdom was known to Jerome only in Greek, and has not left an impress like that of Ecclesiasticus on rabbinic literature – although it is noteworthy that the poems on the figure of wisdom are not represented in the rabbinic quotations of Ben Sira's proverbs collected by Ad. Neubauer.[12] On the other hand, both Jews and Christians began evidently to prize the Song of Solomon.

At the end of the Second Temple period, then, the Song of Solomon seems to have begun to gain the mystical prominence which it thenceforth retained.[13] Rabbinic material suggesting ardour for the mystical interpretation has been clustered round the name of R. Akiba, as noted above. There are likely to be old roots for the application to the deity, in the Shi'ur Qomah texts on the mystical measurement of the divine stature, of the words in Cant. 5.10–16 beginning 'my beloved is white and ruddy', words which are similarly applied in the Babylonian Talmud (Hag. 14a) and the Targum.[14] The period from the destruction of the temple to Bar Kokhba has accordingly been picked out as formative

[12] A. E. Cowley and Ad. Neubauer, *The Original Hebrew of a Portion of Ecclesiasticus (xxxix.15 to xlix.11)*, Oxford: Clarendon Press, 1897, pp. xix–xxx.

[13] Elliott, *The Song of Songs*, pp. 3–5; P. S. Alexander, *The Targum of Canticles Translated, with a Critical Introduction, Textual Notes, and Commentary,* The Aramaic Bible, Edinburgh: T. & T. Clark, 2002, Introduction, §6.

[14] Scholem, *Major Trends*, pp. 63–5; G. G. Stroumsa, *Savoir et Salut*, Paris: Les Éditions du Cerf, 1992, pp. 54–5, 73–4.

for this development among Jews.[15] Comparison of Revelation and 2 Esdras with the passages on the Song of Solomon from the Mishnah and Tosefta quoted above makes a view on these lines plausible, even if the formative period is extended to the end of the second century to allow for uncertainties of attribution to named rabbinic teachers. Correspondingly, by the third century the Christians too have clearly inclined towards mystical understanding of the Song of Solomon.

III

The other side of this coin, however, it may be suggested, was a movement at the end of the Herodian age away from Ecclesiasticus and the Wisdom of Solomon, which had formed a comparable focus of visionary and unitive mysticism. The development of the figure of wisdom in these books and in early Christianity has often been studied, especially in connection with Christology and feminine images of deity, and it has been freshly presented by P. Schäfer since this essay was first written.[16] For the present argument, however, just three aspects can be emphasized. First, a wisdom mysticism connected with Ecclesiasticus and the Wisdom of Solomon prevailed during the period when, as just noted, the Canticle was less prominent; and secondly, the wisdom books and the mystical interpretation of the Song of Solomon are broadly comparable in use of visionary and unitive imagery; yet thirdly, Ecclesiasticus and Wisdom present a figure which is clearly spiritual, for all their evocation of physical beauty, whereas in the Song of Solomon the spirituality of the figures is given mainly by the interpretative tradition.

---

[15] E. E. Urbach, 'The Homiletical Interpretations of the Sages and the Expositions of Origen on Canticles and the Jewish–Christian Disputation', *Tarbiz* 30, 1961, pp. 148–70, ET in *Scripta Hierosolymitana* 22, 1971, pp. 247–75 reprinted in E. E. Urbach, ed. R. Brody and M. D. Herr, *Collected Writings in Jewish Studies*, Jerusalem: Magnes Press, 1999, pp. 318–46 (pp. 247–51).

[16] P. Schäfer, *Mirror of His Beauty: Feminine Images of God from the Bible to the Early Kabbalah*, Princeton: Princeton University Press, 2002, pp. 19–78.

To begin with the prevalence of wisdom mysticism and its general comparability with mystical interpretation of the Canticle, the relevant texts in Ecclesiasticus and Wisdom, books which themselves won approval and influence, belong to a series of such poems in Jewish and early Christian literature. The cosmic and mystical significance of the figure of wisdom is evident in the poems of Proverbs 3 and 8—9, with their Septuagintal renderings, and something of its importance emerges in the third-century Greek rendering of the Pentateuch, when Bezaleel receives *πνεῦμα θεῖον σοφίας*, 'the divine spirit of wisdom' (Exod. 31.3; 35.31 LXX); but it comes to the fore in the second century BC in Ecclesiasticus. Among the hymns concerning wisdom incorporated into this book, that in chapter 24 is wisdom's self-praise, on the model of Proverbs 8, and speaks of her place in the divine assembly, her coming forth from the mouth of the most High, her dwelling in Jerusalem, and her glory and grace; it leads to the invitation 'Come to me, you that are desirous of me' (24.19). At the end wisdom is identified with the Mosaic law (24.23), as in the perhaps roughly contemporary wisdom-poem Baruch 3.9—4.4 (4.1); compare Deut. 4.9 'Keep therefore and do [the statutes and judgements], for this is your wisdom and your understanding'. The last of the hymns in Ecclesiasticus is 51.13–30, a Hebrew alphabetical poem added at the end of the book, and also current separately, as shown by its inclusion in the Psalms scroll from Qumran cave 11.[17] The poet describes his ardent youthful pursuit and attainment of wisdom, who 'came to me in her beauty' (verse 14 in 11Q5); here and elsewhere the Greek version spiritualizes the imagery. These two poems already show that wisdom mysticism, like mystical interpretation of the Canticle, uses the language of courtship and love to signify a spiritual vision and union.

To move beyond Ecclesiasticus, the series of wisdom poems reaches its high point in Wisdom 7—9. Here, in a manner both biblical and Platonic, Solomon reverently praises wisdom as a

[17] Verses 21–29 are lost at the foot of col. xxi; see J. A. Sanders, *The Psalms Scroll of Qumran Cave 11*, DJD 4, Oxford: Clarendon Press, 1965, pp. 79–85.

loving world-soul, infinitely subtle and all-pervasive, an effluence from the divine glory and the giver of all good gifts; he describes his own youthful passion for her ('I loved her above health and beauty', 7.10), and recites his ardent prayer for her. Then the series continues in Christian poetry, for example Od. Sol. 33, especially the lines (5–13) beginning 'But a perfect virgin stood', which recall Proverbs 8, and the poem in Acts of Thomas 1.6–7, beginning 'The maiden is the daughter of light'.[18] In these last two poems the subject is probably the Church, portrayed as the divine wisdom and envisaged as a pre-existent spiritual entity co-ordinate with Christ, as in 2 Clement 14.

This series, beginning from Ecclesiasticus, runs from the second century BC to the second century AD, and shows a continuous preoccupation with this theme which provides a context for the importance of the figure of wisdom in Philo, the synoptic tradition, and the gnostic Christian myths of Sophia reviewed in the later second century by Irenaeus and exemplified in the Apocryphon of John. These may reflect non-Christian Jewish mythological development of material found in Wisdom and Philo,[19] or they may simply be radical Christian reshaping of such material;[20] but in either case they attest the vigour and importance of interpretation of the figure of wisdom at the end of the Herodian age and the beginning of the second century.

The influence of the figure of wisdom during the Herodian age itself is evident in the synoptic tradition of the sayings of Jesus, notably at Lk. 7.35 and parallel, on wisdom's children or works (for wisdom as mother compare Ecclus 15.2, and, in the longer Greek text, 24.18; Wisd. 7.12), and Lk. 11.49, on 'the wisdom of God' as saying 'I will send them prophets and apostles' (perhaps in allusion to Prov. 9.3 LXX, where wisdom's messengers are male). Perhaps the most famous instance is Mt. 11.29 'Come to me . . . and I will give you rest; take my yoke upon you', with its

---

18 E. Preuschen, *Zwei gnostische Hymnen*, Giessen: J. Ricker'sche Buchhandlung (A. Töpelmann), 1904, pp. 10–17, 28–44.

19 Schäfer, *Mirror of His Beauty*, p. 59 inclines to this view.

20 As urged by A. H. B. Logan, *Gnostic Truth and Christian Heresy: A Study in the History of Gnosticism*, Edinburgh: T. & T. Clark, 1996, p. 32.

echoes of the wisdom poems of Ecclesiasticus.[21] In Matthew here and at 23.34, where wisdom's words in Lk.11.49 appear simply as words of Christ, the form taken by the sayings tradition seems already to presuppose an understanding of Christ as the divine wisdom, even though this Christology is not a clear preoccupation of the evangelist.[22]

Lastly, the prevalence of wisdom mysticism in the Herodian age is confirmed by its importance in Philo. A number of his relatively few non-Pentateuchal biblical quotations are linked with the topic of divine wisdom,[23] and prominent among them is Prov. 8.22, from wisdom's self-praise, 'God obtained me first of all his works, and founded me before the world.' This verse is echoed when Moses is imagined as saying, to justify his prayer that the Lord would appoint a man over the congregation (Num. 27.16), that wisdom antedates not only his own birth, but that of the whole cosmos (Philo, *Virt.* 62). Prov. 8.22 is similarly quoted to show that wisdom is mother and nurse of the cosmos, which is the offspring of her union with God (*Ebr.* 30-31); Proverbs can indeed be understood to present wisdom as nurse (8.30), but with regard to union 8.22 'obtained' is here probably further interpreted by Wisd. 8.3, on wisdom's *symbiosis* with the God who loves her.[24] Another great theme of Wisdom 7—9, the *symbiosis* with wisdom sought by Solomon (Wisd. 8.9; cf. 8.2, 18), appears in Philo above all in his interpretation of the marriages of the patriarchs. Thus the wise Abraham with Sarah in her goodness and beauty, when Pharaoh seizes her (Gen. 12.10–20), stand for the union of mind and virtue achieved through wisdom; and Isaac and Rebekah, and Jacob's quest for a wife in 'the house of wisdom', the daughter of God (Bethuel, Gen. 28.2),

---

[21] Ecclus 24.19, quoted above, 51.23–27 and – as stressed by W. D. Davies and D. C. Allison, Jr, *A Critical and Exegetical Commentary on the Gospel according to Saint Matthew*, vol. 2, International Critical Commentary, Edinburgh: T. & T. Clark, 1991, p. 293 – 6.18–31.

[22] Davies and Allison, *Matthew*, vol. 2, p. 295.

[23] W. L. Knox, 'A Note on Philo's Use of the Old Testament', *Journal of Theological Studies* 41, 1940, pp. 30–34 (pp. 31–2).

[24] A debt to the Wisdom of Solomon is suggested by Schäfer, *Mirror of His Beauty*, p. 41.

stand for mystical unions with wisdom (*Abr.* 92–102; *Qu. Gen.* 97, 143, 145–6, on Isaac; *Immut.* 92, *Fug.* 49–52, on Jacob).[25] Such Philonic interpretation, however elaborate, is not altogether removed from the treatment of Sarah in the paraphrase of Genesis 12 in the Genesis Apocryphon found in Qumran cave 1, where a detailed report of her charms to Pharaoh ends 'and with all this beauty, there is much wisdom with her' (1QapGen ar xx 7).

The series of wisdom poems thus corresponds to the continuous prominence of the figure of wisdom in a variety of Jewish and Christian writings, down to the second Christian century; known locations for the works cited range from Jerusalem (the Wisdom of Jesus son of Sirach) to Egypt (his grandson's Greek translation) and Alexandria (Philo). The mystical reflection on wisdom which appears most strikingly in Ecclesiasticus and Wisdom was clearly widespread. In content, it broadly corresponds to the visionary and unitive themes of the mystical interpretation of the Song of Solomon. Thus any shift of mystical focus within the Solomonic books from Ecclesiasticus and Wisdom towards the Canticle with Proverbs, as in the Jewish community, or towards the Canticle alongside a continuing association of Ecclesiasticus and Wisdom with Proverbs, as in the Church, could take place without undue disturbance. Moreover, in the period when the Song of Solomon was less prominent, a largely comparable mystical focus was provided by the figure of wisdom.

Yet, as noted already, this shift of focus meant that a text to which a spiritual interpretation had largely to be brought – the Song of Solomon – often became more prominent than texts which themselves presented a figure envisaged as a divine spirit – in Wisdom, Ecclesiasticus, and also Proverbs. To this extent mystical theology moved away from biblical texts which were themselves rooted in a mysticism, and became still more closely associated with allegory.

---

[25] See E. R. Goodenough, *By Light, Light: the Mystic Gospel of Hellenistic Judaism,* New Haven: Yale University Press, 1935, pp. 157–68.

IV

Within the context of this book it is notable that, as has now appeared, one factor in this development in mysticism was a tendency in biblical interpretation. There was increasing concentration in the Jewish community on the established short collection of biblical books, and, within the Solomonic books of that collection, on the Song of Solomon as a focus of mysticism; widely approved books outside the number of the twenty-two or twenty-four, like Wisdom and Ecclesiasticus, concomitantly became more open to question. These interpretative positions then had their effect on the Christians, still a minority compared with the Jews, although Christian esteem for the Septuagint collection in its full extent was too settled, and often (as in respect of Wisdom and Ecclesiasticus) too closely connected with the Church's Christ-centred teaching and cultus, for the approved books to retreat as they eventually did among the Jews.

Central mystical themes thus came to be connected with a fresh biblical focus. In the Church, however, the presentations of wisdom in Ecclesiasticus and the Wisdom of Solomon continued to be important. Both depict a divine spirit, but broadly speaking Ecclesiasticus appeals to the senses, notably in chapters 24 and 51 as discussed above, whereas in Wisdom (7.22—8.1) the loving disciple gives ardent but intellectually-focused praise to a spirit who is an effulgence of the everlasting light. This emphasis in the book of Wisdom has done something to balance not only Ecclesiasticus but also, particularly in respect of Christ-mysticism, those aspects of dependence on the Canticle which Inge deplored.

This whole development suggests the importance of the Bible for mysticism, but the shift in biblical focus also suggests something of the independent impetus acquired by the great mystical themes of vision and union. Any theological work which takes Jewish and Christian mysticism seriously must also take the Bible seriously; but the biblical exegete must likewise reckon with the mysticism which has helped to shape the wisdom books and other biblical texts, and the mystical impetus which has more broadly and continuously impinged on biblical interpretation.

14. Metaphor, Poetry and Allegory

Erotic Love in the *Sermons on the Song of Songs* of Bernard of Clairvaux

DENYS TURNER

I

Though many authorities in the Latin patristic and medieval periods – from Gregory the Great in the sixth century to Denys the Carthusian in the late fifteenth – seem to suppose that they are working within a common and uniform tradition, constructions of the four senses of Scripture are notoriously diverse, and frequently inconsistently employed, in the medieval practice of exegesis. It is no use attempting to capture medieval exegetical theory or practice within a single clearly defined account of how those senses are to be distinguished. Were we, for example, to take the theoretical exactnesses of Thomas Aquinas concerning the four senses of Scripture as our starting point for the taxonomy of styles of medieval interpretation of the Song of Songs, we might indeed gain a certain clarity of perspective for the nonce, this being what constitutes the main temptation to start there. On the other hand, while clarifying some things, others, I believe, are thereby obscured, among them an important feature of Bernard of Clairvaux's readings of the Song in his eighty-six *Sermons*.

In this essay I want to outline but the shape of a number of linked hypotheses. First, that medieval exegetical strategies vary about as much as they do today, and that they vary principally according to purpose. Secondly, to determine something about what Bernard of Clairvaux is doing in those *Sermons*, by way of setting his purpose in contrast with that which governs the exegetical strategies of Thomas Aquinas and Nicholas of Lyra. This, in turn, will provoke a more general speculation, one which is provoked also by that most striking of impressions gained by anyone in the least acquainted with the standard medieval monastic Song commentary: namely, of the enormous gulf there is between the intense poetic eroticism of the Song itself, and the generally bloodless pedantry of the commentarial tradition. That speculation is that it is a general purpose of nearly all medieval *monastic* exegetical practice to evacuate the Song of its erotic potential, and that it is in the service of that end that most monastic exegetes devised their account of the relations between the 'four senses'; finally, that Bernard of Clairvaux is almost alone in that in his *Sermons* is found some genuine feeling for and some commentarial participation in the eroticism of the Song's discourse.

II

Let us begin with some comments on Thomas Aquinas' distinctions between four senses of Scripture as he formulates them in his *Quodlibet* 7, question 6.[1] The first comment may not seem particularly relevant, though it is in fact, and is that, if Weisheipl is right, this *quaestio* is not a *Quodlibet* at all, but a Disputed Question;[2] that is to say, it is not the Master's response to his audience's agenda, but a question chosen for debate by Thomas himself, presumably because he attached some importance to it within his own priorities. And what importance Thomas may have attached to this particular disputation would become transparent if it were true, as again Weisheipl believes it to be, that this question was one of four chosen by Thomas to debate in fulfilment of a very public and official duty: the requirement to

[1] For the Latin text, see *Quaestiones Quodlibetales*, Rome: Marietti, 1949. For an English translation, see Denys Turner, *Eros and Allegory*, Kalamazoo: Cistercian Publications, 1995, pp. 343–58.

[2] James A. Weisheipl, *Friar Thomas D'Aquino, His Life, Thought and Works*, Oxford: Blackwell, 1975, pp. 105–7.

dispute before the assembled Masters at Paris at his own inception as Master in 1256.[3]

If that is true, then it should provide a clue as to Thomas' purpose in choosing to dispute this issue of the four senses, and perhaps as well some explanation of why he draws the distinctions between them in the way in which he does. For as a question disputed at his inception, we could expect it to have the character, as it were, of a manifesto, a statement of his own programme as theological master at a great theological school. It is not too hazardous to guess, therefore, that his decision to debate the senses of Scripture on this occasion was meant to signal the importance Thomas attached to Scripture as the foundation of the whole enterprise of school theology, a supposition whose plausibility is reinforced by his having situated the parallel discussion in the *Summa Theologiae* within the first article, on the nature and purpose of *sacra doctrina* itself.[4] In short, what we may guess from this evidence is that the standpoint from which Thomas addresses the distinction of senses in the only two texts in which he explicitly discusses it is that, very particularly, of the schoolman of theology at the University of Paris.

If that is a fair supposition, it is probably no more hazardous to guess that this programme of defining the role of Scripture within the theological methodology of the schools influenced not only Thomas' choice of subject for disputation at his inception, but also the manner of his making the distinctions themselves. As a Parisian Master, Thomas was inevitably preoccupied with, among other things, the nature of theology as argument,[5] and therefore with the grounds on which sound argument from Scripture may be based. And this in turn raised the question of which senses of Scripture could serve as a firm enough basis for a

---

[3] Weisheipl, *Friar Thomas D'Aquino*, pp. 105–7. Nearly all recent scholarship dates Quodlibet 7 to Thomas' first regency in Paris and to either 1256 or 1257.

[4] *Summa Theologiae*, 1a q.1, aa 9–10.

[5] In the *Summa Theologiae* discussion the previous article concerns the question of whether *sacra doctrina* may be properly described as *argumentativa*, to which, of course, Thomas replies that it must.

sound theological structure. That this was in fact Thomas' main concern is borne out by the manifest emphasis of both discussions, for in both texts the argument is the same: if the development of *sacra doctrina* involves argument, and if the foundations of *sacra doctrina* lie in Scripture, then Scripture must contain a sense which is without ambiguity, or else the whole theological project is too vulnerable to fallacy, specifically the fallacy of equivocation.[6] But, he goes on, any one passage of Scripture is capable of multiple readings of spiritual sense. For spiritual senses are based on likenesses (*similitudines*)[7] between one thing and another, and any two things can be like one another in many different ways. Therefore, theological argument can be based legitimately only on an unambiguously determinable literal sense and in both texts Thomas quotes Augustine's authority to emphasize the point: 'no argument about doctrine may be based on any but the literal sense, as Augustine says in his letter to Vincentius the Donatist'.[8]

I suspect a polemical point here. If in general terms programmatic and declarative of the schoolman's theological method, these discussions are above all meant to exclude the arbitrary use of Scripture in theological argument, to which habits of neglect of the literal sense, common in the standard monastic commentary, and leading to an excessive reliance on the spiritual senses, left theologians all too vulnerable. And when we come to the detail, in particular of his distinction between the literal and the three spiritual senses, we can observe this concern motivating him again. Two aspects of his discussions show this rather more clearly than others. The first is his insistence that metaphors (*similitudines imaginariae*)[9] are part of the literal sense, and the second is that the literal sense of Scripture is to be found in the things and events (*res*) it refers to, things and events which must be historically true if the spiritual senses are to be legitimately founded upon them.[10]

As to the first, Thomas is determined to be clear about an issue

---

[6] See *Q. Quodlibet.* 7, q6 a1 obj. 2.

[7] q6, a1 ad4.

[8] q6 a1 obj. 4; *Summa Theologiae* 1a q1 a10 ad1.

[9] q6 a2 ad1.

[10] q6 a1 ad1.

on which he evidently regarded many to be confused. The word 'literal' as used of a sense of Scripture does not contrast, as it does in our own usage, with 'metaphorical', for a metaphor is just another, albeit indirect, way of referring, with truth or falsity, to some fact or event in the world. Poetry, he thinks, is entirely written in metaphors,[11] and if we supposed that metaphors always yield a spiritual sense, then we would have to suppose that all poetry is on a par with Scripture in yielding spiritual senses, which, of course, it does not. That being the case in principle, Thomas concludes that even where in Scripture the text is written in metaphors, it is not by virtue of its metaphorical character as such that it possesses a spiritual sense, if, indeed, it possesses one at all. For any old human author can write in metaphors and make poems; but only the Holy Spirit can dispose that Scripture yields up a spiritual sense.

What, then, determines the literal sense as distinct from the spiritual senses? Here again, Thomas seeks clarity where he seems to think others are confused. And I paraphrase his argument in our terms rather than his, though I hope still accurately: the literal sense and only the literal sense is the meaning of the words of the text of Scripture. Hence, whatever devices of speech are used, whatever trope contributes to the meaning of the text, these contribute to nothing but its literal sense. As we might put it, so far as the semantics of Scripture are concerned, they are wholly exhausted by the literal sense. Or as Thomas himself puts it, 'all that is part of the literal sense which can genuinely be got from the meaning of the words'.[12] But, he goes on, it is not just words which are capable of signifying things, for the things which are signified by the words of human authors are themselves capable, through the action of the Holy Spirit, of signifying too. Now if the literal sense is that which is signified by the words, then the spiritual senses are those further senses which are signified by the things the words signify. As he says:

The author of [all] things can not only make use of words to

---

[11] q6 a3 obj.2.

[12] q6 a2 corp.

signify something, but also can arrange for things to be figures of other things. Because of this the truth is made plain in sacred Scripture in two ways. In one way insofar as things are signified by the words: and this is the literal sense. In another way by virtue of the fact that things are figures of other things: and this is what the spiritual sense consists in.[13]

Now it seems to follow from this that, for Thomas, the spiritual 'senses' of Scripture are not senses of the text itself – for only the literal sense is that – but are rather found in the signifying power of the historical events which Scripture, in its literal sense, truly records. Anything at all which belongs to the text of the Book is literal: whereas allegory, tropology and anagogy are senses authored by the Holy Spirit in the text of providential history. From this follows the mistake of those who, confused about this distinction, derive opportunity for freelance and arbitrary allegorizing from the mere presence of metaphor in the language of Scripture, who find in every utterance of poetry in Scripture an alibi for a plurality of meanings which threatens theological discourse with equivocity. In short, for Thomas, poetry as such has no exegetical or spiritual significance.

III

Equally hostile to this partiality for free-range allegorizing, equally committed to the priority of the literal sense, but motivated by different exegetical purposes, is the Franciscan Parisian Master of the fourteenth century, Nicholas of Lyra. Broadly, at any rate in the methodological introduction to his *Postilla Litteralis* on Scripture,[14] his distinction of senses follows Thomas. But for Nicholas the Song of Songs presents a particular problem not raised for his theoretical literalism by other texts of the Old Testament. To all appearances the Song is a collection of bawdy poems about a corrupt sexual liaison between unmarried partners. But a text consisting in so unworthy a narrative cannot

[13] q6 a1 corp.
[14] For a partial translation, see *Eros and Allegory*, pp. 383–90.

be what the Holy Spirit calls for spiritual meanings to be founded in. Hence, the literal referend of the Song cannot consist in the love affair between Solomon and the Shulamite woman.[15] But if not in that narrative, in what can the literal sense consist?

Nicholas' solution is ingenious, and very nearly unique in medieval Christian exegesis. It is to treat the entire first six chapters of the Song as an extended series of metaphors (*parabola*) not for christological mysteries, but for the history of Israel, that history in turn, serving, as on Thomas' account it should, as the foundation in historical fact (*res*), for allegory. Now this solution also depends upon a clear and Thomistic decision to regard all metaphor as part of the literal sense, since it is by metaphor that the Song literally denotes the Jewish history which, in turn, forms the basis of allegory. In turn, this move restores to prominence, from its condition of suppression in standard monastic-allegorical exegesis, the foundation of Christian interpretation of the Hebrew Scriptures in their Jewish truth: the *sensus litteralis* becomes again, as it had once before in Andrew of St Victor, the *sensus hebraicus*.

It does so all the more visibly in the anonymous *Expositio Hystorica*[16] on the Song composed sometime in the late thirteenth century – although Nicholas appears not to know of it. This *Expositio* is written *secundum Salomonem*, that is to say, following the hermeneutical principles of Rabbi Solomon ben Isaac, or 'Rashi', the Jewish commentator of eleventh-century Paris. In fact the *Expositio Hystorica* is an adaptation and paraphrase, as well as a Latin translation of, Rashi's commentary, composed by a Christian scholar. The author's intention was manifestly to follow Rashi as closely as he could, while rejecting anything in Rashi inconsistent with an orthodox Christian interpretation.

There is no need on this occasion to dwell on the necessary Christian revisions of Rashi's text, for what matters is that in principle, of course, any Christian attempt to read the Song in

---

[15] See *Eros and Allegory*, p. 394.

[16] *Secundum Salomonem: A Thirteenth-Century Latin Commentary on the Song of Solomon*, ed. S. Kamin and A. Saltman, Ramat Gan: Bar Ilan University Press, 1989.

Rashi's terms is bound to focus upon the common ground in a literal sense. For there, as in Nicholas, the anonymous Latinizing Christian can readily identify the literal sense with the *sensus hebraicus*. Consequently, following Rashi along a path of theoretical hermeneutics laid down already by Thomas and later to be followed by Nicholas, our Christian author composes an interpretation of the Song which is both in the strict sense 'literal' and at the same time not, in this literal sense, to be understood as the narrative of the mutual love of Solomon and the Shulamite woman. The author manifestly regards his position as consistent: the Song is both *literally 'about'* and *metaphor for* the history of Israel. He says:

> Solomon . . . composed this work in [the guise of] a metaphor of a woman who has been made a widow by her husband's desertion while he was still alive and she desires and longs to be restored to him and to be united to him by love, remembering as she does the love of her youth. The Bridegroom himself suffers for her in her misery, remembering the kindnesses of her youth and her beauty and honest behaviour, which had united her with him by powerful bonds of love; and he does so on this account, that he has not willingly afflicted her, nor has he rejected her unconditionally, for she is still his wife and he her husband.[17]

As the editors of the recent edition of the Latin text argue,[18] this reading of the Song as pure metaphor is consistent with its author's claim to be offering an *expositio hystorica* only on a principle which was first clearly argued for by Hugh of St Victor in the twelfth century and by Thomas more systematically in the thirteenth, namely that metaphor is part of the literal sense. To which one can add, that though Nicholas, as I say, appears not to know the Latin *Expositio*, he certainly does know his Rashi. And between them all agree on the following three hermeneutical propositions as regards the interpretation of the Song: first, that

---

17 *Expositio Hystorica*, 1. 9–16.

18 Kamin and Saltman, *Secundum Salomonem*, p. 12.

the Song is not literally about the love of Solomon and the Shulamite; secondly, that it is a work composed entirely of metaphor; and thirdly that the literal sense of the Song's metaphors lies in their reference to the history of Israel's relationship with her God.

Now the significance of this to our purposes is to remove support for a widespread and mistaken assumption. That assumption is that as medieval commentaries on the Song go, better justice is done to the authenticity of the Song's erotic text and texture the more attention is paid to its literal sense; that it is the remorselessly allegorizing and spiritualizing techniques of the monastic tradition – of Gregory, Bede, Alcuin, Honorius of Autun, Rupert of Deutz or of Thomas Gallus – which is alone responsible for the erotic pallidness of the medieval commentarial tradition. Not so. In point of erotic pallidness, scarcely anything in the whole Middle Ages matches the reduction in sexual tension of Nicholas of Lyra's terse but pedantic historicism; scarcely any medieval commentary provides so stark a contrast as does his between the rich, full-blooded eroticism of the text itself and the commentary upon it.

IV

Nonetheless, on the score of theoretical precision of hermeneutic, Thomas, and Nicholas following him, are, you might say, at least clear. But, I suggest, theirs is a dangerous and misleading clarity in so far as one reads other traditions of medieval scriptural commentary quite generally in the light of those precisions. Above all, we can be tempted to ask of Bernard of Clairvaux, just how clear he is about these things in his *Sermons on the Song of Songs*. And the answer to that question, addressed in any such terms to Bernard, can only be that Bernard is thoroughly confused as to hermeneutical theory and method.

Just how confused Bernard can look if you read his exegetical practice in the light of a Hugh of St Victor or a Thomas Aquinas or a Nicholas of Lyra, is easily illustrated by the following passage from *Sermon* 9.7:

> While the Bride is conversing about the Bridegroom, he, . . .,

> suddenly appears, yields to her desire by giving her a kiss . . . The filling up of her breasts is proof of this. For so great is the potency of that holy kiss, that no sooner has the bride received it than she conceives and her breasts grow rounded with the fruitfulness of conception, bearing witness, as it were, with this milky abundance. Men with an urge to frequent prayer will have experience of what I say. Often enough when we approach the altar our hearts are dry and lukewarm. But if we persevere, there comes an unexpected infusion of grace, our breast expands, as it were and our interior is filled with an overflowing love; and if someone were to press upon it then, this milk of sweet fecundity would gush forth in streaming richness. Let us hear the bridegroom: 'You have received, my love, what you asked for, and here is a sign to show you, your breasts are better than wine; henceforth you will know that you have received the kiss because you will be conscious of having conceived. That explains the expansion of your breasts, filled with a milky richness far surpassing the wine of worldly knowledge that can intoxicate indeed but with curiosity, not charity; it fills but does not nourish; puffs up but does not build up; pampers but does not strengthen.'[19]

Evidently you could ask of this passage, which is it: metaphor or allegory? In more huffily pedantic spirit still, you could ask whether Bernard does not mistakenly suppose that he is giving a properly allegorical reading of the Bride's breasts, when in fact all he is doing is extruding theological and spiritual lessons out of a rather over-worked metaphor. For after all, the connection between the swelling of a pregnant woman's breasts and the expanding bosom of meditative prayer is established only through what Thomas would later call *similitudines imaginariae*, not as he and Hugh thought was required by properly founded allegory, through the Holy Spirit's providential determination of real historical connections between Solomon's love for the Shulamite and the redemptive purposes of God. The 'likenesses' Bernard

[19] *Sermon* 9.7, in *Bernard of Clairvaux, On the Song of Songs*, vol. 1, ET Kilian Walsh OCSO, Kalamazoo: Cistercian Publications, 1977, pp. 58–9.

establishes between the language of the Song and the tropological discourse of his interpretation are abstract, de-historicized and, one has to say, often far-fetched exploitations of metaphors, where they are not mere similes. So you could say Bernard is just confused about that concerning which Hugh and Thomas are determined to be clear, namely, that whereas metaphor is, allegory is not, part of the meaning of the text, and that if you want a properly founded theology, you had better beware of extracting theological conclusions from mere metaphors. And of course you would say this were you to insist on pressing the exigences of Victorine and Thomist biblical method upon Bernard.

But I think it would be wrong to do this and wrong for a reason which goes well beyond the obvious anachronism of forcing a twelfth-century Cistercian's Song exegesis into the mould of a thirteenth-century schoolman of Paris, or even of the twelfth-century master of St Victor. The reason, I guess, is more general and has to do with fundamental differences of exegetical purpose. First, because as I have argued, Thomas' distinctions belong within a methodological project for a systematic theology in the mode of the schools. There, those distinctions are needed and they need to be made with the precision with which Hugh and Thomas make them. Bernard's reading of the Song, however, is made within a quite different, because homilectic, purpose, where the principal concern is not with epistemologically secure foundations for a dialectical theology, but with the practical direction of Cistercian monks. Bernard's concern is therefore not with the literal meanings on which a theological edifice can be built, but with the impact of his speech on lives; he is therefore less concerned with what the words of the Song in some scientific sense of the word 'literal' literally say, but with what it is that his saying them does, not with literal truth-bearing properties of language, but with the character of utterance as speech-act; not with exegetical truth, but with a homilectic and pastoral rhetoric. 'Today', he says, addressing (in fiction or in fact) his Cistercian brethren in chapter, 'Today we read in the book of experience.'[20]

---

[20] *Sermon* 3.1, p. 16.

It is for this reason that Bernard's reading of the Song is much more preoccupied with the erotic quality of the language itself, which he clearly values more in its capacity for spiritual arousal than in any narrative truth it may possess, a matter on which he is altogether silent. At the outset he declares that his fascination with the Song is for its language, not for its truth: he values it because it is a 'figurative language pregnant with delight',[21] thereby nicely eroticizing his metaphor for its eroticism; the Song's language is a 'melody . . . the very music of the heart . . . an inward pulsing of delight . . . [which] only the singer hears . . . and the one to whom he sings – the lover and the beloved';[22] and in more general terms he praises the quality of this language for its spiritual appropriateness:

> No sweeter names can be found to embody that sweet interflow of affections between the Word and the soul, than bridegroom and bride. Between these all things are equally shared, there are no selfish reservations, nothing that causes division. They share the same inheritance, the same table, the same marriage-bed, they are flesh of each other's flesh.[23]

And again he says of the Song's opening words, 'Let him kiss me with the kiss of his mouth':

> How delightful a ploy of speech [is] this, prompted into life by the kiss, with Scripture's own engaging countenance inspiring the reader and enticing him on, that he might find pleasure even in the laborious pursuit of what lies hidden, with a fascinating theme to sweeten the fatigue of research. Surely this mode of beginning that is not a beginning, this novelty of diction in a book so old, cannot but increase the reader's intention . . .[24]

Bernard could hardly be more positive in his welcome for that feature of the Song's language and imagery which, for many another monk, was the chief stimulus to burrow beneath it for alternative, more 'spiritual' meanings: the Song's explicit,

---

[21] *Sermon* 1.8, p. 5.
[22] *Sermon* 1.11, pp. 6–7.
[23] *Sermon* 7.2, p. 39.
[24] *Sermon* 1.5, pp. 3–4.

baroque eroticism. The Song's erotic frankness appears not to worry Bernard at all, on the contrary, he revels in it. But it did worry most monks. And it worried Nicholas of Lyra. Which is why if a Thomas had reasons of systematic theology for a careful distinction of the four senses, the average monk, sharing little of Thomas' scholastic interests, had an equally powerful, if very different reason for distinguishing them: for the average monastic commentator, the eroticism of the Song's language, threatened carnal danger, both personal and exegetical, and the four senses provided an exegetical method for the spiritualization of the Song's carnality. Hardly more different from the rhetorical confidence of Bernard of Clairvaux could be the exegetical timidity of the fifteenth-century Flemish Carthusian, Denys van Rykel, who is much troubled by the temptations which will afflict the minds of the spiritually immature when reading this text which, 'on the surface, seems so very sensual but on a true understanding proves to be very spiritual'.[25] For, he asks,

> What is to be done with those many religious and canons and others in holy orders who in Church and in the divine office will commonly hear or read these words, though not yet purified, who have hardly attained to a true and spiritual understanding and can scarcely read and hear these words at those times . . . without lewd imaginings? I think that they are to be advised to strive as far as possible to understand this book with purity of mind and in its true sense [which for Denys, of course, is anything but the literal] if they are to leave behind them every kind of unbecoming thought.[26]

Connected with this pious scruple there is in Denys, as there is not in Bernard, a very characteristic medieval monastic inversion. Few would have verbally contradicted Bernard's praise for the eroticism of the Song's language *as image*, intensely worrying as it

[25] Denys the Carthusian, *Enarratio in Canticum Canticorum*, art. 2, in *Doctoris Ecstatici Divi Dionysii Cartusiensis Opera Omnia*, vol. VII, Typis Cartusiae S.M. de Pratis: Montreuil, 1898, 296B; trans. in *Eros and Allegory*, p. 420.

[26] *In Cant.*, art. 2, p. 296A'–B', *Eros and Allegory*, p. 421.

was to many and lacking, as most were, in his outright enthusiasm for it. At all costs, however, the Song's carnality has to be denied any literal value and, as Denys insists,

> they are mistaken who think that this work should be read in its literal and historical sense as referring to Solomon and his bride, the daughter of Pharaoh and [only] allegorically to Christ and the Church. If this were so then the subject matter of this book would be of no worth, sensual and prurient and not spiritual, mystical, most excellent and heavenly; nor would it be a prophetic text, but rather a sort of love song.[27]

For which reason, in so far as Denys attaches any value to the erotic carnality of the Song's language it is as pure, but abstract, image. But what that image images is purely spiritual, realized most typically in the monastic way of life itself. Hence the need for a radical inversion of the Song's language and imagery. For a Denys the Carthusian, it is the monk who truly effects by celibacy what the erotic images by its carnality. Carnal marriage between woman and man is the sign, but the monk's mystical marriage to Christ is the reality signified. The sign, thereby, is successfully emptied, by means of allegory, into its spiritual significance. And so, by the device of allegorization, the text is denied its significance as poetry.

But this exegetical inversion is not there in Bernard, not there because he does not need it. Because Bernard appears less threatened by the Song's carnality of image, his *Sermons* differ very markedly in rhetorical tone not only from classical monastic commentary of his own times and later, but also from the standard scholastic commentary of the next century and beyond – as I have indicated, Nicholas of Lyra's literal *Postilla* is every bit as bloodless a thing rhetorically speaking as is Denys' hyperbolical allegorizing. Bernard's discourse resists that de-eroticization of the Song's carnality: on the contrary, he enthusiastically places that carnality in the foreground, emphasizing its erotic density. Bernard, we might say, 'foregrounds' the carnal image, and

---

[27] *In Cant.* Prol., p. 292, *Eros and Allegory*, p. 415.

the subtle interactions of the carnally sensual imagery and the spiritually sensual tropology which so characterize Bernard's *Sermons* quite defies analysis in terms of the hermeneutical schema of the four senses and is, in my view, altogether obscured by the attempt to impose it.

In short, it is my view that though clearly Bernard knows and assumes standard twelfth-century categorizations of literal and spiritual senses and sometimes consciously uses them, his employment of the erotic discourse of the Song is principally in the interests of an homilectic rhetoric of speech-act, not in those of a scientific exegesis of meaning; in the eroticization of the spiritual, not in spiritualization of the carnal; hence, his *Sermons* ought to be read not principally as allegory, but principally as poetry. In consequence, the doctrine of the four senses, as it came to him in the monastic traditions he inherited from Origen and Gregory the Great, could not have served any but the contrary of his poetic purpose, which was, if anything, best served by the rhetorical heightening of the Song's erotic tensions, not their exegetical slackening, by a rhetorical thickening of the erotic densities, not by their spiritualized evacuation. Bernard, in my view, is the poet of the Song's poetry.

15. Historical Criticism and Sacred Text

ROWAN WILLIAMS

The historical criticism of the Bible has found itself increasingly under attack over the last couple of decades, on two fronts. There is the complaint by theologians of very varied complexion that historical criticism, while purportedly neutral in philosophical terms, in fact has an agenda that is at least implicitly hostile to the theological use of Scripture in any serious way. The complaint may come from different sorts of conservative, from those who want to rehabilitate pre-modern methods of exegesis in which doctrinal considerations quite properly play a central role in determining acceptable readings; but equally from the various schools of theology that may broadly be called 'emancipationist' in their focus, liberationist and feminist theologies in particular. For these, the historical-critical method represents a model of epistemological dominance that has to be challenged, the pseudo-neutrality of Western modernity which disallows an 'interested' reading from the perspective of minorities, in the name of a rational discourse claiming universality.

And this relates to the second front of attack, that which derives its energy from different kinds of postmodern critical theory: the authority of origins is one of the themes most regularly contested in such theory, the notion that meaning can be secured and decisively defined by discovering the most primitive layer of a text's historical life – ideally the authorial intention. But texts are not like this; they live in the complex processes of revision, retelling and reception, and (for at least some in this milieu) there can be no decisively 'right' reading of any text. Historical criticism may have an interest as archaeology, but it contributes little or nothing to the business of interpretation.

To take just two fairly recent examples of the former trend, we might look at the 1998 special issue of *Modern Theology* on 'Theology and Scriptural Imagination'[1] and at the first volume of the 'Scripture and Hermeneutics' series sponsored by the Bible Society, *Renewing Biblical Interpretation,* published in 2000.[2] The former includes two essays on figural and allegorical reading (by John David Dawson and Robert Wilken), a long discussion by Alvin Plantinga of the hidden assumptions of historical criticism (it is intrinsically hostile to the miraculous), a novel and provocative argument from Kathryn Tanner for letting the Bible work as a 'popular' text, constantly refusing the standardization of interpretation offered by elites, and a good deal more. The Bible Society volume is a formidable collection (with a strikingly large representation of Old Testament scholars) ranging widely over issues of philosophical presuppositions and historical trends, offering (from Christopher Seitz) a groundbreaking discussion of some aspects of the history of nineteenth- and early-twentieth-century hermeneutics, to which I shall be returning, a helpful analysis of the methodology of 'critical realism' adopted by Tom Wright in his monumental project on the New Testament, a good deal on what sense we can now make of any theological reading of the Old Testament, and some spirited responses to the essays from John Riches (noting how some of the attacks ignore the actual development and rationale of the critical method) and Walter Brueggemann (observing a certain distance in the discussions from the actual business of interpreting in concrete circumstances). To read both these symposia is to realize that in the eyes of a good many the historical critical method is in crisis; though this is a conclusion that might be reached by plenty of students of current critical scholarship, especially in regard to the Gospels, where it is far from clear any longer what *counts* as a serious argument (the Jesus Seminar has a lot to answer for).

---

1 *Modern Theology* 14.2, April 1998.

2 Craig Bartholomew, Colin Greene and Karl Möller, (eds.), *Renewing Biblical Interpretation*, Carlisle: Paternoster Press, 2000.

On the postmodern side, we can look back to Frank Kermode's *The Genesis of Secrecy*[3] as an early contribution from quite outside the theological world; and a number of studies from other scholars whose basic formation is also in literary criticism and critical theory, especially in the USA, writers like Elizabeth Castelli[4] and Regina Schwartz,[5] both of whom have been active in developing biblical commentary of a new kind untrammelled by doctrinal or ecclesial interest (though, I should say, replete with theological interest). Here the concerns are with what some theorists have called the world in front of the text, and the text's role in concealing, reinforcing, subverting, inverting (sometimes all at once) the dispositions of ideological power in its environment. We are dealing not only with a hermeneutic of suspicion, but also with the further stage of making a text of real or potential oppressiveness, moral ambivalence, yield an internal suspicion towards its own process. We are very far here from any conventional concern with original intentions.

From both sides of this assault on the centrality, even the integrity, of the historical critical method, it is possible to see what a substantial task is opened up for theology. In this essay, my intention is to consider these two critiques as posing two distinct, though obviously related questions, tackling which gives us some sense of what the theological task will involve. Very broadly: the postmodern agenda prompts the question, 'What is a *text*?'; the postcritical theological agenda asks, 'What is a *sacred* text?' If we can hold those questions together, I believe that some useful illumination may be gained in our thinking about the future of theologically serious hermeneutics.

---

[3] Frank Kermode, *The Genesis of Secrecy: On the Interpretation of Narrative*, Cambridge, MA: Harvard University Press, 1979.

[4] See, for example, her essay on Romans in *Searching the Scriptures: A Feminist Commentary*, ed. Elisabeth Schüssler Fiorenza, vol. 2, New York: Crossroad, 1994; London: SCM Press, 1995, pp. 272–300; and her involvement in editing *The Postmodern Bible* with the Bible and Culture Collective.

[5] See especially Regina Schwartz, *The Curse of Cain: The Violent Legacy of Monotheism*, Chicago: University of Chicago Press, 1997.

What is a text?

To begin with generalities: a text is a *representation*, in two obvious senses. It is writing that claims to represent the world; or a train of thought; or a 'structure of feeling' (Walter Davis's phrase).[6] It claims attention; it proclaims itself as a mediation of reality that requires assent. But it is also a representation of the conditions of its own production; and the task of interpretation is to make plain the contradictions between what the text says it represents and what it represents of its own conditionedness. When Derrida makes his famous claim that there is nothing outside the text, he is simply registering (as Kevin Hart spells out in his admirable essay on Derrida, *The Trespass of the Sign*)[7] the omnipresence of mediation and therefore of the task of deconstructive reading (reading so as to bring to light the contradiction between the two levels of representation). This does not imply that the 'real' meaning is the second kind of representation; that is the error of modern rationalism (Freudian or Marxist, for instance), which identifies interpretation with genealogy. Rather the process of interpretation is a dissolution of what we might initially or instinctively expect 'meaning' to be – the transparency of text to what it represents. 'Culture is often the site of our reification in structures of feeling that are insidious; but it is also the site of struggles for liberation that are uniquely revelatory. The trick is not to see it as solely one or the other. Every text potentially involves both things, in unstable relationship.'[8]

Thus, between the poles of authorial intention and cultural conditionedness there opens up another territory for interpretation, potentially limitless: what is going on in the exchange between author and context that allows the product of that exchange (the text) to offer itself or invite in ways that do not wholly depend upon either factor? Against the background of

[6] Walter Davis, *Inwardness and Existence: Subjectivity in/and Hegel, Heidegger, Marx and Freud*, Madison: University of Wisconsin Press, 1989, p. 229.

[7] Kevin Hart, *The Trespass of the Sign: Deconstruction, Theology and Philosophy*, Cambridge: Cambridge University Press, 1989, pp. 25ff.

[8] Davis, *Inwardness and Existence*, p. 228.

social and ideological constraint, what is the *diference* of the text? This may reveal itself dramatically in the breakdown of a received or conventional form, a breakdown of which the author may not even be aware; less dramatically in the generation of new metaphors or conceptual structures. And for the interpreter the implication is that the text as it stands is first and foremost a *product* – not a neutral archaeological site. The concern with redaction within orthodox critical scholarship reflects this, of course; but it has often been limited by excessive or exclusive interest in the conscious intent of an author or group, and a model of rewriting that does not give adequate consideration to what might be called intra-textual strain as a motive for exploring new idioms or images. Furthermore, the interpreter does not simply look at what strains or contradictions the text seeks to overcome and which the text, consciously or unconsciously, represents; he or she will also be alert to the fresh contradictions or strains set up by the text, inviting further textual elaboration – the unfinished business of any and every text. Understanding this is a precondition for beginning to see how or why a text escapes its authorial and social/ideological context.

One striking fact about the biblical text in this respect is that it proclaims unambiguously its own 'produced' character. It is visibly a collection of discrete compositions; it abounds in cross-reference; for the Christian reader, it is in a very strong sense a re-visioning of a textual tradition, it is already itself an act of interpretation (rereading Hebrew Scripture); it displays an inner literary history (narrative texts reworking other narrative texts, from Chronicles and Kings to Matthew and Mark). Precisely because it displays its character in this way, however, we cannot simply begin from a finished textual synthesis: we are always confronted with the material for synthesis in its relative textual integrity. In plainer terms, Chronicles does not replace Kings, nor Matthew Mark. It means that it is possible to see the history of rewriting as both response to existing tensions and evasion of existing tensions. We are not licensed to relegate earlier strata in a textual history to hermeneutical irrelevance.

This, I take it, is the point being made by Christopher Seitz in the essay already cited,[9] where he complains that early-twentieth-century Anglican exegesis replaced a theology of the text with a theory of religion, a narrative in which the text's history was subsumed in a story of developing understanding or maturity in a religious community – the implication being that earlier strata had no more than evidential significance for this story, rather than raising issues of meaning in their own right (and, more specifically, issues of the meaning of God). The nature of the biblical text allows us to give due weight to what we might call a pathos of reading: the new textual moment emerges from the unmanageable contradictions of available speech in a changing situation; but it is also, in its attempt to resolve or remove a contradiction, potentially a moment of *loss*, diminution of meaning. We read this composite biblical text to understand not only the proposed resolutions, but to be aware of what losses occur as text responds to text; to be aware of how the question may be 'fuller' than the answer, or at least the articulated answer.

In all this, the tools of the historical critical method are in fact essential – so long as they are clearly separated from an interpretative method mortgaged to genealogy, an assumption that the earlier is the authentic, or to evolutionism, an assumption that the later is the finished, the definitive. Part of our problem is that such separation has not been all that common. To read, say, Deuteronomy is to acknowledge both its unfinished business, what it was that ensured Deuteronomy was not the last word in Scripture, and its integrity as posing the question of the meanings of God in its own terms. Its status and claim do not depend upon what it generates in later textual reflection: to stay with its inherent stresses and aporiai as well as its achievement as text, and not to relegate it to a stage in a longer story is fundamental to a reading that grasps what sort of composite text Scripture is overall. But at the same time its posing of the question of the meanings of God is not quite the same thing as its statement of

[9] Christopher Seitz, 'Scripture Becomes Religion(s): The Theological Crisis of Serious Biblical Interpretation in the Twentieth Century', in Bartholomew, Greene and Möller, *Renewing Biblical Interpretation*, pp. 40–65, especially pp. 46–52.

what it intends to 'represent'. We read with an eye to tensions within the text, to the voices on its edge, to what it opposes or suppresses, so far as we can discern. It takes its place within the entire composite text of Scripture as an element already communicating the meanings of God through its inner conversations and stresses and self-reflection or self-subversion. And the same is true, *a fortiori,* of the whole of Hebrew Scripture over against Christian: to quote Seitz, 'It speaks of God as God is, and does this through its own literary form, without necessity of the construction of religious history.'[10] When we say that Scripture must be interpreted by Scripture, we must not take this as a licence to subordinate the meanings of Deuteronomy to meanings that are 'better' or more fully articulated elsewhere. Only when the meanings of Deuteronomy have been explored fully in their own right can we do justice to the convergence of scriptural meanings; but more of that later.

So the point of considering first the question, 'What is a text?' is to remind us that textual representation is intrinsically complex and tense. The classical historico-critical approach, with its interest in origins and its compulsive tendency to reduce textual material to evidence for a developmental narrative, misses something of this complexity. Texts are preserved because they speak of more than the circumstances that produced them; to see this, we also need as full a conspectus as possible of those circumstances – but we need a sensitivity to what in the text is 'excessive' and therefore unsettled, to its representation of a question, of a tension for which the words are not yet clear. That representation has to be pondered and absorbed at one level *independently* of the way in which an 'answering' or 'completing' text offers to resolve its difficulties. A text within the overall text of Scripture must, then, be read simultaneously as creating the conditions for another textual element and as standing in its own terms unresolved (and posing the meanings-of-God question in its own right).

---

[10] Seitz, 'Scripture Becomes Religion(s)', p. 62.

What is a sacred text?

In what has been said so far, I have already begun to move into this second area by introducing talk about the meanings of God. Let us try to spell this out further. Any text, according to the sort of theory I have espoused here, is engaged with its context in a way that produces both a representation of that context's contradictions and an attempted representation of a way beyond those contradictions. A good reading of any text involves seeing how the text establishes its difference from the context (its excess over already available meanings), thus setting up a new chain of textual reflection and response, as well as seeing how it repeats what is received, consciously and unconsciously. What is distinctive about reading Scripture is the conviction that it is a sacred text; and a sacred text, I suggest, is one for which the context is always more than the social-ideological matrix. This cannot be established, of course, by historical study or phenomenological analysis. It arises from a reading context that assumes a continuity between the world of the text and the world of the reader, and also assumes that reader and text are responding to a gift, an address or a summons not derived from the totality of the empirical environment. In other words: what the text represents is not only the conversation between writer and social-ideological environment, but also a conversation with a presence that is not a rival speaker, a participant in the exchange and negotiation of empirical speakers (which makes it a very strange conversation, of course). We read *this* text as sacred because it represents the possibility and actuality of relation with more than a competing speaker – a relation which, in so far as it takes us beyond the world of negotiating speakers and rival exercises of power and determination, has the character of grace or liberation.

Thus the question that will arise from reading a sacred text as sacred (as opposed to a pragmatic recognition that this text is sacred for somebody) is, 'How is the text unsettled, made "tense", driven into contradiction, by the address of God, as well as by the tensions of the social-ideological context? In what way is the active, transcendent other "inscribed" in its workings?' Again, there is a longstanding problem in exegesis: interpretation that takes this question seriously has habitually assumed that the answer must be in terms of a simple representation of the divine mind or will (leading to unsustainable doctrines of biblical inerrancy). This is very close indeed to the characteristic problem of rationalist interpretation of any kind, the desire to find in the text a transparency to what it represents (as if there could be what amounts to a knowledge without representation, without mediation). A theological exegesis is not one that assumes such transparency in the text, but one that looks for those contradictions between intention and performance, those marks of excess and of intra-textual strain that might have to do not only with immediate ideological context but with God.

Deuteronomy, to be specific, can be read as an essay in moralizing the history of ancient Israel, developed against the background of an historical context where 'reform' of the kingdom's institutions repeatedly fails; at this level, it is an ideological enterprise like others. But if we go a little further in our reading, we might pick up the cognate themes in Deuteronomy and the Deuteronomic literature which assert that God's creation of a people is in the first instance an act of pure, gratuitous will and that therefore God's relation with any specific order in Israelite society is at best contingent and at worst adversarial. In the treatment of these themes, Deuteronomy and the related literature leave an 'excess' of strangeness, as it were a refusal to put the question in terms of how God's interaction with the kingdom can be morally explicated. This, the theologian might say, is the excess of grace, the placing of the social-ideological context in the wider context of divine agency. To read this as *witness* of course requires more than hermeneutical skill in the ordinary sense; it requires what I have elsewhere[11] called analogical skill, making a connection between the context of the scriptural process or narrative and

---

[11] Rowan Williams, 'The Discipline of Scripture', in *On Christian Theology,* Oxford: Blackwell, 2000, pp. 44–59; cf. idem, 'The Unity of the Church and the Unity of the Bible', *Internationale Kirchliche Zeitschrift,* 91.1, January/March 2001, pp. 5–21.

the context of the reader. More plainly, in this case, it requires the contemporary sense of belonging in a community existing by gift and incapable of guaranteeing grace by its own good order, and recognizing in the scriptural text the source and rationale of such a community identity as the effect of the pressure of God. The text represents the priority of divine action in various ways – not by being undialectically transparent to God's self-imparted meaning, but by exhibiting the reality of divine pressure in the unfinished character of its theological rationalizations, the excess of reference to divine election and judgement which tends to relativize its systematic solution to the moral puzzle of Israel's history.

The analogical skill itself presupposes something further: a principle of assumed unity between textual world and reader's world that is not simply a continuity of ideas or a simple subordination of reader's world to the surface categories of textual world. For the Jewish reader of Jewish Scripture, this is primarily the sheer continuity of the people's identity: for the Jew now and the Jew in the 'then' of the text, the common factor is the givenness of divine choice and call (once again, Deuteronomy illustrates this by its assimilation of the ritual hearers of the text in the present to the Israelites in the desert with Moses). For the Christian, a similar structure is at work; but in this case the choice and call are anchored in the act of God in Jesus. Those who read this text as sacred from the Christian point of view thereby identify themselves with those who first encountered the incarnate Saviour, with those who first heard the proclamation of his resurrection; and, by a further turn in the argument, with those who heard the call of God in Israel's history, since it is understood that the God who calls is not only in general terms 'the same God' but more specifically the God who is made flesh in Jesus, so that the reading of Jewish Scripture is shaped by what is heard in Jesus. And this analogical structure and the quite complex unity it suggests tell us that the hearing of God at any one point does not exhaust God's speaking. The actual historical process in which Scripture is produced does not, in its attempt to respond to the gift of God, contain or confine that gift. Equally, the response we make now to the text does not contain or confine the meanings of

God – which is why we read alert for deeper 'senses' of the text, and why we never finish reading Scripture.

The sacred text thus enacts its sacred character not by its transparency but by its nature as unresolved, unfinished, self-reflexive or self-questioning. It is through these things that its 'excess' appears – its character as not determined by the matrix from which it historically comes or by the conceptual frameworks it constructs. After all, if God is as the narrative presents God, it will not be possible to translate God without remainder into either narrative or conceptuality. The only 'translation', for the Christian reader, is the action of Jesus, who is 'transparent' to God not as a speaker of unmediated divine truths, but as an agent who effects the purpose or desire of God without interruption. It is against this background, I think, that Peter Ochs, writing from a Jewish perspective, can describe Scripture as a 'performance' of the divine Name.[12] God names God in Scripture as the unconditioned and uncaptured, apprehended as such only in the upheavals and new beginnings of the history of those God encounters in grace and freedom.

Conclusions

It will be fairly clear that I am not by any means advocating a suspension or rejection of historico-critical scholarship; but its use within theology, I suggest, needs to be considered in the light of some of the questions raised about what a text is and what a sacred text is. Otherwise, theology itself (returning to the point made by Seitz) puts itself in thrall to a theory of religion, phenomenological and historical in character, for which the analogical contemporaneity (forgive the jargonish shorthand) of the text has no real meaning. The challenging theological task is something to do with making sense of the unity presupposed between generations of hearers; with having a way of explaining how and why we suppose the same God to be at work, in a way that is more

[12] Peter Ochs, 'Scriptural Logic: Diagrams for a Postcritical Metaphysics', *Modern Theology* 11.1, 1995, pp. 65–92.

than strictly a matter of conceptual compatibility. Thus, as has often been said, there can be no sensible Christian theology of Scripture without a careful Christology and an ecclesiology to match – a way of construing the unity-as-called of God's people, comparable to the categories that Jewish faith can deploy in setting out its continuity across contexts. Critical work crucially exposes for us, in greater richness than in a pre-critical age, the specific tensions and constraints, what Davis calls 'the breaks, gaps and binds in the text',[13] which constitute its 'difference'. It imposes also, I believe, one simple discipline on the interpreter: while history will not settle issues of meaning, interpretation that is strictly *incompatible* with what we can know of the history of a text's production will not do, to the extent that it trains us to look away from the actual difference of the text.

It is not just premature, it is theologically wrong-headed to write off the historical-critical method and its relevance for constructive theology. We may look for a postcritical theology, but it will not be one that ignores the critical moment. If we do proceed theologically in a way that – at least – assumes a bit of critical distance about the deliverances of critical analysis, and does not wait nervously for the critical consensus to be established beyond reasonable doubt (an uncomfortably long wait, on any showing) we need to make sure that this is not an attempt to secure a place beyond mediation and history; and for this we need more candid and imaginative work on the nature of the reading community – which means, ultimately, on the nature of the agency that creates and nurtures that community. Put as briefly as possible, a doctrine of Scripture requires a doctrine of God.

---

[13] Davis, *Inwardness and Existence*, p. 230.

16. 'Salvation History': The Truth of Scripture and Modern Theology[1]

MARTIN HENGEL

The term 'salvation history' (*Heilsgeschichte*) is not in favour in modern theology. Although it denotes a fundamental theological problem, namely the relationship between salvation and history, many people are not happy with it. And with good reason. The term is relatively recent. It was introduced into theological discussion by Johann Christian Hofmann with his work *Weissagung und Erfüllung* (Prophecy and Fulfilment), published in 1844. For him the whole of Scripture was prophetic history leading up to the salvation brought by Christ, a history the truth of which is recognized only by those who have been 'born again'. His scheme broke both with orthodoxy and with the theology of idealism stamped by Hegel and Schleiermacher, but proved unable to establish itself. However, the term 'salvation history' continued to be influential, above all in biblicism with a pietistic character, which discovered in Holy Scripture the stages of a universal and harmonious divine plan of salvation. No wonder that this preferred use of the term provoked antipathy elsewhere.

There are fewest reservations when the term is used in the Old Testament. For who will doubt that there a series of schemes of 'salvation' history exist side by side and interwoven? Indeed the scheme of the whole Old Testament canon from the creation to the book of Daniel tends in this direction – regardless of whether the stories told in it are historical or mythological. They remain

[1] For the translation I thank the Revd Dr John Bowden.

part of the historical experience in faith of God's people with their one God.

However, outside the Old Testament the term is largely rejected.

In the new fourth edition of *Die Religion in Geschichte und Gegenwart* my friend and colleague from the Tübinger Stift, the Erlangen theologian Friedrich Mildenberger,[2] recommends that the term should not be used because of the difficulties associated with it, since here 'the modern construction of history takes the place of the biblical discourse'.

In the third edition Heinrich Ott,[3] Karl Barth's successor in Basel, saw the term as a problem: here 'the content of faith is *objectified* . . . which goes against the nature of faith', and the 'object of faith is developed in the scheme of a succession, whereas . . . faith . . . is an act of present-day experience'. He also argues that the linear understanding of time is 'questionable in view of the eternal, eschatological reality of God'.

The term 'saving facts' (*Heilstatsachen*) has been dropped completely: here, according to the Marburg theologian Hans Grass, 'revelation is falsified so that it becomes a fact of the past that can be ascertained objectively'.[4]

The new *Theologische Realenzyklopädie* (*TRE*) does not have a separate article and refers the reader to the composite article on history.[5] Whereas in the Old Testament Klaus Koch[6] has no problems in using the term, in the New Testament it causes difficulties for Ulrich Luz.[7] As early as 1968, in his monograph on Paul's understanding of history,[8] in a critical discussion of

---

[2] *Die Religion in Geschichte und Gegenwart*, fourth edn, Tübingen: Mohr (Siebeck), 2000, vol. 3, pp. 1584–6.

[3] *Die Religion in Geschichte und Gegenwart*, third edn (*RGG*³), Tübingen, Mohr (Siebeck), 1959, vol. 3, pp. 187–9.

[4] *RGG*³, vol. 3, pp. 193f.

[5] *TRE*, Berlin: de Gruyter, vol. 12, 1984, pp. 565–698 with different authors.

[6] *TRE* 12, pp. 571–86.

[7] Ibid., pp. 595–604.

[8] Ulrich Luz, *Das Geschichtsverständnis des Paulus*, Münich: Christian Kaiser Verlag, 1968, pp. 14f.

Oscar Cullmann's work he described the term as 'unhelpful' and avoided it. At that time he was less interested in history than in the 'historicity' (*Geschichtlichkeit*) – in the sense of the historical character of the existence of the individual and his existential experience of salvation.[9] Moreover he claimed that, for Paul, from Adam to Christ the whole of history is not salvation history (*Heilsgeschichte*) but a history of ill (*Unheilsgeschichte*). Although in his *TRE* article written fifteen years later Luz agreed with Gadamer now against Heidegger (and Bultmann) that 'history comes before the historicity (*Geschichtlichkeit*) of the individual',[10] he avoids the term 'salvation history', which he continues to find questionable, and emphasizes, against Cullmann, that 'Paul's theology (cannot be) depicted as a scheme of salvation history',[11] because Paul speaks of God's saving action only at a particular point in time.

In the systematic theological section of the *TRE* article Wolfhart Pannenberg[12] attempts initially to pass a positive judgement on the concern of the 'theologians of salvation history'. However, since his heart is set on the bold programme of a 'theology of world history'[13] which comprises both religions and cultures, he too avoids the term and emphasizes that these conservative theologians could not really take up 'the results of modern historical criticism', and opened up a gulf between the historical reconstruction and their salvation-historical view. He argues that 'a theology of salvation history' must come to grief on this dualism, which he finds in Barth and Cullmann.

One could, though, ask whether the attempts at a comprehensive theology of history can be described as a universal synthesis of culture and whether there are historical facts which do not have an associated 'interpretation', since human memory itself and thus historical tradition selects in accordance with

---

[9] Luz, *Das Geschichtsverständnis des Paulus*, p. 17.

[10] Ibid., pp. 204ff.: Even Abraham could here only 'appear as an isolated person in the sea of the history of ill' (p. 206).

[11] *TRE* 12, p. 595.

[12] Ibid., pp. 668–74.

[13] Ibid., pp. 669ff.

'significance'. And should we dispense with the term salvation history altogether because it is wrongly used in an 'unhistorical uncritical way' (what theological term has not suffered that fate?) and because today above all circles close to fundamentalism wrongly appeal to it? I know of no better word to denote what has been a burning problem since the Enlightenment. Perhaps the mistake in early usage lay in the attempt to use it to build a closed system, a tendency which is also evident in Cullmann, as is already shown by the German title of his magnum opus *Heil als Geschichte*.[14] This seems to have been pointed out to him, since he insisted that the title of the English translation should be *Salvation in History*. It is not a matter of building systems but of seeing the problems which lead up to this controversial concept.

After this short anthology of critics I want to point out a feature of biblical history and church history. From Genesis 1 to Revelation 22 the Bible is the book of the universal 'salvation history'. This shows that the Christian religion and its Jewish mother religion are *bound up with history* – in a universal and individual sense. At the beginning comes the 'primal history' of the world and humankind and at the end its consummation. The former ends by being radically reduced to one person, Abraham, from whom the history of God's chosen people Israel unfolds. The latter again concentrates on a single figure, Jesus Christ, the incarnate Son of God, who reconciles humanity with its creator, from whom it has fallen away, and leads to perfect communion with God.

Why should we not be able to use the term *Heilsgeschichte*, 'salvation history', as a description of such a body of writings? That is how the Bible has been understood from the beginning. The fact that there is always also a 'history of ill', an *Unheilsgeschichte*, under the domination of sin is no objection, for it is the ill that calls for God's saving action in his Son, and this too always happens only in judgement and grace. It is the conclusion to Paul's gospel in Rom. 11.32: 'God has consigned all to dis-

---

[14] Oscar Cullmann, *Heil als Geschichte. Heilsgeschichtliche Existenz im Neuen Testament*, Tübingen: Mohr (Siebeck), 1965.

obedience, that he may have mercy on all.' Melanchthon in his *Apologia* can boldly term the forgiveness of sins the *causa finalis historiae*, the final cause of history.[15]

No wonder that up to the time of the early Enlightenment the Bible became the key to world history. I need recall only Irenaeus's economy of salvation and Augustine's City *of God*, a work which dominated the Christian picture of history for more than 1000 years. For Luther and Melanchthon, Scripture, Church and world history formed a unity. 'In its ultimate significance history was salvation history', which, as in Augustine, from the beginning was 'steeped in a metaphysical dualism' that will only really become manifest at its end.[16] In other words, it is primarily the sphere of action of the *hidden God*, which human beings cannot see through. Therefore what happens in the world can seem to Luther to be 'God's mummery, under which he conceals himself and rules and rumbles so wondrously in the world'.[17] Only in faith, that is, in the perspective of the crucified Christ and his salvation, can the Christian recognize God's action in the present and in history as judgement and grace. Is not this statement still fundamentally true today – in view of the terrible twentieth century that lies behind us, and the twenty-first century that is so uncertain?

This unity fell apart in the seventeenth- and eighteenth-century Enlightenment. A secular science of history developed which Ernst Troeltsch describes like this: 'It demolished the previous picture of history, orientated on the Apocalypse or on Augustine; it discovered a hitherto unknown world, opened up incalculable periods of time and dismissed the fall [of Adam the protoplast] from the focal point of history . . . In it individuals are now the focal points of history and social structures develop from their

---

15 'Apologia Confessionis Augustanae', in *Die Bekenntnisschriften der evangelisch-lutherischen Kirche*, Göttingen, 1930, p. 170 §51: Itaque non satis est credere, quod Christus natus, passus, resuscitatus sit, nisi addimus et hunc articulum, qui est causa finalis historiae: remissionem peccatorum. Ad hunc articulum referri cetera oportet.

16 G. A. Benrath, *TRE* 12, p. 630.

17 Luther, WA 15, 373, as quoted by Benrath, *TRE* 12, p. 631.

calculating interaction.'[18] Here I want to mention one English name, Lord Bolingbroke, whose *Letters on the Study and Use of History* (1753) according to Troeltsch provided 'the decisive thrust' and of whom Voltaire said that he had 'destroyed the insanities of theology' (*les demences théologiques*). From now on, 'Man is the subject of every history'.

From the second half of the eighteenth century on, the Protestant faculties of theology in Germany more and more became the arena of a fight over the truth of the Bible, a fight in which those who claimed to represent philosophical and thus theological progress regarded themselves as the victors. There was no longer any room for a *historia sacra* and it was replaced by 'immanent' movements: the 'education of the human race' guided by reason, or the absolute Spirit becoming conscious of itself in human thought. Among theologians who laid claim to 'intellectual honesty', any concrete activity of God in history or even a 'miracle' which destroyed the coherence of nature might no longer take place. 'Supernaturalism' became the theological term of abuse. Revelation could take place only within the pious subject. To a progressive theology, Hofmann's attempt to develop a theology of salvation history, which I mentioned at the start of this paper, or the attempt by his contemporary Vilmar[19] to set 'the theology of facts' over against a 'theology of rhetoric' inevitably seemed unscholarly supernaturalism.

As an example, here is the judgement of Albert Eichhorn, one of the fathers of the history-of-religions school, on two leading nineteenth-century thinkers in the article *Heilige Geschichte* ('Sacred History') in the first edition of the *RGG*, published in 1910:[20] 'Schleiermacher quite deliberately ignored all saving facts: for him the Christian religion was the absolute strength of the awareness of God in Christ and the stimulating effects

[18] *Realencyklopädie für protestantische Theologie und Kirche*³, Leipzig, vol. 2, 1897, p. 231.

[19] On A. F. C. Vilmar (1800–68) see *RGG*³, vol. 6, pp. 1401ff. His main work was *Die Theologie der Tatsachen wider die Theologie der Rhetorik* (1856; fourth edn 1876; new edition by H. Sasse 1938).

[20] *RGG*¹, vol. 2, 1910, pp. 2023–7.

that this has on us.' 'And for Hegel Christianity was the *idea* of the unity of God and man, God-humanity, an idea which, given in Christ, then developed on all sides.' In conclusion Eichhorn confessed: 'The answer can only be: "Science in its strictness and religion in its depth can no longer allow a special activity of God to be demarcated externally from everything else that happens in the world. The primal source of religion lies within the religious person."'

A turning-point came with the exposition of the Letter to the Romans by a Swiss village pastor at the end of the First World War. This must be described as a 'prophetic' work, which made clear the crisis in what thought itself to be progressive liberal theology, its cultivation of the religious individual and its radical criticism. However, initially Karl Barth hardly had the term 'salvation history' in mind. In the nineteenth century, history itself had been understood too much as a religious and moral way towards realizing the kingdom of God within this world. Karl Barth had grown up in the milieu of this theology.

His concern now was with the invasion of this world by God's eternity 'vertically from above'. Jesus Christ alone 'is the meaning of history'.[21] So theology must be wholly and utterly eschatology. And therefore the real 'salvation history' is only 'the ongoing crisis of all history, not a history *in* or *alongside* history'.[22] Like Kierkegaard, Barth was concerned with the 'infinite qualitative difference between man and God'.[23]

However, around twenty years later Karl Barth deliberately retracted his views in his *Church Dogmatics*. Now he could use the problematical term openly and in many senses. Here are just a few examples.[24]

The starting-point is the man Jesus. He is the 'human central

---

[21] Karl Barth, *Der Römerbrief*, 2nd edn, Münich: Christian Kaiser Verlag, 1922, p. 5.

[22] Ibid., p. 32.

[23] Ibid., p. 73. From all authors he quoted Kierkegaard most.

[24] See Karl Barth, *Kirchliche Dogmatik* (*KD*), Registerband, Zürich: EVZ Verlag, 1970, p. 246: Heilsgeschichte; p. 240: Geschichte; p. 225: Bundesgeschichte.

fact' of history.[25] So 'his history' is 'the covenant-, salvation- and revelation-history inaugurated by God';[26] indeed it can 'be the salvation history of all (human beings)', because 'in it God reconciles the world with himself'.[27] When he speaks of God as creator, Barth emphasizes that God is at the same time 'subject and lord of salvation history'. So in the mythical primal history sinful human beings become God's partner in dialogue. This means selection, separation, election and call. Barth concludes: 'The meaning and the mystery of the creation and preservation of the world becomes evident in salvation history. And the meaning and mystery of salvation history itself is Jesus Christ.'[28]

Karl Barth was the most important German-speaking theologian of the twentieth century. As such he became the spiritual father of the Confessing Church. Without him the Church would hardly have come to resist. We may count this among *his* 'salvation-historical influences'.

Over against him stood Rudolf Bultmann as the most influential exegete. Both had the same teacher, Wilhelm Hermann, in Marburg. However, whereas Barth broke rigorously with his 'liberal' past but did not become conservative in the traditional sense and went new ways, Bultmann attempted to adopt a middle course. Impressed on the one hand by 'dialectical theology', he wanted to take up the basic concern of the message of primitive Christianity and Reformation, but at the same time to preserve the critical legacy of liberal theology. This is true above all of his programme of demythologizing. He had to reject the notion of a salvation history decisively. That is evident from his argument with Oscar Cullmann.

Cullmann drew a salvation-historical line in time extending from creation, through the Christ event and the time of the Church, to the end of the world. He claimed that at the centre

---

[25] *KD* III/2, p. 191 relates to a sentence from A. Harnack, *Das Wesen des Christentums*, that Jesus Christ stood in the centre of the history of humanity.

[26] *KD* III/2, p. 192.

[27] *KD* IV/2, p. 38, see p. 91.

[28] *KD* II/1, pp. 569–76, quotations pp. 570, 576.

of this time was the saving event in Christ, through which the powers hostile to God are defeated and there is the dawn of the hidden rule of Christ which becomes manifest in his parousia. Thus the time between stands under the sign of the 'already and not yet'. The resurrection is the anticipation of the eschaton. So salvation in Christ presents itself as history.[29]

Bultmann accused Cullmann of transforming the primitive Christian message of salvation into a supranaturalistic, objectifying philosophy of history. He claimed that Cullmann's apocalyptic picture of history was no longer acceptable to modern thought. According to Paul and John, Christ is not 'the middle' but the 'end of history', and in being addressed by the kerygma believers are called on to gain a new understanding of themselves as God's creatures The notion of 'salvation history', Bultmann argued, required faith to hold objective 'worldly' saving facts to be true, but that was not appropriate for faith. The decisive thing was not 'salvation history' but the punctual 'saving event' and the 'detachment from the world' (*Entweltlichung*) which is given by it: this takes place in the constantly new decision for the kerygma. Jesus has risen into the kerygma.[30]

---

[29] R. Bultmann wrote a very critical review of O. Cullmann, *Christus und die Zeit. Die urchristliche Zeit- und Geschichtsauffassung*, Zürich: Zollikon, 1946 (ET *Christ and Time*, London: SCM Press, 1951; rev. edn, 1962), under the title 'Heilsgeschichte und Geschichte', *Theologische Literaturzeitung* 73 (1946) = *Exegetica*, Tübingen: Mohr (Siebeck), 1967, pp. 356–68. O. Cullmann reworked his former thesis in *Heil als Geschichte. Heilsgeschichtliche Existenz im Neuen Testament*, Tübingen: Mohr (Siebeck), 1965 (ET *Salvation in History*, London: SCM Press, 1965). On his theology see now Karl-Heinz Schlaudraff, *'Heil als Geschichte'? Die Frage nach dem heilsgeschichtlichen Denken anhand der Konzeption Oscar Cullmanns*, Beiträge zur Geschichter der biblischen Exegese 29, Tübingen: Mohr (Siebeck), 1988.

[30] On Bultmann's sharpening criticism against all forms of 'Heilsgeschichte' see the index of the recently published volume: R. Bultmann, *Theologie als Kritik. Ausgewählte Rezensionen und Forschungsberichte*, ed. M. Drescher and Klaus W. Müller, Tübingen: Mohr (Siebeck), 2002, Index p. 597 s. v. 'Heilsgeschichte'. He even criticized C. H. Dodd sharply in Dodd's own 'Festschrift' (!) (W. D. Davies and D. Daube, (eds.), *The Background of the New Testament and Its Eschatology*, Cambridge: Cambridge University Press, 1954, pp. 402–8 = *Theologie als Kritik*, pp. 477–

We get the impression that here we have a confrontation between two closed systems with two different forms of faith. Cullmann calls more for the *fides quae*, Bultmann for the *fides qua creditur*. However, faith is not just an act, but also has a content. Nor may it be reduced to a mathematical point. It is based on the *history* of Jesus Christ; otherwise primitive Christianity would not have produced any narrative gospels.

I now want to make some fragmentary references to the problem of 'salvation history' which we cannot want to evade if we are concerned about the future of a *Christian* theology and its truth.

I shall begin with some basic presuppositions:

God, the creator of the world, is also the Lord of its history. However, we must speak of *God's action* as *hidden action*; his omnipotence remains enigmatic. In other words, God is primarily the *deus absconditus*. History in itself does not yield any deeper meaning, and for human eyes it does not contain any saving goal. This goal becomes visible only because God, in his sovereign freedom, out of fatherly love for his creatures, has revealed himself in history, i.e. *in concrete places in space and time which can be completely objectified*. For that reason *we have to talk of 'salvation history'*. However, this event can be seen as an *act of God* or heard as a form of his address only by faith; as a mere historical event within the world it remains ambivalent and open to misinterpretation. It evades any stringent proof of its meaning and can therefore be doubted. Miracle is included here: we cannot maintain that miracles are impossible in principle, but

---

81) because his 'heilsgeschichtliche' approach in which 'theologische und geschichtsphilosophische Betrachtung . . . vermischt (sind)'. In the New Testament 'Heilsgeschichte' is not understood as development: 'denn mit Christus hat die Geschichte der Welt ihr Ende erreicht' (*Background*, pp. 404f. = *Theologie als Kritik*, pp. 478–9). But is the story of the Gospels not a dramatic story also as some sort of 'development' from Galilee to Jerusalem and from the baptism (or birth) of Jesus to the cross and resurrection, a 'development' in time and space, and is the apostolic sending for mission and the growth of the Church (Mk 13.10) not also a 'development' – and a sign of God's grace? For Bultmann has 'als Leib Christi die Kirche gar keine Geschichte, sondern ist ein eschatologisches Phänomen' (pp. 481–508). Does this opinion not draw near to docetism?

they are ambivalent. For a long time miracle has ceased to be 'the dearest child of faith'; now for some theologians it has become 'the greatest stumbling-block to faith'. The decisive even unique miracle is the revelation of God for the salvation of mankind in time and space and the possibility that this gives of truth in faith, love and hope. This includes specific *thaumasia,* actions which make us 'wonder', but only faith recognizes that they are acts of God. Here from an external perspective salvation history presents itself as a small segment of a world history that we cannot survey, though it embraces the whole. It culminates in the mystery of the incarnation of God in a human being, Jesus of Nazareth. From him and through him God's will for salvation seeks to embrace the whole world.

The modern concept of history governed by 'immanent' causalities need not trouble us here; in particular it does not see through the riddles of history and therefore cannot solve them. Those who deny the possibility of God's action and give themselves over wholly to immanence must also subject their own existence to it. The end of this immanent existence is nothingness. Even religious introspection (*Innerlichkeit*) no longer offers any free space.

We could also use other terms for God's 'saving' action: revelation-, election- or covenant-history; however, the term 'salvation-history' is to be preferred because it is always concerned with God's will for the salvation of the fallen creature, i.e. with God's faithfulness to himself. From the outside the term 'history of ill' could often be more appropriate, since it time and again relates human apostasy and unfaithfulness right up to the centre, the passion of Jesus, with the betrayal, the denial and the cowardly flight. It is nevertheless salvation history because God's faithfulness, God's love to the sinner is stronger: *amor vincit omnia.*

Salvation history resists all harmonization; it is no 'self-contained organism', but is full of oppositions, conflicts, bitter battles over the truth, tribulation and desperation. There is as much room in it for a poem like the book of Job as there is for a sceptical, 'enlightened' Koheleth. Here, too, time and again the *deus absconditus* appears, in the most terrifying way in the godforsakenness of Jesus between Gethsemane and his cry of prayer in Mk 15.34. All these texts combine testimony and confession with a dialogue between God and man within the people of God which God has chosen. Quite a number of 'mythical' constructions and accounts appear in it, above all in the histories of the beginning and the end, including sagas and legends, historical narratives of terrifying profanity – and yet as a whole these texts are about *God's will for salvation in election, judgement and redemption*, and about the praise of his people in response.

However, can we still call this 'history'? Is it not simply a literary collection of texts of differing content and quality? Certainly: one could also speak of a *word-of-God-history*[31] and a *faith-history*,[32] for all these texts stand in a *historical* connection and seek to testify to God's action, i.e. what God does and says. It is the belief in the one God of Israel, who is confessed in primitive Christianity as the Father of Jesus Christ, that holds all these texts together.

For me as a Christian theologian *this history receives its unity and its foundation from its centre and its goal, the person of Jesus Christ*. In it the 'history of the word of God' or 'salvation history' attains its consummation – but not its end, for it goes on in a new, universal way. In the prologue to the Gospel of John this 'history', which has its very first beginning 'in God' is described in a precise, concentrated form.[33] The climax of the prologue, Jn 1.14, describes its consummation in a single sentence: God (1.1, 8) has become man. The statement *ho logos sarx egeneto* embraces the whole spatial existence of the Incarnate One to the

---

[31] Cf. Rom. 9.4–5 and 3.2–3: 'The Jews are entrusted with the oracles (λόγια) of God.'

[32] Cf. Gal. 3.23: πρὸ τοῦ δὲ ἐλθεῖν τὴν πίστιν, 25: ἐλθούσης δὲ τῆς πίστεως.

[33] See Hartmut Gese, *Zur biblischen Theologie. Alttestamentliche Vorträge*, BEVTh 78, Münich: Christian Kaiser Verlag, 1977, pp. 152–201. For the Johannine understanding of time see Jörg Frey, *Die johanneische Eschatologie* I–III, WUNT 96, 110, 117, Tübingen: Mohr (Siebeck), 1997–2000.

point of his 'It is accomplished' on the cross. Even the early Karl Barth in his commentary on Romans described 'the years 1–30', the time of Jesus, as a 'time of revelation', in which the 'divine determination of *all* time is *seen*', for 'Jesus Christ *our Lord* is the meaning of history. In this name two levels intersect. The well-known level of human history is cut by an . . . unknown level, that of the Father . . .'[34]

But, as the author himself later recognized, this Jesus is not a mere 'point on the line of intersection', without 'extension';[35] he is not 'the end of time', nor is it completely impossible to envisage him.

The earliest Christian author, Paul, already knows this. So he reports this 'history' of the Son of God which embraces eternity and time: his mediation at creation, his being sent into the world, his descent from David, his birth from a Jewish woman, his obedience 'under the law', his last meal with the disciples in the night when he was betrayed, his representative atoning death on the cross which brings freedom from the curse pronounced on the sinner by the law, his tomb and the miracle of the resurrection with his appearance to many witnesses.[36]

This 'history of Jesus' forms a unity and has a goal, the kenosis of the Incarnate One for the salvation of the whole world: for the world he has vicariously taken God's judgement upon himself. On Golgotha, the place of disaster, God's 'salvation history' for the whole of humankind is disclosed in the fate of this one man.

Certainly Paul expects the parousia of Christ in the very near future, but a new 'history' has opened up between it and its anticipation in the Easter event which proclaims the salvation made manifest *en Christo*. Time and 'history' certainly cannot be at an end, for the risen Christ himself has called messengers to proclaim all over the world, 'to all peoples', the revolutionary new message which promises salvation *sola gratia*, the gospel.

---

[34] Barth, *Der Römerbrief*, p. 5.

[35] Ibid.

[36] Gal. 3.13; 4.5; 1 Cor. 15.3–4. See M. Hengel in F. Avemarie and H. Lichtenberger, (eds.), *Auferstehung – Resurrection*, WUNT 135, Tubingen: Mohr (Siebeck), 2001, pp. 119–83.

God himself has appointed this *diakonia tes katallages*, this 'ministry of reconciliation'.[37]

Thus on the basis of the 'history of Jesus' a new 'period' of the Holy Spirit, the apostolic messengers and the communities of Jesus Christ which they founded begins. Their testimony is summed up by the New Testament writings.

From the beginning the Church rightly accorded a central place to the salvation-historical perspective in theology. Even today we cannot want to evade it, for the sake of the truth of the gospel. Only in this way do we remain bound up with our Lord as the 'wandering people of God', as the body of Christ.

However, this history cannot be understood in a unilinear way. Already in the Old Testament a number of lines run side by side, sometimes even running into one another, all of which seek to bear witness to what God says and does. There are breaks, new beginnings and clashes. The manifest God can conceal himself and appear as a *deus absconditus*.[38] And yet in the chronological sequence of the Old Testament texts we can see a tendency which has in view not only the salvation of the people of God but also that of all peoples; in other words, the individual theological schemes of history point beyond themselves. I shall quote only one sentence from Ps. 98.3 and Isa. 52.10: 'All the ends of the world see the salvation of our God.'

Jesus and the primitive community really understood themselves to be the fulfilment of the prophetic prediction of Scripture and in so doing proclaimed something new and unprecedented: 'The law and the prophets went up to John; from then on the kingly rule of God is proclaimed.'[39] That is also true of Paul, his doctrine of the law and his mission to the peoples. The Marcionitism of neo-Protestantism since the Enlightenment and German Idealism were a pernicious wrong turning.

As a source for the history of Jesus and the apostles the New

---

[37] 2 Cor. 5.18, cf. the διακονία τοῦ πνεύματος and τῆς δικαιοσύνης 3.8–9. Paul and his co-missionaries are 'servants of the new covenant' 2 Cor. 3.6.

[38] G. v. Rad, *Theologie des Alten Testaments*, Münich: Mohr (Siebeck), 1965, vol. 2, pp. 406ff. with reference to Karl Barth.

[39] Lk. 16.16.

Testament is no less full of conflict, indeed of contradictions. Primitive Christianity, the age of the apostles, was no ideal primal period. The circle of disciples itself lived completely by the forgiveness of sins, the certainty of which had been brought by Jesus. The Reformation formula *simul justus et peccator* applies to them all. Melanchthon's formulation which I have already mentioned, that the *remissio peccatorum* is the *causa finalis historiae*, sounds astonishing, but it is accurate.

The way from the promise of Abraham, from the God who justifies the godless,[40] to Golgotha, and the way of the message of the cross to the peoples, is 'salvation history'.

By comparison, any apologetic fundamentalist biblicism which appeals to the verbal inspiration and inerrancy of the canonical Scriptures goes wrong. It is basically a disguised rationalism which contradicts the nature of Scripture as the testimony of human faith to God's words and actions that create salvation. Historical and philological exegesis, which is therefore always also critical, first discloses to us the depth and diversity of this 'history' grounded in Christ, with its wealth of perspectives embracing the language of myth and legend, and seeking with it to express the last and deepest things which lie beyond the limits of our language and our ideas. I need only recall Genesis 1—3, Revelation 21 and 22 or the christological hymns.

The reduction in existentialist theology of the saving event to the individual decision of faith in the here and now and the *Entweltlichung*, the 'detachment from the world' by which one achieves one's 'authenticity' (*Eigentlichkeit*) that is bound up with it, also deprives this 'history' of its reality and power of conviction, since only it preserves the indispensable *extra nos* of the revelation of God in Christ, who was active and died for our salvation at that time in Galilee and Jerusalem. What God does and says in the Old Testament is illuminated by this history and through it attains its fulfilment and its goal; and the history of the Church as the 'people of God made up of Jews and Gentiles' which begins afresh receives from it its foundation and direction

---

[40] Rom. 4.5 about Abraham: πιστεύοντι δὲ ἐπὶ τὸν δικαιοῦντα τὸν ἀσεβῆ.

for the future. It will be fulfilled for each of us at the end in Paul's words of comfort in 1 Thess. 4.17, 'and so we shall always be with the Lord'.[41] This certainty makes us grateful and hopeful, for it gives us courage and confidence for our theological work and the service of love, today and tomorrow.

---

[41] On the Christian hope see M. Hengel, 'Paulus und die frühchristliche Apokalyptik', in *Paulus und Jakobus*, Kleine Schriften III, WUNT 141, Tübingen: Mohr (Siebeck), 2002, pp. 302–417 (pp. 346ff., 391ff., 410ff.).

17. Reading Scripture Eschatologically (1)

JOHN WEBSTER

This essay offers a dogmatic sketch of the human activity of reading Holy Scripture. The dogmatic sketch is what it says it is: sketchy and dogmatic. It is sketchy because it contains a good deal of unfinished business. In particular, it presupposes a much larger account of the nature of Holy Scripture whose defence would take me well beyond the essay's limits; and it also presupposes a critical appraisal of a good deal of recent theories of reading and interpretation, criticisms which once again I do not have space to substantiate here.[1]

The sketch is dogmatic, in that it attempts to describe the reading of Holy Scripture *sub specie divinitatis*, as an instance of how reconciled sinners, sanctified by the Spirit, are engaged by God's communicative presence. Dogmatics is the delightful activity in which the Church orders its thought and speech in accordance with the gospel; a dogmatic account of the reading of Holy Scripture tries to offer an orderly depiction of that creaturely activity as an episode in the economy of divine grace.

Briefly stated, a dogmatic account of Holy Scripture is an account which displays the ontology of Scripture by talking of divine activity, and above all, by talking of God's communicative presence, of which presence the creaturely reality which we call Holy Scripture is the textual auxiliary. A dogmatic account of the

[1] For an attempt to spell out some of the issues, see J. Webster, *Word and Church: Essays in Christian Dogmatics*, Edinburgh: T. & T. Clark, 2001, pp. 9–110; idem, *Holy Scripture*, Cambridge: Cambridge University Press, forthcoming.

creaturely activity of *reading* Holy Scripture does not entail the suspension or retirement of this language about divine action, but rather its furtherance. The burden of most recent theological accounts of reading has been to treat the act of reading as a quasi-independent theme, one in which talk of the prophetic activity of Christ and the Holy Spirit recedes somewhat into the background, its place taken by an anthropology of interpreters and their acts. Such accounts are characteristically only loosely secured to the topics of revelation, inspiration, canon, and so forth, offering, in effect, a rather thin account of the reader's illumination in which the act of interpretation is the primary concern.

My suggestion, by contrast, is that when we turn to give an account of reading Scripture we do not start a new topic, one in which we leave behind the theology of revelation and its ramifications and in which we appeal to fresh sources; still less do we shift into an area where theology has to take its lead from a theory of history or interpretation. We simply extend the dogmatic principles established in the locus *de sancta Scriptura*, for theological talk of the reading of Scripture is a subsection of what theology has to say about revelation and the fellowship with humankind which God's revelatory presence establishes. In this respect, we best give a theological account of the reading of Holy Scripture by attending to what the older Protestant divines called the 'right use' of Scripture. By that, they meant something very different from ethnographic analysis of the reading-practices of the Christian community to which the term 'uses of Scripture' normally refers nowadays. They meant fittingly obedient and faithful reading of Scripture as divine judgement and consolation, a reading in which we keep company with the holy God. Behind this notion of right use there lies, of course, a dogmatic ontology of Holy Scripture, one in which the term 'Holy Scripture' refers not to the Church's approbation and employment of the biblical text, but rather to that which Scripture *is*: a collection of human writings, sanctified to be the servant of God's communicative presence. What is involved in reading this text is determined by this text.

Put differently: the ontology of the text – its nature as the creaturely servant of the revelatory presence of the Holy Trinity – is to condition the acts of its readers. One implication here is that 'text' and 'reader' are only minimally useful as general categories; the common features of 'textuality' and 'reading' are less important than the particularities of specific text-acts and reading-acts. Although both the historicist and hermeneutical strands of modern theology have been somewhat slow to take the point, it is not very important that the Bible be read like any other book (or, at least, it is only important if the general categories of 'text' and 'reader' are deployed as part of a strategy of naturalizing Holy Scripture). It is more fruitful to try to spell out what might be involved in reading the scriptural text as a reconciled sinner, that is, as a participant in the history of reconciliation in which we come to know, love and fear God above all things. A full account of the matter would again require extensive treatment of the doctrine of Holy Scripture, in relation to topics such as revelation, the sanctification and use of creaturely media in the service of God, inspiration, authority, clarity, sufficiency, and much besides. Here I simply go straight to the final topic of any such account, namely, the nature of the act of reading, which, I suggest, may helpfully be described as 'eschatological reading'.

A word, first, on each of the terms. First, *reading*. The term 'reading' is chosen deliberately in preference to the term 'interpretation'. 'Reading' is a more practical, low-level term, less overlain with the complexities of hermeneutical theory, less patent of exposition through a theory of the human subject, and less likely to be overwhelmed by psychological or philosophical abstraction. Moreover, as a more modest term, 'reading' is more fitting in view of the self-presenting or self-explicating character of the divine revelation which Scripture serves. The term 'interpretation', on the other hand – at least as it has been shaped in the mainstream of theological hermeneutics since Schleiermacher – tends to devote much more attention to immanent explication of the activity of the interpreting subject as that through which the text achieves its 'realization': for this reason, 'reading' is much to be preferred.

Second, *eschatological*. To say that the activity of reading

Holy Scripture is an eschatological activity is to indicate its place in the comprehensive history of regeneration in which all human acts are caught up. To act humanly in any sphere is to act in the presence of, in response to, and under the tutelage of the new reality which has been established definitively in Jesus Christ, which is now being realized through the Holy Spirit, and which awaits its final manifestation at the parousia. Christian existence is eschatological in that, as existence in Christ and in the Spirit, its fundamental structure is the setting aside of the old order of sin and death and the embracing of the new creation. Holy Scripture's place is thus not only in the natural and cultural history of humankind, in which it is certainly a visible feature, but also in the new, spiritually visible, history of the new creation. Metaphysics, ethics and hermeneutics all stand under the same rule: 'the old has passed away, behold, the new has come' (2 Cor. 5.17). How does this rule work itself out in the activity of reading Holy Scripture?

Reading Holy Scripture is an activity of reconciled creatures. To speak of this activity as 'creaturely' is to say a good deal more than would be said if the activity were described simply as 'natural', for 'natural' may suggest that the activity in question can be accounted for exhaustively without reference to God as the origin, preserver and end of human acts. 'Creaturely', on the other hand, underscores the immediate reference of human being and activity to the being and activity of the creator, from whom and for whom the creature is, and by whom the creature acts. Reading Holy Scripture is a creaturely undertaking, then, in that it occurs within the domain of the creator's rule and guidance, and in that its human subject exists and moves under the divine determination. The creatures who undertake this activity in this domain are, moreover, *reconciled* creatures. The creaturely activity of reading Holy Scripture is an episode in the history of God's revelatory self-giving to humankind. As an aspect of the history of revelation, reading Scripture is equally an episode in the history of reconciliation. This is because revelation and reconciliation are the self-same reality, viewed under different aspects. Revelation is God's communicative self-presence which restores fellowship with estranged creatures. God's communicative self-presence always takes its stand in the midst of the creature's estrangement from God. Coming to know God, and reading Holy Scripture as a means of coming to know God, can only occur through the overcoming of fallenness.

In this particular context, the forms of fallenness to which attention must be drawn are the sins of ignorance and idolatry. Sin as ignorance means that the divine address is strange to the sinner; our complicity in sin is such that the matter of the gospel is alien. Reading Scripture is thus not a matter of merely applying our interpretative skills to one more set of texts, and involves much more than extending the range of our affections, sympathies or spiritual taste, still less of our historical and religious knowledge. It is to encounter that which we resist with all our powers, that which we will not know. Likewise, sin as idolatry means that we are busy about the production of images to hold down, reject or alter the matter of the gospel, in the hope that its gracious judgement can somehow be averted or neutralized by replacing it with something of our own invention. Reading Holy Scripture is thus a field of human rebellion. We do not read well. And we do not read well, not only because of technical incompetence, cultural distance from the matter of the text, or lack of readerly sophistication (though all these, too, are hindrances to reading), but also and especially because in Holy Scripture we are addressed by the *viva vox Dei*.

If, therefore, we are to read well, we have to be made into certain kinds of readers. This 'making' of the reader occurs as we and our acts of reading are taken up into the eschatological history of reconciliation. Like all our moral and rational activity, reading, too, must be regenerated if it is to attain its end. Reading Holy Scripture is an eschatological activity because it is part of reason's regeneration; the founding condition for good reading of Scripture is reason's separation by God and its being taken by God into his service. Like all other aspects of human life, reason is a field of God's reconciling and sanctifying work. Reason, too – along with conscience, the will, and the affections

– must be reconciled to the holy God if it is to do its work well. And good Christian theology can only happen if it is rooted in the reconciliation of reason by the sanctifying presence of God. Clearly this does not sit well with some deep intellectual and spiritual conventions of modern culture, which regard reason as a 'natural' faculty – a standard, unvarying and foundational feature of humankind, a basic human capacity or skill. As a natural faculty, reason is, crucially, not involved in the drama of God's saving work; it is not fallen, and so requires neither to be judged nor to be reconciled nor to be sanctified. Reason simply *is*; it is humankind in its intellectual nature. Consequently, 'natural' reason has been regarded as a transcendent and sovereign intellectual legislator, and as such answerable to none but itself. Such conceptions of reason have become so deeply embedded in modern culture and its most prestigious intellectual institutions that they are scarcely visible to us. But for the Christian confession, these conceptions are disordered, because they extract reason and its operations from the economy of God's dealings with his creatures. To think of reason as 'natural' and 'transcendent' in this way is, by the standard of the Christian confession, corrupt, because it isolates reason from the work of God as creator, reconciler and perfecter.

A Christian theological account of reading Holy Scripture must beg to differ, because the confession of the gospel by which it governs its life requires it to say that humankind in its entirety, including reason, is enclosed within the history of sin and reconciliation. And so exegetical reason stands under the divine requirement that it be holy to the Lord its God. Reading Holy Scripture is a particular instance of reason's holiness. Here, too – as in all truthful thinking – we are to trace what happens as reason is transformed by the judging, justifying and sanctifying work of the triune God. Holy reason is eschatological reason, reason submitting to the process of the renewal of all things as sin and falsehood are set aside, idolatry is reproved, and the new creation confessed with repentance and delight.

What this suggests is that an account of the creaturely activity of reading Holy Scripture will be inseparable from a Christian theological anthropology: the activity of reading will exemplify the fundamental pattern of all Christian existence, which is dying and rising with Christ through the purging and quickening power of the Holy Spirit. Reading is an aspect of our mortification and vivification; to read Holy Scripture is to be gathered into the divine work of reconciliation in which we are slain and made alive. Reason's conformity to the matter of the gospel which is announced in Holy Scripture therefore entails both a brokenness, a relinquishment of willed mastery in the encounter with God of which the text is an auxiliary, and also a renewal of the office of exegetical reason, its reintegration into the divine service. Near the beginning of the magnificent seventh chapter of book III of the *Institutes*, Calvin writes that the rubric under which Christian existence in its entirety is set is this: *non nostri sumus, sed Domini*. And he continues:

> Let this therefore be the first step, that a man depart from himself in order that he may apply the whole force of his ability in the service of the Lord. I call 'service' not only what lies in obedience to God's Word but what turns the mind of man, empty of its own carnal sense, wholly to the bidding of God's Spirit. While it is the first entrance to life, all philosophers were ignorant of the transformation, which Paul calls 'renewal of the mind'. For they set up reason alone as a ruling principle in man, and think that it alone should be listened to; to it alone, in short, they entrust the conduct of life. But the Christian philosophy bids reason give way to, submit and subject itself to, the Holy Spirit so that the man himself may no longer live but hear Christ living and reigning within him.[2]

In that exquisitely concentrated paragraph, we can find an entire anthropology of reading or exegetical reason, organized around the reader's mortification and vivification.

Reading Scripture involves, first, a 'departure from self'.

---

[2] J. Calvin, *Institutes of the Christian Religion* III.vii.1. ed. J. T. McNeill and trans. F. L. Battles, Philadelphia: Westminster, 1960, vol. 1, p. 690.

For Calvin, this relinquishment is one of the chief fruits of the activity of the Holy Spirit. The 'spiritual' life – including spiritual reading of Scripture – is a matter of the turning of the mind, once it has been emptied of its carnality, to the bidding of the Spirit. Thus reason's regeneration, its eschatological transformation, involves the overthrow of one 'ruling principle' – reason as an autonomous guide to the conduct of life – and its substitution by the personal presence and activity of the Spirit. And so 'the Christian philosophy' (that is, gospel wisdom in the conduct of human life) is characterized above all by giving way, submission, subjection to the Spirit. So radical is this that Calvin alludes to Gal. 2.20 and sums up the Christian philosophy by saying that its end is that 'the man may no longer live', and goes on to say that the fundamental life-act of the Christian is that of 'hear[ing] Christ living and reigning in him'. 'Hearing' is always a key word in Calvin's anthropology, and its proximity to what Calvin will elsewhere say of deference to Scripture is worth noting in our present context. It would, indeed, not be pressing Calvin too far to say that this hearing of the living, ruling Christ is the fundamental work of reason, and therefore fundamental to the act of reading, for reason's end is 'obedience to God's Word'.

The reader of Holy Scripture is thus a mortified reader. A couple of delimitations may help specify this point. The first concerns the importance of reference to Christ and the Spirit. Calvin's account of reason's mortification is christologically and pneumatologically dense; without immediate reference to Christ and Spirit as agents of regeneration, mortification would be contentless. One consequence here is that a theological account of the mortified reader of Holy Scripture is very different from other accounts of readerly self-negation. The difference lies in the unsubstitutability of the agents of this mortification and vivification (not the reader, but the risen Christ and the Spirit), in the domain in which mortification takes place (the history of reconciliation), and in the person of the reader (who is defined by the Spirit-effected presence of Christ within). My account of this matter differs substantially from Wesley Kort's account of 'centripetal reading' which, although it is developed in conversation with Calvin, is heavily dominated by Kristeva's understanding of 'abjection'.[3] Kort writes:

> Reading the Bible involves first of all movement away from self and world and toward their divestment and abjection. In centripetal reading the coherences and identities of the reader's situation are dissolved, and biblical coherences and identities, rather than be appropriated, are followed as indicators of an exit and then bypassed on the way to it . . . Biblical locations, plots, characters, and theological themes, when taken as directives toward this kind of reading, are invaluable and authoritative because they clarify the act of divestment and abjection, of departure and exit, and because they ask to be left behind.[4]

The difference of this from the account offered here stems partly from direct use of christological categories to describe what Kort describes immanently: *mortificatio* and *vivificatio*, as the extension into human life of Christ's death and resurrection by the power of the Spirit who unites the believer (and therefore the believer as reader) to Christ, are *toto caelo* different from readerly self-divestment. Furthermore, for Kort the divestment which occurs in centripetal reading involves 'the divestment not only of one's world and sense of self but of biblical worlds and identities as well'.[5] In effect, the cognitive content of Scripture is simply an exit sign, that which one passes on the path to radical abjection. But, once again, the mortification of the reader is unavailing unless it is occasioned and sustained by the objective and transformative reality which presents itself to the reader through the service of Holy Scripture. Without such roots in christological and pneumatological considerations, centripetal reading remains abstract self-negation.

---

[3] See W. Kort, *'Take, Read': Scripture, Textuality, and Cultural Practice*, University Park: Pennsylvania University Press, 1996; J. Kristeva, *Powers of Horror: An Essay on Abjection*, New York: Columbia University Press, 1982.

[4] Ibid., p. 128.

[5] Ibid.

A second delimitation concerns the moralism which easily afflicts accounts of reading which make heavy use of the conceptuality of character and virtue. Readerly virtues are not a sphere of unaided human competence. The virtues of the godly reader through which right use is made of Scripture cannot be crafted, whether through a private process of spiritual self-cultivation or through appropriation of the habits and patterns of living which are acted out in the public life of the Christian community. Reading Scripture is an episode in the history of sin and its overcoming; and overcoming sin is the sole work of Christ and the Spirit. The once-for-all abolition and the constant checking of our perverse desire to hold the text in thrall and to employ it as an extension of our will can only be achieved through an act which is not our own. The reader's will needs not simply to be called to redirect itself to appropriate ends, but to be reborn. Reading Scripture is inescapably bound to regeneration; only after a drastic reworking of spiritual psychology can the language of virtue have its place. What is therefore fundamental in giving an account of hermeneutical conversion is not a theory of moral virtue or the reader's 'character', but a soteriology and a pneumatology. Through the incarnate Word, crucified and risen, we are made capable of hearing the gospel, but only as we are at one and the same time put to death and raised to new life. Through the Spirit of the crucified and risen Christ we are given the capacity to set mind and will on the truth of the gospel and so read as those who have been reconciled to God.

What of the reader's vivification? How is regenerated exegetical reason to be characterized? We may recall that, in Calvin's summary of Christian existence, to the negative of mortification there corresponds the affirmation: *sumus Domini*, we are the Lord's. This ontological determination of Christian existence entails the imperative: 'Let his wisdom and will therefore rule all our actions.'[6] The human shape of this ruling of the divine wisdom is summed up by Calvin as *service*: the Christian not mortified to no purpose, but rather with the end 'that he may apply the whole

---

[6] Calvin, *Institutes* III.vii.1.

force of his ability in the service of the Lord'. One important consequence of this for a Christian account of reading Scripture is what might be called 'focused attentiveness'. The Christian act of reading Holy Scripture is to be characterized by a certain exclusiveness, a deliberate directing of attention to the text and an equally deliberate laying aside of other concerns. Negatively, this involves a refusal to allow the mind and the affections to be seized by other preoccupations. Reading Scripture thus involves mortification of the free-range intellect which believes itself to be at liberty to devote itself to all manner of sources of fascination.

To this negative, there corresponds positive attentiveness to the text. The vivification of the reader's reason involves the Spirit's gift of a measure of singularity or purity in which Scripture is not one of a number of possible objects of attention, even the most important in a panoply, but the one word which is to absorb us into itself. Reading Scripture well involves submitting to the process of purification which is the readerly counterpart to the *sufficiency* of Scripture. We can, says Kierkegaard, be 'deceived by too much knowledge'.[7] One of the diseases of which the reader must be healed is that of instability, lack of exclusive concentration; and part of the reader's sanctification is ordered simplification of desire so that reading can really take place. 'Let us always hang on our Lord's lips,' counsels Calvin,

> and neither add to His wisdom nor mix up with it anything of our own, lest like leaven it corrupt the whole mass and make even the very salt which is within us to be without savour. Let us show ourselves to be such disciples as our Lord wishes to have – poor, empty, devoid of self-wisdom; eager to learn but knowing nothing, and even wishing to know nothing but what He has taught; shunning everything of foreign growth as the deadliest poison.[8]

---

[7] S. Kierkegaard, *Purity of Heart is to Will One Thing*, New York: Harper, 1938, p. 204.

[8] J. Calvin, *Psychopannychia*, in *Tracts and Treatises in Defence of the Reformed Faith*, vol. 3, Edinburgh: Oliver & Boyd, 1958, p. 418.

Thus, however important the mortification of the reader, it must not be abstracted from the reader's vivification. 'Faithful reading' is not only characterized by brokenness, but also by the restoration and reconstitution of exegetical reason; to stop short of this point would be to risk denying that sin has been indeed set aside. One of the functions of a genuinely operative pneumatology in this context is to articulate grounds for the reader's *confidence* that it is possible to read Holy Scripture well – having in mind the true ends of Scripture, with false desire and distraction held in check, and with reason and spirit quickened into alertness to the speeches of God. This confidence is not the antithesis of fear and trembling: like all truthful human action, it emerges out of the fear of God. And, because it is wholly dependent upon the illumination of the Spirit, it is hesitant to trust other lights (especially its own, from which it has been set free). Yet: the Spirit has been and continues to be given to illuminate the reader, and so exegetical reason may trust the promise of Christ to lead into truth by the Spirit's presence and power. In the matter of reading Holy Scripture, too, disorder and wickedness have been overcome and reason's reconciliation to God has begun.

18. Reading Scripture Eschatologically (2)

CHRISTOPHER ROWLAND

At roughly the time that Lady Margaret Beaufort was endowing the Lady Margaret chairs of divinity in Oxford and Cambridge five hundred years ago, Sandro Botticelli was painting pictures which evoke the effects of the prophetic preaching of Girolamo Savonarola who was hanged and burnt at the stake for heresy for prophesying 'new doctrines'.[1] Savonarola's remarkable career reminds us that, far from being out of the ordinary, eschatological conviction had been a central component of medieval religion. If most modern theological syllabuses were any guide, one would have little inkling of the importance of Savonarola, and his earlier prophetic predecessors Joachim of Fiore and Peter Olivi.[2] Many theology students will have come across, and may have studied in detail, Aquinas' theology and perhaps they may have heard of the philosophy of Olivi. What they will probably not know is that, alongside Olivi's philosophical work, is his role as an interpreter of the Apocalypse and as an advocate for the radical Franciscans, whose influence was far-reaching in popular religion in parts of southern Europe in the fourteenth century.[3] I hope the importance of all this for the discussion of the theme of this volume will become apparent in what follows.

---

[1] D. Weinstein, *Savonarola and Florence: Prophecy and Patriotism in the Renaissance*, Princeton: Princeton University Press, 1970.

[2] R. K. Emmerson and B. McGinn, *The Apocalypse in the Middle Ages*, Ithaca: Cornell University Press, 1992.

[3] D. Burr, *Olivi's Peaceable Kingdom: A Reading of the Apocalypse Commentary*, Philadelphia: University of Pennsylvania Press, 1993.

This essay focuses on eschatology and the peculiar contribution it makes to the broad field of 'wisdom' by exploring the distinctive insight made by 'living at the end of the ages'. There are many aspects which could be covered, but the focus in the first part will be on the perspective on the reading of Scripture enunciated in Coleridge's 'Confessions of an Enquiring Spirit':

> With such purposes, with such feelings, have I perused the books of the Old and New Testaments, each book as a whole, and also as an integral part. And need I say that I have met everywhere more or less copious sources of truth, and power, and purifying impulses, that I have found words for my inmost thoughts, songs for my joy, utterances for my hidden griefs, and pleadings for my shame and my feebleness? In short, whatever find me, bears witness for itself that it has proceeded from a Holy Spirit, even from the same Spirit, 'which remaining in itself, yet regenerateth all other powers, and in all ages entering into holy souls, maketh them friends of God and prophets' (Wisdom 7.27).[4]

I want to suggest that the eschatological reading of Scripture, within the Joachite tradition, echoes the importance of a divinely initiated insight into the meaning of both events and of Scripture in New Testament writings. In this section a particular focus will be the way in which the word 'apocalypse' betokens a wisdom 'from beyond'. There is something about the form of the Apocalypse which makes it more opaque than Daniel, where the meaning of the visions is set out for the seer by an angelic intermediary. The lack of explanation in the Apocalypse means that the reader is drawn into the task of engaging with the text. Luther recognized this difference between the Apocalypse and Daniel when he wrote in his 1530 Preface to the book that 'it does without either words or interpretations and deals exclusively with images and figures'.

---

[4] S. T. Coleridge, *Confessions of an Enquiring Spirit* (1840), Philadelphia: Fortress Press, 1988 and on the importance of the visionary dimension in biblical interpretation, see M. Lieb, *The Visionary Mode: Biblical Prophecy, Hermeneutics and Cultural Change*, Ithaca: Cornell University Press, 1991.

The lack of explanation in the Apocalypse means that the reader is drawn into the task of engaging with an allusive text.

Secondly, using the Joachite material as a starting-point, I shall more briefly outline the emphasis on life in the penultimate age in the New Testament writings. The concern here will be the way in which writers seek to communicate to their readers that they are in a time of historical transition in which the coming age of salvation is not imminent but intrudes into and already affects life in the present, but with the important proviso that the time of perfection in knowledge, insight and practice is still to come. The point of using the analogy with medieval apocalypticism is to make a historical point about early Christian belief and practice. A distinctive genius of New Testament theology is the puzzle of the 'now' and the 'not yet' and the sense which accompanies that of being on the brink of something important, an anticipatory mode if you will. In this sense, the Joachites and the New Testament writers want people to live in the light of that conviction.

Joachim of Fiore describes an important moment in his life when he was struggling to make sense of the Apocalypse and how in the middle of the night, as he was meditating on the text of the Apocalypse, 'the fullness of this book and of the entire agreement of the Old and New Testaments was perceived by a clarity of understanding'.[5] By means of this gracious insight, which was replicated in more dramatic form in Savonarola's prophetic visions three hundred years later,[6] Joachim describes how he found in the Apocalypse the key to the inner meaning of Scripture and the whole history of salvation,[7] an experience which echoes Hildegard's earlier and very similar claim to insight in her 'Scivias',[8] and later Joachim's major interpreter Peter

---

[5] B. McGinn, *Visions of the End: Apocalyptic Traditions in the Middle Ages*, New York: Columbia University Press, 1998, p. 130.

[6] Weinstein, *Savonarola and Florence*, pp. 67–111, 163–5.

[7] B. McGinn, *Apocalyptic Spirituality: Treatises and Letters of Lactantius, Adso of Montier-en-Der, Joachim of Fiore, the Franciscan Spirituals, Savonarola*, London: SPCK, 1979, p. 99.

[8] Columba Hart and Jane Bishop, *Scivias / Hildegard of Bingen Scivias*, New York: Paulist Press 1990, p. 59; P. Dronke, *Women Writers of the*

John Olivi.[9] For all of these writers the Apocalypse was not a book to be tolerated or politely ignored, but was the key to the interpretation of the whole of Scripture. In the meditation upon the Apocalypse the spiritual insight which informed the prophets of old was again at work, as Joachim elsewhere writes: 'God who once gave the spirit of prophecy to the prophets has given me the spirit of understanding to grasp with great clarity in his Spirit all the mysteries of sacred scripture.'[10]

This approach to the meaning of Scripture is something which is characteristic of many strands within the New Testament, where insight into the divine mystery does not always come by means of ingenious or sophisticated scriptural exegesis. The wisdom to understand the mystery of Christ is a gift from God. In the Gospel of Matthew, for example, according to Peter's confession perception of the identity of Jesus comes through divine revelation (16.17), and in the infancy narratives, dreams open the mystery of the divine purposes (1.20; 2.13; 2.19; 27.19). The theme of divine reversal which runs through the Gospel means the 'the babes' are recipients of insight into the identity of the messiah. Children (along with the impaired) are the ones who recognize Jesus in the Temple (21.16; cf. 11.25–27), a passage peculiar to Matthew.[11]

Elsewhere in the Gospels and Acts, the accounts of Jesus' baptism and the transfiguration (Mk 9.2ff. and par.) remind us of the apocalypses and the call-visions of the prophets and are part of the cycle of revelatory moments in which the status and character of Jesus is disclosed. Jesus' report of seeing 'Satan fall like lightning from heaven' (Lk. 10.22) suggests a visionary

Middle Ages: A Critical Study of Texts from Perpetua to Marguerite Porete, Cambridge: Cambridge University Press, 1984.

[9] Burr, *Olivi's Peaceable Kingdom*, pp. 122–4.

[10] Joachim of Fiore, *Ten Stringed Psaltery*, 10, in McGinn, *Apocalyptic Spirituality*, pp. 99–100.

[11] C. Rowland, 'Apocalyptic, the Poor and the Gospel of Matthew', *Journal of Theological Studies* 45, 1994, pp. 504–18 and idem ' "Open thy Mouth for the Dumb": a Task for the Exegete of Holy Scripture', Inaugural Lecture as Dean Ireland's Professor of the Exegesis of Holy Scripture, 11 May 1992, *Biblical Interpretation* 1, 1993, pp. 228–41.

anticipation of all that was being experienced in the struggle with the evil powers in the actions of both himself and the disciples, an indication that a moment of ultimate apocalyptic importance has happened with Jesus and his immediate companions.[12] In the Acts of the Apostles, as with the dreams in the opening chapters of Matthew's Gospel, visions provide the dynamic for the spread of the gospel. Paul's experience on the Damascus road, repeated three times, emphasizes the providential nature of this event in the divine economy. Likewise Peter's vision of the descending sail and the instruction to sacrifice and eat animals without regard for their ritual cleanness prepares him for his journey to Cornelius, explanation of which is required by the elders in Jerusalem in Acts 11.

Such passages are symptomatic of the decisive moments of visionary insight in which insight into the divine wisdom comes by revelation.[13] In his letter to the Galatians Paul emphasises the importance of visionary elements as the basis of his practice (Gal. 1.12, 16; cf. Acts 22.17). It is the mysterious world of apocalyptic vision which best explains that shattering moment in Paul's life. He believed that Jesus of Nazareth, seated at the right hand of God who will be manifested in glory at the close of the age (1 Cor. 1.7), had been revealed to him already in the old age.[14] The decisive revelation of God's righteousness had come in the gospel of Christ (Rom. 1.17). This revelation had ceased to be something just for a learned elite but was available to all who could discern the wisdom of God in the crucified Christ (1 Cor. 1.18; Mt. 11.25–27). Paul sees himself and his companions as stewards in the divine palace with the privilege of administering the divine secrets (1 Cor. 4.1). In this age when one can only see in a glass darkly one needs Scripture as assistance in the search for the

---

[12] C. Rowland, *The Open Heaven: A Study of Apocalyptic in Judaism and Early Christianity*, London: SPCK, 1982.

[13] J. Ashton, *The Religion of Paul the Apostle*, New Haven: Yale University Press, 2000.

[14] M. de Boer in J. J. Collins, *Encyclopedia of Apocalypticism*, vol. 1, New York: Continuum, 2000, pp. 345–83; and further M. Bockmuehl, *Revelation and Mystery*, Tübingen: Mohr (Siebeck), 1990.

gateway to divine truth. Scripture points to this greater truth and provides a resource for the discernment of the character of life 'at the end of the ages' (1 Cor. 10.11; Rom. 15.4). Nevertheless its meaning is opaque, and it might also be a veil which may prevent understanding (2 Cor. 3). This kind of hermeneutic should not surprise us given Paul's description of what he describes as an allegorical use of Scripture in Gal. 4.24, where the literal sense of Scripture points to a 'deeper', 'transcendent', 'allegorical' meaning in the contrast between two cities and two covenants and challenges readers to identify with the Jerusalem which is above which is also that which is to come.[15]

A rather different perspective on apocalyptic mystery emerges in the Gospel of John.[16] Wisdom and the knowledge of God come not through the information disclosed in visions and revelations. Jesus proclaims to Philip, 'The one who has seen me has seen the Father' (14.8), and at the conclusion of the Prologue, the Evangelist speaks of the Son in the following way: 'No one has ever seen God; the only Son, who is in the bosom of the Father, he has made him known' (1.18). Suggestively, John Ashton has written of the Gospel of John as an apocalypse – in reverse, upside down, inside out.[17] By this I take him to mean that the way in which apocalypse is focused on the incarnate son of God rather than dreams, visions and the quest for angelic mysteries reflects something very important about the theology of the Gospel of John. The Scriptures bear witness to this decisive, eschatological revelation, though they cannot entirely explain it (Jn 5.39).

In the Gospel of John the revelation of the divine glory comes with none of the fire and light which attends Ezekiel's vision or for that matter the apocalypse to the disciples at the Transfiguration. (The promise to Nathanael in 1.48–51 that he will see greater

---

[15] D. Boyarin, *A Radical Jew: Paul and the Politics of Identity*, Berkeley: University of California Press, 1994.

[16] J. Ashton, *Understanding the Fourth Gospel*, Oxford: Clarendon Press, 1991.

[17] Ashton, *Understanding the Fourth Gospel*, p. 387; J. Kanagaraj, *'Mysticism' in the Gospel of John: An Inquiry into the Background of John in Jewish Mysticism*, Sheffield: Sheffield Academic Press, 1998.

things and the heavenly voice in 12.28 are rare exceptions.) The eschatological tabernacling of God with humanity has occurred in the incarnation of the divine Logos. There is no need for waiting for the heaven on earth in the new Jerusalem as in the Apocalypse (Rev. 22.4). Nevertheless the recognition of that divine glory is hidden from many, save those like the Samaritan woman, Martha and Mary, and the healed blind man. Even close disciples like Philip, as we have seen, do not see the Father in Jesus. The immediate recognition of divine glory is still awaited, to use the words of 1 John, until such time as we shall see him as he is (1 Jn 3.2). Meanwhile the Gospel of John offers the opportunity through the enigmatic words of Jesus and his suggestive but ambiguous signs that the one sent from the father embodies the divine glory. The Gospel text functions as a pedagogy guiding the readers or hearer to the moment of disclosure. As Wayne Meeks has put it so well, readers have an experience rather like that of the dialogue partners of Jesus: either they will find the whole business so convoluted, obscure, and maddeningly arrogant that they will reject it in anger, or they will find is so fascinating that they will stick with it until the progressive reiteration of themes brings, on some level of consciousness at least, a degree of clarity: 'The book [the Gospel of John] functions for its readers in precisely the same way that the epiphany of its hero functions within the narratives and dialogues.'[18] The Gospel of John, like other parts of the New Testament, attaches great weight to the Spirit as a mark of the eschaton. What role there is for the Spirit in the process of reading the Gospel is not clear, though the major role of the Spirit Paraclete to bring to minds Jesus' words as well as revealing that which is to come suggests that there is a link between reading the Gospel and the activity of the eschatological Spirit.

The particular approach to Scripture has its context in Second Temple apocalypses which offer examples of those moments when there are opened up perceptions of other dimensions of

---

[18] W. Meeks, 'The Man from Heaven in Johannine Sectarianism', in J. Ashton, (ed.), *The Interpretation of John*, Edinburgh: T. & T. Clark, 1997, pp. 169–206.

existence and another perspectives on ordinary life.[19] At first sight they suggest modes of reading which may differ from those typical of the various midrashic methods in which interpretative ingenuity is required to 'penetrate the subtleties of parables, seeking out the hidden meanings of proverbs and being at home with the obscurities of parables' to quote Jesus ben Sirach's sketch of scribal activity (Ecclus 39). With some forms of apocalyptic interpretation he was obviously much less comfortable, however: 'Do not meddle in what is beyond your tasks, for matters too great for human understanding have been shown you' (Ecclus 3.23). Among such matters too great for human understanding might be a hint of the visionary exegesis of the first chapter of Ezekiel, in which the meaning of the text, at least in some quarters, involved a 'seeing again' what Ezekiel saw.[20] The mystical interpretation of Scripture is known as merkabah mysticism, whose importance in Second Temple Judaism has been illuminated by the Songs of the Sabbath Sacrifice from Cave 4 at Qumran.[21] The most explicit example of this visionary appropriation of Scripture in the New Testament is the vision of John on Patmos.[22] Ezekiel's vision is a crucial part of a John's vision and is the means whereby John sees the eschatological role of the Lamb who opens the book with seven seals. John's vision is itself an interpretation of the biblical text, in which the language of Ezekiel merges with other parts of Scripture as well as, possibly, aspects of a merkabah tradition which are now no longer extant, to offer that particular amalgam of images in John's vision of heaven. It resembles, and yet differs in several respects from, contemporary visions of God in the

---

[19] M. Fishbane, *Biblical Interpretation in Ancient Israel*, Oxford: Oxford University Press, 1985.

[20] D. Halperin, *Faces of the Chariot*, Tübingen: Mohr (Siebeck), 1988, pp. 70–8.

[21] C. Newsom, *The Songs of the Sabbath Sacrifice*, Atlanta: Scholars Press, 1985; idem et al., *Discoveries in the Judaean Desert XI Qumran Cave 4. VI*, Oxford: Clarendon Press, 1998.

[22] C. Rowland, 'The Visions of God in Apocalyptic Literature', *Journal for the Study of Judaism*, 10, 1979, pp. 138ff.; idem, *The Open Heaven*; idem, *The Book of Revelation*, New Interpreter's Bible 12, Nashville: Abingdon, 1998.

apocalypses. A key difference, however, is the decisive impact of Jesus Christ on the visionary's imagination in the insertion of *ἀρνίον ἑστηκὸς ὡς ἐσφαγμένον* (Rev. 5.6), into the merkabah scene and the eschatological judgement, which ensues from that heavenly event.[23] Whatever way we approach Revelation 4—5 it offers us an example of 'reading Scripture eschatologically'. Apocalypse and eschaton converge in the Lamb's vindication in the heavenly court and the opening of the sealed scroll, which, according to a whole series of interpreters down the centuries, marks the critical effect of the gospel on the world. Let me add in parenthesis: we may not be in a position to know exactly whether Paul as a Pharisee may have been schooled in the divine mysteries but if one wanted an analogy to what might have happened to Saul on the Damascus road, which he describes as an apocalypse of Jesus Christ (Gal. 1.12), I would turn to the other Apocalypse of Jesus Christ and its christological shape of the merkabah vision as an example of that which has begun to turn Paul's religious world upside down.[24]

In pursuing one form of eschatological reading of Scripture I have concentrated on a hermeneutical method in which the text opens up new meanings and functions as a gateway to a greater reality. The kind of interpretation one finds in 1QpHab at Qumran and in the fulfilment quotations in the Gospel of Matthew evince a different approach in interpretation, however, in which there is a greater sense of closure suggested either by eschatological fulfilment or authoritative interpretation. This may be dominant in the New Testament but not to the exclusion of other modes of reading. Throughout the New Testament there is a strong sense of being part of the penultimate, being on the brink of fulfilment of anticipated eschatological events which are seen as already, at least in part, taking place. That sense of anticipation qualifies certainty in a situation for there is still waiting to be done

[23] Rowland, *The Book of Revelation*.

[24] Ashton, *The Religion of Paul the Apostle*; S. Kim, *The Origin of Paul's Gospel*, Tübingen: Mohr (Siebeck), 1981; C. Rowland, 'Apocalyptic, Mysticism and the New Testament', in P. Schäfer, *Geschichte und Theologie*, Tübingen: Mohr (Siebeck), 1996, pp. 1–23.

before knowledge and fulfilment finally comes. The sense of the 'not yet' does not allow the complete closure of hermeneutical possibility in engaging with the scriptural narratives, therefore. Eschatological reading of Scripture does have a tendency to exclusivity. But even in a passage like 1 Corinthians 10 there may be hints of a more inclusive way of reading Scripture, but that is something that needs further reflection.[25] The sense of fulfilment and anticipation brought their own problems. It is not surprising that in various texts the need for discernment (1 Cor. 12.10, 30; 14.5, 13), testing the spirits (1 Jn 4.1; 1 Thess. 5.21; 1 Tim. 4.1) and a communally balanced reading are all stressed (if that is what is meant by 2 Pet. 1.20).

This brings me, more briefly, to the second theme of the essay. In Joachim's and Olivi's interpretations of the Apocalypse the sixth, penultimate, age, assumes great importance as a time of anticipation and struggle.[26] This penultimate period represents a space for renewal and conflict with the forces of Antichrist, which evokes an outburst of spiritual activity in the form of spiritual renewal. In this penultimate period persecution and renewal, exile and prophetic witness jostle one with another. The sense of anticipation prompted various patterns of moral renewal,[27] and this should remind us that Olivi's eschatological reading of Scripture was not about learned prognostications but intimately linked with the renewal of the Church as the witness to the coming kingdom.

The link between the eschatological reading of Scripture and moral renewal is akin to that in New Testament writings from Matthew to the Apocalypse.[28] A characteristic of the theology of the New Testament is precisely this sense of anticipation, of the present as a decisive moment in God's saving purposes and

---

[25] C. Rowland, 'The Engraver, the Chandler and the Trades Unionist: Reflections on the Grassroots Reading of Scripture', *Political Theology* 2, 2000, pp. 11–32.

[26] Burr, *Olivi's Peaceable Kingdom*, pp. 91, 117–18.

[27] G. L. Potesta in B. McGinn, *Encyclopaedia of Apocalypticism*, vol. 2, New York: Continuum, 2000, p. 110.

[28] C. Rowland, *Christian Origins: The Origin and Character of the Most Important Messianic Sect of Judaism*, rev. edn, London: SPCK, 2002.

the opportunity, which exists for the people of God to act in the present as they wait for the coming of the messianic reign. It is the time when the Spirit of prophecy offers testimony to the 'now' of the day of salvation (2 Cor. 6.2). On the negative side in 1 John the presence of dissent and separation marks out the identity of Antichrist as an all too human presence in the midst of the community. The present is a penultimate time when there is the groaning and travail which must precede the messianic age. The theme of witness in the period of penultimacy is expounded in Revelation 11. The vision of the two witnesses comes immediately after a renewed commission to John to prophesy again about 'many peoples and nations and languages and kings' (Rev. 10.11).[29] In the space between the sixth and seventh trumpet blasts John is called to prophesy. Like the Lamb, he is instructed to take a scroll though this time he consumes it. The character of the prophetic witness is exemplified by the two witnesses who offer their testimony in the midst of the time of the trampling of the holy places by the nations. In the penultimate period prophetic witness is necessary, as a central part of the life of the community, though the letters to the angels of the churches reveal the extent of their incapacity to fulfil this role and John and his companions function as a prophetic remnant, an example of endurance as they keep the commandments of God and the faith of Jesus (Rev. 14.13).

Messianic and eschatological doctrines are central to Christianity (e.g. 1 Pet. 1.11–12; Heb. 1.1–4). The first Christians in their diverse social settings were encouraged to believe that *they* were privileged to be 'the ones on whom the ends of the ages had come' (1 Cor. 10.11).[30] The present had become the critical moment; history and eschatology had become inextricably intertwined. Jesus of Nazareth proclaimed the present as decisive in God's purposes and himself as the messianic agent. In similar vein, Paul regarded himself as God's agent whereby the nations are offered their part in the last days, possibly a role which made Paul such

[29] R. Bauckham, *The Theology of the Book of Revelation*, Cambridge: Cambridge University Press, 1993.

[30] Rowland, 'Apocalyptic, the Poor and the Gospel of Matthew'.

a problematic figure to some of Paul's Jewish and Christian contemporaries. That sense of present history as one pregnant with eschatological opportunity waned. By the time the Montanist movement appeared,[31] which was in effect a recrudescence of the earliest Christian practice and expectation, such an outlook proved to be incompatible with an understanding of history in which the eschatological agency was a matter of past and future but not of the present.

The subject of apocalypticism and eschatology is crucial in discussing the relationship between Scripture and theology. The heart of early Christian self-understanding was its realized messianism authenticated by the apocalyptic insight. Eschatological conviction is the content of the message, but the means whereby individuals came to apprehend its meaning came through claims to visions from God. What we find in earliest Christianity is apocalyptic functioning as the basis of its messianic convictions. One feature of the struggles in early Christianity seems to have been claims to authority which were authenticated by appeal to direct divine mandate, a feature which rapidly became more circumscribed in a later age which was more suspicious of the prophet and visionary. At the heart of the New Testament are instances of individuals with an understanding of the ultimate significance of their historical actions. Christian theology has been in part an attempt to articulate that basic datum in theological intricacy and practical exemplification. In the New Testament we have documents which are saturated with hope and the conviction that an insight of ultimate significance has been vouchsafed which relativizes all other claims. The New Testament, rooted as it is in apocalypse and eschatology, also breathes the spirit of accommodation, domestication and stability. Christianity found ways of translating its messianic drive, which would blur the boundary between heaven and earth into a religion which would enable those who aspired to perfection to go on living in the midst of the old age imperfection. It is no accident

[31] C. Trevett, *Montanism*, Cambridge: Cambridge University Press, 1995 and more generally on early Christian eschatology, B. Daley, *The Hope of the Early Church*, Cambridge: Cambridge University Press, 1991.

that a major statement of the compromise, Augustine's *City of God*, has at its heart the epistemology of apocalyptic, though its solution served the interests of the alliance of secular and spiritual power which was the heart of post-Constantinian Christendom. Early Christians had to wrestle with the messianic inheritance not by rejecting it but by using it as the basis for explaining how the beyond could manifest itself amidst the obscurities of the present. In perhaps the boldest example in the New Testament, the Gospel of Matthew in the Last Judgement in 25.31–46 offers an interpretation of the eschaton which abruptly interrupts the preoccupation with the eschatological future.[32] The occupant of the judgement seat decides between the righteous and unrighteous, not on the basis of theological rectitude, but of service to the needy. The scope of the eschaton is brought into the present in dealing with the suffering and insignificant. Life is imbued with eschatological significance, though not in the sense of the outworking of some grand utopian design. It is particularly ordinary acts of charity which are given the aura of ultimate significance.

Lady Margaret's context prompted the initial reference to aspects of medieval eschatology. Medieval texts may be used in a heuristic way, so that study of messianism in later Christianity and also Judaism[33] might be a complement to the Second Temple sources in the study of the New Testament. Such perspectives remind us of the importance of the claim that reception history has on exegetical attention.[34] An initial excursion into the reception history of the Apocalypse over the last year or so has been a fascinating journey and a much-needed addition to my theological education. Of course, there is something peculiarly appropriate about this form of study for the exegesis of a visionary text like the Apocalypse, the interpretation of which has been in the hands of those who receive it, whether the visionary recipient, or the

32 Rowland, 'Apocalyptic, the Poor and the Gospel of Matthew'.

33 M. Idel, *Messianic Mystics*, New Haven: Yale University Press, 1998.

34 U. Luz, *The Gospel of Matthew 1–7*, Edinburgh: T. & T. Clark, 1989; and the forthcoming Blackwell's Bible Commentary series whose focus is on reception history.

readers of the vision, ancient and modern. Like Botticelli's extraordinary 'Mystic Nativity', the Apocalypse and indeed other New Testament Scriptures point to a hinterland of eschatological meaning.

The medieval apocalyptists in the Joachite tradition understood something about the eschatology of the New Testament. They took seriously aspects of the early Christian reading of Scripture, in which God's address to humans, and the inspiration of the Spirit were central to their appropriation of Scripture. What characterized early Christianity was its genius of allowing the immediate and the inspirational to be tested with the 'scientific'. That seems to me to be going on all over the place in the New Testament (not least in the way in which visions, prophecy, dreams and the like are 'tested' in the Acts of the Apostles). The various layers of the theology and ethics of the New Testament are saturated with this perspective (not a realized eschatology, to be sure, but one which has been termed 'penultimate'). In different ways the New Testament writers marry apocalyptic and eschatological convictions with a social and ecclesial pragmatism which have given the Christian religion its distinctive identity. Even the mature Augustine reflects this (even if in key respects he turns his back on early Christian eschatology), for in *The City of God* the apocalyptic shape of a Christian view of history, akin in many respects to both Matthew and the Apocalypse, is set forth in a form which has been determinative for much later theology. Within the broad range of interpretations in the reception history of the Apocalypse, I have offered two aspects of that history from the golden age of eschatological reading which I believe only echo the New Testament texts themselves in the way in which they read Scripture eschatologically.

Index of Names and Subjects